spooky trails and tall tales

MASSACHUSETTS

Hiking the State's Legends, Hauntings, and History

STEPHEN GENCARELLA

FALCON

GUILFORD, CONNECTICUT

An imprint of Globe Pequot, the trade division of
The Rowman & Littlefield Publishing Group, Inc.
4501 Forbes Blvd., Ste. 200
Lanham, MD 20706
www.Falcon.com

Falcon and FalconGuides are registered trademarks and Make Adventure Your Story is a trademark
of The Rowman & Littlefield Publishing Group, Inc.

Distributed by NATIONAL BOOK NETWORK

British Library Cataloguing in Publication Information available
Library of Congress Cataloging-in-Publication Data
Names: Gencarella, Stephen Olbrys, 1971– author.
Title: Spooky trails and tall tales Massachusetts : hiking the state's legends, hauntings, and history /
Stephen Gencarella.
Description: Guilford, Connecticut : Falcon, 2021. | Includes bibliographical references and index.
Identifiers: LCCN 2021017013 (print) | LCCN 2021017014 (ebook) | ISBN 9781493060429
(paperback) | ISBN 9781493060436 (epub)
Subjects: LCSH: Hiking—Massachusetts—Guidebooks. | Trails—Massachusetts—Guidebooks. |
Ghost stories, American—New England. | Massachusetts—History.
Classification: LCC GV199.42.M4 G46 2021 (print) | LCC GV199.42.M4 (ebook) | DDC
796.5109744—dc23
LC record available at https://lccn.loc.gov/2021017013
LC ebook record available at https://lccn.loc.gov/2021017014

For Charlie Johnson.

And to the memory of Clifton Johnson.

Contents

CONTENTS

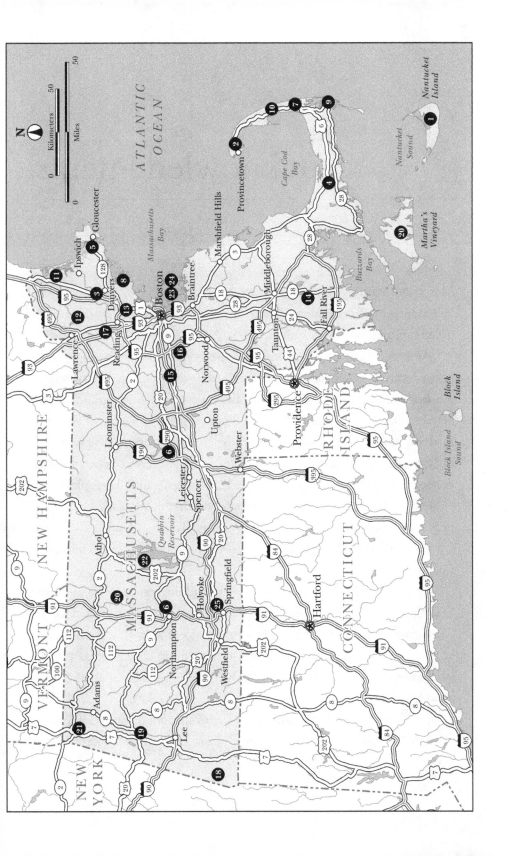

Acknowledgments

Massachusetts has been very kind to me. I met the love of my life there and together we welcomed all four of our children to the world. And I have buried beloved dogs in its soil.

As a teenager growing up in Rhode Island I would borrow my grandfather's station wagon, drive to Alewife with friends, and wander throughout Boston. (He took the blame for the mileage when my grandmother asked too many questions.) I hold fond memories of Fenway and Foxboro Stadium and of sites stretching from the Berkshires to the Cape. In my early twenties, I had the pleasure of teaching Latin at Norwood High School. And for the past two decades I have been gainfully employed as a professor at the University of Massachusetts, Amherst. These and other opportunities allowed me to live in towns as diverse as Salem, Uxbridge, Charlemont, and Montague. I will forever be grateful to the Commonwealth and its people.

I am thankful, above all, to my favorite hiking companions: my wife, Winnie, and our children, Salvatore, Angeline, Antonio, and Marcella.

Although fate—in the form of a pandemic—has kept us from hiking together, I have traveled a long way with my editor, Dave Legere, and all to my benefit. I am profoundly grateful for his guidance, patience, and good humor.

I will thank my friend and fellow critical folklorist Ray Huling as often as I am able. Ray's advice is never incorrect, and this book was made better by it.

I have the good fortune to call Chris Dobbs, Erik Ofgang, and Anthony Bak Buccitelli friends. Their leadership, scholarship, and impeccable writing are a constant source of inspiration.

A book of this sort is only possible with the support of friends and colleagues. I would like to thank all of them for their encouragement and contributions to our world: Katie Abbondanza, Pam Adams, Robin Andreoli, Meir Yishai Barth, Nick Bellantoni, Lauren Bergnes, Lisa Bernardi, Dotty Snow Bicknell, Bingk (Sharon Houle), Dan Bolognani, Daniel Bosques, Tanya Bourgoin, Rachel Briggs, Rosa Briggs, Marge Bruchac, Lois Bruinooge, Ryan Conary, Tary Coppola, John Coston, Joe Cote, Chloe Deeley, Heather and John DiPaolo, Ed Dombroskas, Eliza Donhauser, Greg Dorchak, Shara and Neal Drew, Davis Dunavin, Eddie Guimont, Alannah Finlay, Steph and Alex Foulkes, Jill Fritzsche, Chris Gilbert, Katie Gohde, Sal Gencarelli, Wick Griswold, Pete Haase, Evan Helmlinger, Sharon Hill, Scott Jauck, Karl Johnson, Fran Kefalas, Donna and Neal Kirk, Ann and Felix Kloman, hari stephen kumar, Allie Kyff, Debra and John Lawless, Caleb Lincoln, Tony Lupinacci, Ange Lussier, LRB (Linda Reilly-Blue), Michael Lee-Murphy, Mary Mazur, Troy Medinis, Russ Miller, Atticus Nischan, Daniel Nischan, Brenda and Bob Osborn, Glenn Ostlund, Tyra Penn-Gesek, Deryn Pomeroy, Maureen Quintin, Mark Rampmeyer, Cordelia and Andy Roth, Carl Ruck, Juliet Rutigliano, Rachel Sayet, Rita Schmidt, Kate Schramm, Bird Stasz, Becky Townsend, Molly Turner, Porntip Twishime, Greg Wharmby, Jen White-Dobbs, Anya Wilczynski, Dave Williams, Gary Williams, Rachel Wood, Dave Worthington (and old blue), and Dottie Zellman. I'm grateful to senior production editor Jehanne Schweitzer, typesetter Joanna Beyer, and proofreader Paulette Baker for their work seeing the book through production.

Twenty years ago, I wrote a dissertation that concluded with my imagining the composition of a guidebook that would promote responsible tourism. In many ways, this present volume is an attempt at that devilish plan. And the gratitude to my mentors John Louis Lucaites, Dick Bauman, Bob Ivie, and John McDowell is inexhaustible.

ACKNOWLEDGMENTS

I would like to thank the staff, volunteers, and board members of all National Heritage Areas and Corridors in Massachusetts: Blackstone River Valley, Essex, Freedom's Way, Last Green Valley, and Upper Housatonic Valley. I would also like to salute the exemplary work of all of my colleagues in FINE (Folklorists in New England).

I am, as always, grateful to my colleagues in the Communication Department at the University of Massachusetts, Amherst. And I cannot tire of expressing the great honor it is to have worked with all the students—thousands now—and the privilege it will be to work with all those in the decades ahead.

One of the pure joys of writing this book was the excuse to read the work of masterful storytellers who themselves clearly admire Massachusetts and its folklore. Please take my advice. Your life will be better if you read every word written by Clay Perry, Elizabeth Reynard, Marilynne Roach, and Edward Rowe Snow. Likewise, the dedication to the study of Massachusetts folklore by George Carey and William Simmons should never be forgotten. And the scholarship and activism of Gladys Tantaquidgeon will forever remain a model to inspire us all.

The older I am—I turn a half century this year—the happier I become that I chose my intellectual heroes wisely. And every day that I wrote another line of this book, I hoped that it would echo in some way what I have learned from Clifton Johnson. Although Johnson (1865–1940) has long been praised in small circles, he has never received the accolades he deserves as a monumental figure for the folklore of New England. Discovering his work was a watershed moment in my career. It convinced me that the life of a cloistered academic would be a useless endeavor and that the best folklorists write to be read by the public. I regard this book as a letter of respect and indebtedness to all his contributions.

Meeting Clifton's grandson, Charlie Johnson, was a cosmic gift. Charlie's generosity at our first meeting was transformative. As he drove us to sites throughout the area and shared copious stories of folklore and his family, I simply could not believe my dumb luck. I've written elsewhere that it was the single best day in my career as a folklorist. But it turned out that I was incorrect. It stands on equal ground with the day that Charlie and I met at the Jones Library in Amherst and combed through his father's scrapbooks, spoke on the phone with his equally accomplished nephew, and chatted at length yet again about all the rich contributions to folklore and to folklore studies that his family has given us.

I hope to be around for many more decades doing the work of an honest folklorist. No other day will be as rewarding as those two that I shared with Charlie Johnson—that is, until we meet again.

This book is dedicated to those two remarkable teachers, Charlie and Clifton Johnson.

Introduction

"From manuscripts and printed accounts I could collect
as many prodigies in one part of the country and another,
at different times, as would fill a small volume."
—Thomas Hutchinson, *The History of Massachusetts*

Be careful! The book you hold in your hands may not be the book you
desire it to be.

Although I share copious legends from Massachusetts throughout its
pages, sometimes in my own words and sometimes in the words of others,
this is not solely and strictly a collection of eerie tales. You will also find
no evidence in these pages for the existence of ghosts, monsters, or other
things that go bump in the night except as captivating characters in fascinating folk narratives.

This is a book written for those who enjoy learning, those who enjoy
hiking, and ideally those who enjoy some combination of both. Stories
have genealogies—some even have archaeologies—and as a professional
folklorist, I hope to show you those histories and explain why they matter.
The stories we pass on, the stories we hear, and the stories we believe all
help shape the people who we are. They help us understand our place in
the social world and in the cosmos. So this is a book that intends to honor
storytellers and storytelling. It follows their tales like a good hike, always
on a path but wandering where they take us.

This is also a book that is not afraid to hope that some stories gain strength and that others pass away. Many tales composing Massachusetts folklore exude prejudice, xenophobia, and misogynistic, classist, or racist tendencies. I do not hide that information in these pages. I trust that readers want to be educated and to make ethical judgments based on expansive rather than limited knowledge. I am of the opinion, furthermore, that if such awareness detracts from entertaining practices, it might be time for serious reflection as to how our society expects to be entertained. In other words, folklore matters significantly, and we must courageously examine its ugly manifestations as readily as we celebrate its sublime contributions.

In each chapter, I share at least one folkloric tale, often citing directly from original sources, which are listed in the Works Cited. I then explain the stories behind the story—that is, the tale's genealogy and cultural history—to the best of my ability. Each chapter closes with a proposed site for an activity that folklorists call *Legend Tripping*—traveling to a place in order to experience or even to become part of the tale. I attempt to provide information regarding a suitable trailhead and maps available online. In some cases I recommend a specific hike, and in others I recommend visiting the area in general with its plentiful hiking opportunities.

There is a problem in approaching this task in such a manner, as much as one can call the thoroughly enjoyable indulgence of writing a book about Massachusetts folklore either a problem or a task. There are many places in the Commonwealth associated with great stories but not great hikes. The abundant ghost stories and haunted houses in the Berkshires leap to mind, but there are numerous other places well deserving of genealogical investigation that were not included in this book. Similarly, there are many—far too many—great hikes with no folklore, at least not yet. And there are places that tempt with the hint of grand narratives to match their rewarding hiking but that come up short upon investigation. Purgatory Chasm in Sutton is a prime example with its litany of inviting infernal names and no major tales to give flesh to their hellish delights.

Please be forewarned that the stories are the emphasis in this book. Use this guide as an introduction to twisted trails and tall tales, but do your homework before heading out. Some locations are challenging even for the seasoned hiker, and some are deceptively so on account of rapidly changing natural conditions. Some are in very remote areas. Many allow seasonal hunting where it is important to dress accordingly. Hikers may also need to take precaution against the weather or tides, shifting trail conditions, and wildlife ranging from black bears to the ubiquitous ticks and mosquitoes. Be aware that as with folklore, the Commonwealth is also embarrassingly rich in poison ivy. And always be trailhead smart.

One-quarter of the royalties from this book will be shared with the Upper Housatonic Valley National Heritage Area and the Essex National Heritage Area, two remarkable nonprofit organizations that have improved the lives of all of us who love Massachusetts and its cultural heritage. I pledge to contribute to both of them additionally as I am able, and I intend to support other heritage organizations in future publications. I hope that you will support the range of federal, state, and local organizations that protect our natural and cultural resources with donations of time or money, or simply by thanking the volunteers who make safe, clean, accessible trails available for us today and for future generations.

Finally, I invite you to reach out to me with suggestions, corrections, additions, and recollections of folkloric stories. No tale is insignificant. It would be particularly helpful to learn if these stories are still being told in your community. Please contact me through email at my UMass address at solbrys@umass.edu. I look forward to hearing from you.

I hope that all of these stories give you something to think about as you head out and hit the trails. And to borrow—yet again—the words of Charlie Johnson, hiker and storyteller extraordinaire, happy legending!

1

His Snakeship Returns

AY, WHAT IN the world is that?"

Something appeared quite suddenly to disturb the serenity of Ipswich Bay. It was Tuesday, July 28, 1896. William Henry Sargent was hauling in his lobster pots as he had countless times before. His dory rested on the water about two hundred yards from Plum Cove in the village of Lanesville. Sargent was accustomed to the sounds of the sea and the shore, but he was not prepared for the eerie whistle that pierced the air and seized his attention.

He turned his head in the direction of the noise. And there, barreling at him with tremendous speed, "was the most hideous-looking thing he had ever seen in his experience on the water." It was a marine monster, fifty feet in length, with three gigantic humps, all chalky white, and spread at intervals along its serpentine spine. The creature passed within forty feet of his boat as his bones froze with fear. It slid under the water, remained submerged for several minutes, and then broke the surface a half mile away and sped off past Halibut Point.

Unharmed but shaken, Sargent pulled to shore. There he found fellow fisherman gathered in a crowd, all astonished at what they had just witnessed in the shadow of Folly Cove.

In the grip of panic, Sargent did not look at the creature's head. But others less fortunate came close to its hideous visage that day. All agreed that it was the size of a washtub that could fit a full-grown man. And from that titanic head peered out two great, glaring, bulging eyes.

Word spread like a hurricane: His Snakeship had returned.

This story of a monster swimming off Gloucester appeared on the front page of the venerable *Boston Globe* for two consecutive evenings. With a touch of ironic timing, the *Fall River Daily Evening News*—seemingly unaware of the northern encounter—asked the question "Where is the sea serpent this year?" in its pages on July 30. An abundance of replies would not take long. "No More a Myth" ran the headline in the *Globe*—"Sea Serpent Seen by Scores in the Bay."

If the reports were true, the sea serpent was busy announcing its return that day. From Halibut Point, it rounded Cape Ann and soon appeared undulating hastily in the waters of Marblehead, heading for Boston. It paid no attention to the startled boats that it passed.

By early evening the ophidian beast was off Nahant, poised to surprise a yachting party from Beachmont out for an evening of deep-sea fishing. This time the creature obliged its witnesses. It lingered on the surface for five minutes, never showing head or tail but revealing just enough for those aboard the sloop to stare with amazement and trepidation.

The next morning, lobstermen from Duxbury and Plymouth had their turn with His Majesty. They were in the lower harbor pulling in their pots when they spied a humped mass charging ferociously toward them. Captain A. G. Faye of *The Clio* saw it, too, and bravely started in hot pursuit.

The Clio ran the monster toward the shallows of the inner harbor, but the serpentine lord knew his waters well. He cut a swift turn, crossed over the shoals at Browns Bank, and escaped into the freedom of Cape Cod Bay—chastened, perhaps, but not done with his display of raw and royal power.

On July 31 the *Boston Globe* reported the following account from Sandwich:

It was long before sunrise when the fishermen who operate the fish traps off this shore left their rude shanties and proceeded in their boats down the narrow and crooked channel to the bay this morning.

There was not breeze to even cause a ripple and the broad expanse of Cape Cod Bay was like a mirror, reflecting and magnifying the big fishing boats as they were propelled far out from the shore to where the traps are set.

As is the custom of the fishermen, they gazed upon the traps as soon as they came within seeing distance, and much speculation was indulged in as to the amount of fish which had been caught during the night.

Suddenly one of the fishermen espied something far beyond the trap, moving in the direction of it at a rapid rate and churning the water with a milky white foam.

The men ceased rowing and viewed the monster of the deep with a mingled feeling of awe and security as it came rushing toward them.

For fear that the frail boat would be demolished or swamped the crew resumed rowing and quickly got along side of the big trap.

As the monster closed in with the unstoppable rage of the sea, the hapless crew realized it was a hundred feet in length. No prayers climbed to heaven for their safety. Fear had stolen their breath.

All things considered, 1896 was late in the reign of His Snakeship. Tales of a serpentine marine monster patrolling the waters of New England first arose in the 1600s and continued unabated into the early twentieth century. The Great New England Sea Serpent is one of the most significant characters for storytelling in the Bay State. It is arguably the monarch of Massachusetts folklore. And its stories are essentially countless. June Pusbach O'Neill's admirable attempt at such a collection only scratches the surface.

There are hints of serpent lore among the Indigenous people of the region at the time of European colonization. There is a glimpse of this tradition in an account from John Josselyn, an Englishman who visited the New World in the mid-1600s. Josselyn reported a serpent—although not necessarily a sea serpent—"that lay coiled up like a cable upon a rock at Cape Ann; a boat passing by with English aboard, and two Indians, they would have shot the serpent, but the Indians dissuaded them, saying, that if he were not killed outright, they would all be in danger of their lives."

European folklore of the fabled creature was readily imported into the Colonies. And as the wilderness of the New World gave way to coastal civilization and its accompanying industries, the sea serpent proved a valuable canvas for the projection of numerous concerns. The prominence of commercial whaling from the 1600s until the mid-1800s and the constant reliance upon fishing meant that numberless young men would leave the safety of terra firma to risk life at sea. Far too many did not return.

The earliest stories of a monster lurking out in the briny deep speak to that very real—and often realized—anxiety of losing loved ones to unforgiving waters. I use that term "monster" deliberately. It is a word related to "admonition." It means something that warns—and especially something that warns from being out of place beyond mortal knowledge—something quite capable of reminding humans that nature is not theirs to control. For centuries the sea serpent, the great monster of Massachusetts, was an apt symbol of the dangers awaiting those whose livelihood depended on the ocean and its fickle waves.

Although fishing is forever, the great age of whaling in New England had come to a close by the late 1800s. His Snakeship's reign outlived those of sea captains and whalers in Boston and New Bedford, Nantucket and Provincetown. This longevity should surprise no one. As with all good stories, tales of the sea serpent evolved over time.

Two cultural shifts in the nineteenth century were inspired by and shaped sea serpent stories. The first was the rising tide of modern science. Discoveries of dinosaur fossils revolutionized zoology. Theories of evolution ignited global debates. The budding field of psychology investigated human perception and its relation to belief. These advances often coalesced around the question of the sea serpent's existence.

The creature occasionally cooperated with these efforts. In 1817, for example, the scholar William Bentley wrote in his diary of August 15: "We have heard from Gloucester that a Narway Kraken had visited the harbor within Ten Pound Island. We have had letter upon letter. Many attempts have been made to kill him. The general representation is that his head is like a horse and that he raises it several feet out of the water. That his body when out of the water looks like the buoys of a net, or a row of kegs, or a row of large casks."

The appearance garnered headlines throughout the young nation. The scientifically-inclined rushed to investigate. David Humphreys, the honored solider who served both Israel Putnam and George Washington, interviewed several witnesses and wrote detailed letters to Joseph Banks of the Royal Society of London. Their collection, appropriately entitled *Some Account of the Serpent of the Ocean*, holds up two hundred years later as a harrowing narrative of "a monstrous Serpent" and unsuccessful attempts to ensnare it.

A month later, felicitous news broke that one of its spawn was in captivity. A farmer in Rockport gathering hay with his sons in Loblolly Cove came upon an aggressive snake of an unknown species. It fought the pitchfork that pierced its belly with unholy fury to its death. Soon thereafter it was in the possession of the Linnaean Society of New England, a learned organization dedicated to natural history. Eventually they identified it as a new species—*Scoliophis atlanticus*—and the credible offspring of the larger beast.

The triumph did not last. Subsequent investigations revealed that the unusual creature was nothing more than a black snake afflicted with tumors.

Scientific attempts to explain the sea serpent did not curtail the widespread desire to see it and to share its stories. A wave of storytelling gripped Nahant after the creature was spotted in 1819. Egg Rock, that impenetrable testimony of earth against the waves, became a favored location for the inquisitive serpentine traveler. Stories of his annual sojourn to Nahant proliferated throughout New England.

In 1823, for example, the *Connecticut Mirror* published "Sonnet to the Sea Serpent" from the poet John Gardiner Calkins Brainard:

> Welter upon the waters mighty one—
> And stretch thee in the ocean's trough of brine;
> Turn thy wet scales up to the wind and sun,
> And toss the billow from thy flashing fin;
> Heave thy deep breathings to the ocean's din,
> And bound upon its ridges in thy pride,
> Or dive down to its lowest depths, and in
> The caverns where its unknown monsters hide,
> Measure thy length beneath the gulf stream's tide,
> Or rest thee on the naval of that sea
> Where floating on the Maelstrom, abide
> The krakens sheltering under Norway's lee;
> But go not to Nahant, lest men should swear,
> You are a great deal bigger than you are.

Brainard's playful tone was prescient of the yarns that would follow throughout the nineteenth century, which relate to the second cultural shift.

As tourism increased in importance—and overtook commercial fishing as a source of income for maritime communities—so did wondrous tales of the sea serpent. Newspapers reported on its first appearance each year. Hotels and other tourist accommodations routinely advertised as the ideal location for a viewing.

Beckoning tales of His Snakeship's visitation inspired fandom. Sea serpent clubs became popular at the turn of the century. Whether dedicated to observe the waters in the name of science or to toast his name in the decades before Prohibition, these organizations were shining signs of pride of association with a monster.

The sea serpent became so ingratiated into coastal New England tourism that it inspired numerous hoaxes to dupe the gullible and to delight the faithful. One such practical joke occurred on Nantucket in July 1937. It began when an exasperated fisherman informed the island's newspaper that he had witnessed an enormous serpent hunting in nearby waters. Gigantic footprints then appeared on Madaket Beach. A photograph of incredulous men stretching a tape measure across their four-to-five-foot span sent newspapers throughout the region into upheaval.

And then the monster emerged from its aquatic abyss and came to shore on crashing waves.

Or more appropriately, the monster floated over Nantucket Harbor to South—now Francis Street—Beach from Coatue Point, where it had been inflated.

The leviathan was an enormous balloon designed by puppeteer Tony Sarg. Hundreds of people were (admittedly gleefully) taken in by this sensation of the summer.

It was a thoughtful prank. All of Nantucket had been a haunt for the sea serpent. It had been spotted, for example, off South Shore in 1821, Great Point in 1835, and Siasconset in 1854. And genuine applause is warranted for Sarg's joke in fulfilling an idea hatched a century earlier. In 1833, the "Java Mermaid"—likely the Fiji Mermaid, a mummified combination of a monkey and a fish—was touring New York to large and curious audiences. An editorial in the *Nantucket Inquirer* sensibly argued that if New Yorkers were such easy marks, it was the responsibility of Nantucket to separate fools from their money.

"We shall build a glorious skeleton of a sea serpent," the editorial proposed, "out of old whale bones, oil casks, and tarpaulins—with a buffalo's skull at one end, and a sea-devil's tail at the other. This we can contrive to set adrift upon the south shoal, so as to get it stranded at Siasconset in the first southeasterly storm. Then away it goes to market."

While this scheme did not quite unfold as planned, Sarg's sea serpent was honored with a journey from Nantucket to New York City to participate in the Macy's Thanksgiving Day Parade.

In addition to hoaxes, actual skeletons have appeared on beaches throughout Massachusetts, awakening old stories and provoking new tales. One such skeleton—a purported eighteen feet in length—washed ashore Wood End in Provincetown in 1939. To the disappointment of many, scientists at Harvard concluded that it was a basking shark. They argued the same in 1970 when a monstrous body was discovered in the sands of Mann Hill Beach in Scituate. Dubbed "Cecil the Seasick Sea Serpent" after a then-popular cartoon character, that carcass inspired souvenir hunters as readily as it did storytellers.

Not everyone relishes the notoriety of an encounter with His Snakeship. Henry David Thoreau recorded an anecdote, for example, that the renowned politician Daniel Webster once saw it in the bay between Plymouth and Manomet Beach. "For God's sake," Webster instructed his companion, "never say a word about this to anyone, for if it should be known that I had seen the sea serpent, I should never hear the last of it, but wherever I went I would have to tell the story to everyone I met."

On the other hand, some raconteurs fully embrace the opportunity. George Washington Ready of Provincetown was such a man who, in 1886, "was going from the town to the backside of the Cape, and in crossing one of the sand-dunes, or hills, saw a commotion in the water, about a half mile from the shore in the Herring Cove. It looked like a whirlpool and from his standpoint appeared to be twenty feet in diameter, from the center of which jets of spray, looking like steam, were ejected to the height of fifty feet. Intently watching this strange phenomenon, he presently saw a huge head appear above the surface, and point for the shore."

Ready hid in a clump of beach plum bushes and observed the monster. Its head, he reported, was as large as a two-hundred-gallon cask, concave on the underside and convex on the other. He estimated the beast was three hundred feet long and twelve feet in diameter at the thickest part of its body, which was covered in large scales alternately colored green, red, and blue.

In its open mouth Ready spied four rows of teeth, each two feet long and glistening like polished ivory. A tusk extended from its nose for a length of eight feet. Six eyes, all the size of dinner plates, perched on stalks protruding three feet from the head. Three were fiery red and three were pale green.

The creature sported a V-shaped tail, twenty feet long and only ten inches thick but studded with hard bony scales that mowed smooth anything over which it dragged. The monster was less sea serpent and more denizen of an infernal realm. It reeked of sulphur, Ready claimed, and scorched the grass beneath its massive frame.

The beast lumbered from the shore inward to slither into Pasture Pond. It disappeared there, draining the freshwater with it. And when Ready summoned the courage to examine the hole, he found that the creature had burrowed so deep that it left a barren tunnel for at least 250 fathoms—that's 1,500 feet to landlubbers—and still no bottom could be found.

By all accounts, "Professor" George Washington Ready was quite a character in Provincetown. He was one of its last town criers, a position he held until his death in 1920, and took very seriously the responsibility to regale visitors with remarkable tales. It earned him the honor of being called "the town's best story teller" by the *Boston Globe* in a celebratory essay in 1915.

There is one final component of the lasting folklore of the sea serpent that bears mention. Every few decades some authority laments that interest in the creature and its stories are about to disappear. In 1923, for example, the *Boston Globe* queried, "Where Has the Sea Serpent Gone?" In 1948 the same paper asserted that "Seeing Sea Serpent Slipping." As I write these lines, we are in another period of neglect.

But fear not, dear reader. It is only a matter of time. We forever remain subjects to the monarch of Massachusetts monsters and his storied reign. And His Snakeship always returns.

Legend Tripping

In pursuit of the sea serpent, all that is necessary is to get to the coast or any shoreline in the Commonwealth. For the sake of following the hunt laid out in this chapter, there is no hiking per se in Lanesville, although the one acre of Harvey Reservation technically offers a walk. It is part of Greenbelt, Essex County's Land Trust (https://ecga.org/Property/Harvey-Reservation), which even publishes a map. **Trailhead GPS: N42 40.44 / W70 39.38**

Halibut Point State Park in Rockport is overseen by the Department of Conservation and Recreation (https://www.mass.gov/locations/halibut-point-state-park), which also offers a map for this small site with breathtaking views. Seasonal fees apply. It is adjacent to Halibut Point Reservation, a property of the Trustees of Reservations (https://thetrust ees.org/place/halibut-point-reservation/), which offers a map. **Trailhead GPS: N42 41.11 / W70 37.53** And technically, there is a space for parking at the end of Old Penzance Road in Rockport with a trail that leads to Loblolly Point. **Trailhead GPS: N42 38.25 / W70 35.34**

It is not feasible to list all of the minor sites around Nahant Bay or to wrestle with the various rules for hiking the beaches in this book, but the reader's investment in doing so would be rewarding. A visit to Nahant, especially looking out toward Egg Rock, is medicine for the folkloric soul. The same can be said for various sites around Gloucester Harbor looking out at Ten Pound Island.

Although not detailed above, historically one of the major and constant sites for sea serpent sightings is Nantasket Beach in Hull. Nearby, Gunrock Beach had one of the most active sea serpent clubs at the turn of the twentieth century. Mann Hill (Egypt) Beach in Scituate is not far from there. The beaches of Manomet in Plymouth are a bit farther off from that group and look across Cape Cod Bay. All of these sites, although remarkable, require planning to visit, especially during the summer season.

All of Nantucket warrants attention. And fortunately the entire island boasts sea serpent sightings at one point or another, so the reader should find a way to get there and start hiking. In addition to the beaches, visit the properties managed by the Nantucket Conservation Foundation (https://www.nantucketconservation.org/) and the Nantucket Land Bank (https://www.nantucketlandbank.org/). Coskata-Coatue Wildlife Refuge, overseen by the Trustees of Reservations (https://thetrustees.org/place/coskata-coatue-wildlife-refuge/) offers another option.

The hike that should not be missed in order to celebrate Professor George Washington Ready's amazing encounter is in Provincetown. With free but limited parking at the Province Lands Visitor Center, head to Race Point Beach. Heading east toward Truro, the beach hike will pass the site of the Peaked Hill Bar, occasionally referenced in tales of sea serpents and mooncussers. But for this hike, head west toward the Race Point Lighthouse. The Hatches Harbor Trail starts there and heads inland. At the intersection of Province Lands Road, across the street, is the Province Lands Bike Trail. It travels directly past Pasture Pond. Hikers could retrace back to Province Lands Road and return to the visitor center or continue on the Bike Trail. It's not really possible to get lost this close to Provincetown. To round out this popular place of legends concerning His Snakeship, visit Herring Cove Beach and Wood End at low tide as well as the harbor. To do all of this, of course, requires planning, especially during the tourist season. As with any fruitful sea serpent hunt, do not attempt it on a whim. **Trailhead GPS: N42 04.25 / W70 12.20**

2

"Ain't We to Provincetown?"

WHEN JEREMIAH SNAGGS realized that he was dead, a sly grin grew across his face.

"I ain't in Hell yet," he chuckled. Although, Captain Snaggs was quite sure he was bound for it given the life he had lived on the sea and, truth be told, on the land as well. He had not, as the religious say, died in the odor of sanctity.

Out of an old habit, Captain Snaggs paused to catch his breath. But no air filled his ghostly lungs. He laughed at the humor of it all.

The silence of the coffin was pleasing, he thought, much like the sound of cooperative waves. But at last Captain Snaggs heard something in the distance. It was not the rustle of wings come to lift him to heaven. It was the slow but steadfast pace of a single set of legs walking with purpose and determination. Near to the casket they stopped.

Silence again. And then the eruptive hum of a match and the puffing of a pipe just lit. Captain Snaggs never smelled such fine tobacco when he was alive. He knew that some infernal dignity had entered to pay respects and escort him to his new home.

Taking one more drag of breath out of an old habit, Snaggs hoisted his spirit straight out of his body.

There were no mourners in the sullen room. Few, indeed, mourned his passing. But standing there with a sly grin of his own was the Old Gentleman in Black, come to claim debts he had rightfully won when Captain Snaggs bet the Devil his head.

The captain was a wily man when he was alive, but there was no trick to help him escape Old Nick. So he did the one thing a lively dead man could do: flee like a harpooned whale in a Nantucket sleigh ride. Down Cape he flew from the breakers at Barnstable to the beach in Brewster where a mermaid once washed ashore.

Pausing at a kettle pond, Captain Snaggs listened to the still air. Far off in the distance he heard the steady sounds of the Old Gentleman's steps grow closer by the second. So off he spirited east to Orleans, just in the nick of time. There he hid in a makeshift barque behind the bark of a hollow tree. But soon the Old Gentleman's steps closed in. And the scent of fine tobacco told Captain Snaggs it was time to set sail again.

He raced to Wellfleet, where a stroke of genius struck. Captain Snaggs found a sagging jack-o'-lantern, the spitting image of his tired face, and summoned his spectral strength to heave it into a tree. Grinning with an old salt's charm, the fleshy pumpkin caught Old Nick's eye. But when the Old Gentleman tapped his pipe upon its hollow head, he grinned and knew the game continued.

By that time Captain Snaggs had reached the farthest reach of Provincetown, past Hatches Harbor and round to Race Point. With nowhere else to go, it was only a matter of time. The sound of cloven steps soon reached the sea captain's ears. The smell of fine tobacco filled the air like a sea breeze in July. The Old Gentleman had arrived.

Old Nick handed his pipe to Captain Snaggs to help him calm his nerves.

He exhaled and the smoke danced in the salty air like rum-soaked, drunken witches gathered at Clam Pudding Pond.

"All right," said Captain Snaggs, finally willing to face his fate. "You caught me fair and square. Where do we go from here?"

"Go?" replied the Old Gentleman with a sly and fiendish grin. "Nowhere. Ain't we to Provincetown?"

Forgive the bad pun, but the spirit of this story follows a tradition that was popular in the first half of the twentieth century. The specific tale here is based on Mary Heaton Vorse's brief account in her 1942 *Time and the Town: A Provincetown Chronicle*, but a far lengthier example awaits the reader in Elizabeth Reynard's *The Narrow Land*. I'll admit that I took some poetic license to smuggle in Brewster, where there is a hike that no one should miss.

Reynard's story is entitled "Jedidy and the Devil." It entails Captain Jedidy Cole, who rises from the burying box and encounters the Devil even before he can get his ghost legs on. Cole petitions for a ten-minute head start. The Devil consents because he was impressed that Cole had convinced four women to marry him during his less than saintly life.

On his way out the door, Cole snatches four corpse candles and heads straight to a gourd patch. There he seizes four pumpkins and with a bowie knife, carves a jack-o'-lantern into one. He leaves that pumpkin with its glowing grimace on a picket fence and heads off to Hawes Tavern in Chatham for a drink of rum.

Once in pursuit, the Devil seemingly mistakes the jack-o'-lantern for Cole. He teases the orange captain, who hears the insult—ghosts can hear faraway, just as the Devil can hear anyone who talks about him—and replies in kind, thereby alerting the Adversary to his bibulous location.

The ruse continues several times. Cole leaves another jack-o'-lantern at the tavern but again cannot resist replying to the Devil's taunting comments. Cole flees to Treat's Burying Lot in the South Parish of Eastham and there places a third jack-o'-lantern on a tombstone, but the Devil outsmarts him again. In Wellfleet, Cole places his final jack-o'-lantern high in an oak tree.

This provides a comical turn. The Devil scrambles up the tree thinking it is Cole, but slips and falls. A branch catches the Devil by his pants and he swings indecorously, prompting Cole to taunt the Prince of Darkness for being closer to Heaven than he.

In response, the Devil sets his pants aflame to free himself from the snare and sets off full speed after Cole. They race to the tip of Provincetown, where the Devil finally catches up with the captain. Cole surrenders and asks where the Devil will take him next, assuming it to be Hell. The Devil answers that they are already home, in Provincetown.

In her notes, Reynard explained that this narrative—in the language of folklorists it is called a shaggy dog story—was taken from oral tradition, although she does not cite her immediate source. She does mention that there are several variants with different captains and different towns as starting points, with the final scene always in Provincetown.

We can assume that the names of real captains often graced this jocular tale, perhaps by their own crew, but I cannot find any evidence of a Jedidiah Cole or a Jeremiah Snaggs in the typical annals of the Cape. The latter appears in a few minor literary works of the nineteenth century, and it is possible Vorse borrowed her protagonist's name from the titular character of a 1914 silent film, *The Captain's Chair*, starring Joseph Hazelton. That film is a comedy in which the death of Snaggs, a sea captain, leads to a moral treasure hunt of sorts.

It is also plausible that this tale reflects the vestige of a fascinating element of Provincetown's history, Helltown. Although many people today believe the moniker refers to the entire town, Helltown was a fishing hamlet near Hatches Harbor on Cape Cod Bay. It emerged in the late 1800s and was, according to early commentators, first established as a rude gathering of primitive huts for fishermen who did not want to face the sometimes uncooperative and time-consuming sailing conditions necessary to navigate from Provincetown Harbor around Long Point. Helltown fell into ruin—well, more ruin—after gasoline-powered craft solved that problem.

Its demise paved the way for folklore to emerge concerning its name. In 1928, for example, newspapers throughout the Northeast published an interview with an aging fisherman originally posted in the *Boston Evening Transcript*. The man professed that the site was called Helltown because no women were present there, nor bunks, cots, hammocks, or anything for comfort. In the 1930s, reports proffered that it was named in the colorful language of fisherman who returned empty-handed to taunting sands. A decade later brought proposals of hellish work or of raising hell after a day of intense labor.

By the 1960s rumors teased that it was so named because of the strange people who frequented P-Town across the centuries, including pirates and witches who escaped the noose on Gallows Hill. In the 1980s it took on a sense of drunkenness and a red-light district, one made all the more hardened in public consciousness thanks to Norman Mailer's depiction in *Tough Guys Don't Dance*. It is not difficult today to find proponents of an anecdote that the Puritans christened it as a place of people unwilling to live in fear of the wages of sin.

Even if Helltown were not the final stop for the sea captain and the Devil, Provincetown's wanton reputation for the supernatural thrived in the early decades of the twentieth century. The combination of storytelling fisherman and tourists seeking stories made for a powerful alliance. Jeremiah Digges, in his 1937 *Cape Cod Pilot*, recalls one such story reportedly set in 1898, the year of the Portland Gale, a storm with hurricane winds that sank the SS *Portland* and killed the two hundred people aboard.

John Santos was a fisherman who once lost his limb to a shark and replaced it with a buoyant wooden peg leg. He was, however, from that moment on, forever "shark-jonahed." The rest of his body would follow that leg if he kept returning to sea. And John Santos did just that: return to the salty sea.

The sharks feasted well when he fed them that night the winds swept him straight overboard. Days later, his wooden leg washed ashore, the only part of John Santos to survive the hurricane. A fellow fisherman returned it to his grieving widow, Mary. She kept it close to her, lovingly, for a year until the night of November 26, 1899—the anniversary of the Portland Gale.

John's ghost visited her in the night and asked her to leave his leg out for him. He pinched her cheek and disappeared. Dutifully she took out the skipper's leg from their spice cupboard and placed it in the corner of the room upon the weary fireplace.

When Mary came downstairs the next morning, the leg was leaning in the same spot. Yet it was strangely soaking wet. It had rained hard during the night so, sensibly, she thought water had dripped down the chimney, but the sight of her dead husband's wooden leg made her grow more uneasy by the hour.

She summoned the village doctor. He listened to her tale and then inspected the wooden leg. As any sound scientist would do, he placed his tongue upon the wood. His eyes grew wide. And then he announced he would have a fisherman take the wooden leg out to sea, weigh it with heavy net leads, and cast it into the briny deep. "I'm a doctor," he explained, "and I don't listen to stories. But Mrs. Santos, I put my tongue to that wood. *It don't rain salt water!*"

It is not clear if the real John Santos, a Portuguese fisherman who lived in Provincetown in the 1930s and was captain of the *Mary Madeline*—and occasionally fined for flounder dragging off-season—appreciated the jesting reference.

Among its many fascinating contributions to Massachusetts folklore— page constraints prohibit exploration of the haunted Harlow house and the Black Flash from the 1930s or the more recent ghost train—Provincetown is one of the few places that could boast fishermen with the skills to land the sea serpent.

In May 1893, word spread quickly that His Snakeship had been captured on the bayside weir between Provincetown and Truro. The description intimates a deep-sea denizen: a thirty-foot-long, eel-like creature, with five rows of teeth, a serrated fin down the entire back, and smooth instead of scaly skin. It fought relentlessly and would have made several widows were it not for a well-placed bomb lance from a whale gun in its neck. Lifeless, the sea serpent was hauled into Provincetown to await transportation to Boston and then to the Smithsonian or the Chicago Fair.

Who could have guessed that the sea serpent thought dead was merely stunned? Who could imagine that it would revive mere moments before a photographer arrived, dive back into the bay, and elude a photograph that would prove its existence once and for all?

Yet such surprising news struck the headlines of newspapers throughout the region one day after they announced its capture. It was as if the rising tide of Provincetown Harbor poured life into its saline veins! The serpent headed seaward, passing directly under the vessel that would carry it to Boston. It wrapped into the cables and began to drag the panicked boat under the waves. The ship would have sunk and the crew been lost had the captain not cut the line with a mere second left to spare.

His Snakeship surfaced at Wood End, raising his neck ten feet out of the water to flaunt his sovereignty once again. Swimming forty miles an hour, he made Herring Cove in seconds. Fishermen at Helltown pulled for shore for fear of their fatigued lives. The sea serpent made one last show and then dove under at Race Point. He was spotted, minutes later, surfacing at Peaked Hill, where he joined an expectant second member of his kind. They were last seen from Truro's Highland Lighthouse heading south and out to sea.

Truro has its own tales to tell. If the uncanny experiences of Provincetown are not enough to tantalize, readers may wish to hunt—or be hunted by—the Beast of Truro. Its story begins in September 1981 when a few chickens went missing from their flock. A few cats followed soon thereafter, and according to reports they were discovered where felines should not be, without their heads. Soon a dog, a deer, and three pigs were among the victims of a shadowy, slinking thing. Some heard catlike cries shatter the calm night air. And then, on cue, came the suspects: a mountain lion, a bobcat, an escaped ocelot, or a pet Bengal tiger whose owner had some explaining to do. Whatever the beast was, the sandy soil of Truro was its benefactor; it never left clear footprints for the skeptic to solve the mystery.

The beast was the talk of the town and for a brief time the talk of the nation. The *New York Times* covered the incident in January 1982. It interviewed one couple who had taken a leisurely stroll on the bike path near Head of the Meadow Beach. There they encountered the beast.

The couple estimated the creature stood a mere fifty feet from them. It appeared to be sixty to eighty pounds with short ears and a ropelike tail shaped in the letter J. They were certain it was a mountain lion. Rumors, after all, had mentioned that the beast's victims were slashed, the way a carnivorous cougar kills its prey. The husband armed himself with a branch, but the creature disappeared into the woods without introducing itself and the certainty of its species.

It didn't need cheap certainty to enter Massachusetts folklore. The Pamet Puma had arrived.

Unfortunately, the same forces that conspired to make the Truro Beast a cause célèbre ushered its untimely death. I do not mean that the searches and attempts to track the creature ended in vain. They did, but lack of evidence hardly puts a good folkloric story down; to the contrary, it often heightens the luring mystique. Nor was it the estimation by town officials, animal control, and scientists that the culprit was a dog or a pack of dogs. New Englanders are a tenacious people. They have been told by government authorities since the late 1800s that mountain lions have been extirpated. And yet those great felines continue to be seen routinely, at least by desiring eyes conditioned to spot them in a blur.

No, what killed the Beast of Truro was explosive, Icarian fame. By March 1982 it was being covered by the National Geographic News Service—not as an animal but as a legendary creature akin to Bigfoot, the national folk hero of monsters. Whatever the beast was, it simply could not compete with that notoriety. Having been crowned the next great monster by the national press, when it couldn't deliver it was simply wiped away and never mentioned again. Bigfoot quickly reclaimed his hairy crown.

It is a shame that legends of the Truro Beast never had the opportunity to thrive in a local environment that could have nourished those yarns. One can only imagine what could have been if the residents of Truro and Provincetown had a few months to polish their anecdotes, rumors, and harrowing tales before the summer arrival of the off-Capers and their voracious appetite for a good story.

But all is not hopeless. Sightings of the beast occasionally occur— CapeCast, the video news branch of the *Cape Cod Times*, reported one as recently as 2008—and Truro residents have playfully integrated Pamet Puma iconography into their community. So perhaps with a little luck and the desiring eye of a good storyteller, the Truro Beast will someday again help make a trip to Provincetown an exquisite devil of a task.

Legend Tripping

The joy of this legend is that it invites hikers to take any route they would like as long as they keep moving and end at Provincetown. Although there are many gems hidden throughout the Cape, this itinerary recommends some of the best-known hikes on route from Brewster to P-Town. Do not attempt all in a single day even if you are a ghost; linger and enjoy these sights.

An excellent place to start is the Cape Cod Museum of Natural History (http://www.ccmnh.org/) in Brewster, which boasts the 1.5-mile lollipop John Wing Trail. Parking is for museum visitors, but who would not visit this museum when hiking there? The museum website has a pamphlet and map. **Trailhead GPS: N41 45.12 / W70 06.56**

Next is Nickerson State Park (https://www.mass.gov/locations/ nickerson-state-park), also in Brewster, which includes a large kettle pond, Cliff Pond. There are a number of well-marked hikes throughout. The 3-mile Cliff Pond Loop is a standard hike for visitors to the Cape, but all of the paths warrant attention. Be aware that there are active bike paths throughout. The state website has a pamphlet and map. Seasonal fees apply. **Trailhead GPS: N41 46.08 / W70 01.52**

Next is the Wellfleet Bay Wildlife Sanctuary overseen by Mass Audubon (https://www.massaudubon.org/get-outdoors/wildlife-sanctuaries/wellfleet-bay), which offers a pamphlet and map. There are 5 miles of meandering trails throughout, including two ponds, a pine forest, and views of Cape Cod Bay. Park at and visit the Esther Underwood Johnson Nature Center—and donate! **Trailhead GPS: N41 52.56 / W69 59.41**

Next is Great Island in Wellfleet, part of the Cape Cod National Seashore (https://www.nps.gov/caco/index.htm). There are several out-and-back hikes here, including the 3.9-mile tavern loop and longer 8.8-mile hike out to Jeremy Point. Parking is free on Chequessett Neck Road. **Trailhead GPS: N41 55.58 / W70 04.09**

Next is Beech Forest in Provincetown, also part of the CCNS. This easy walk loop is a nice place to catch your breath before the Old Gentleman catches you. The free parking lot is off Race Point Road. **Trailhead GPS: N42 03.59 / W70 11.39**

Finally, there is Race Point Beach and Hatches Harbor Trail in Provincetown. Parking is at the Province Lands Visitor Center, also part of the CCNS. Walk to the beach from there and head toward the Race Point Lighthouse. Pick up the Hatches Harbor Trail, which will intersect with the Province Lands Bike Trail and Province Lands Road and return to parking, a hike that would entail at least 6 miles. **Trailhead GPS: N42 04.25 / W70 12.20**

If you wish to risk the lair of the Beast of Truro, check out the Pamet Area Trails and Head of the Meadow Beach, also both of the CCNS. The parking lot for the first is located on North Pamet Road at the Environmental Education Center. **Trailhead GPS: N42 00.05 / W70 01.29** The parking lot for the second is at the end of Head of the Meadow Road; use the CCNS parking lot. Seasonal fees apply. The quest for the sea serpent is covered in another chapter. **Trailhead GPS: N42 03.10 / W70 04.57**

3

The Salem Witch Trials

THE SALEM WITCH Trials of 1692 were a horrific period in history. As Samuel Adams Drake aptly summarized, Salem was the scene of a tragedy in which the guilty escaped and the innocent were punished. They were not the first executions on the grounds of witchcraft in the New World, but the magnitude of their delusion forever changed society. In conveying folkloric stories that evolved from the trials, I intend no insult those who suffered momentous injustice.

Today Salem is a bustling tourist destination. "Witch City" has become internationally renowned, especially for Halloween activities under the umbrella of "Haunted Happenings." It is also a place dedicated to robust discussions about religious tolerance and the exploitation of history. I speak from personal experience, having lived in Salem from 1993 to 1995 and writing my dissertation on it twenty years ago.

As many readers will know, the Salem Witch Trials were not restricted to the contemporary city, which was called Salem Town in the late 1600s. The trials and executions took place there, but Salem Village—now Danvers and Peabody—was the site of considerable dramatic action. Other towns in Essex County were also involved. Of the twenty people executed, eleven came from Salem Town or Village. The nine others were from Amesbury, Andover, Marblehead, North Andover, Rowley, and Topsfield. Still others who were accused or died in jail lived in Beverly, Billerica, Boxford, Gloucester, Haverhill, Lynn, Malden, Reading, Salisbury, and

Wenham. The jails of Boston and Ipswich held prisoners when Salem was full. No municipality in the area was untouched.

It is impossible to explain the trials in detail here, but for sake of introduction, Salem in 1692 was a hotbed of religious, political, and cultural anxieties. Puritan folk belief regarded the Devil as a genuine threat. Many Old World superstitions regarding witches remained ingrained in the Massachusetts colonies. Accusations of witchcraft were infrequent but occurred in the decades leading up to Salem. In 1688, for example, Ireland-born Ann Glover was hanged as a witch in Boston.

Around the same time, Samuel Parris became minister of Salem Village. It was a contentious appointment that stirred controversy within the agrarian community. In January 1692, Parris's daughter Elizabeth and her cousin Abigail Williams began to exhibit erratic behavior, the type and reasons for which are debated still. The two young women eventually accused Parris's slave Tituba of bewitching them. Soon thereafter Sarah Good and Sarah Osborne, both social outcasts to some degree, similarly stood accused.

Dozens of others joined in making accusations. Local magistrates commenced examinations and established a special court to try those accused of being in league with the Devil. When the trials came to a close in 1693 following the intercession of Governor William Phips, nineteen people had been hanged at Gallows Hill in Salem and one man had perished in an equally unthinkable manner. Several others died in prison. More than 150 people stood accused, and untold scores had their lives upended.

Folklore was at the heart of the Salem Witch Trials. It took a repugnant shape in the admission of "spectral evidence" during court cases. As the name implies, it is the use of purported supernatural evidence of criminal activity, based on the belief that a witch's specter could leave its physical body and do harm to living beings. Witnesses offered the content of their dreams and related claims of contact—usually painful—with the presumed witches. Accusers often fell into fits in the presence of the accused and claimed they were under attack.

Each of the accused deserves to have their story told, but some victims of the trials became folk characters in legends after their executions. This chapter will focus on those folkloric traditions.

At the time of the trials Susannah Martin lived in Amesbury. She was a widow, essentially impoverished, and as an outspoken woman, a ready target. She had been accused of witchcraft before and countersued for slander. When hauled before the afflicted girls in 1692, she laughed derisively at their antics. Her response was interpreted as a sign of allegiance with the Devil.

Martin maintained her innocence throughout her ordeal. The depositions and testimonies against her are difficult to read as an egregious miscarriage of justice, but they reveal numerous ideas about witchcraft that entered later folk narratives in Massachusetts. Cotton Mather, the Puritan minister, included a transcript of Martin's trial in *The Wonders of the Invisible World*.

Several witnesses claimed that Martin's apparition tormented them physically and mentally. Others testified that she would appear to them at night, perch on their chest, and choke them. Numerous people reported cursed cattle, including cows that died, drowned, or ran away. Strange lights in the woods were attributed to her presence. An attack by spectral dogs and a black cat were as well. One witness claimed that a dog in her possession transformed into a wooden keg. Another testified that she could walk through wet weather and keep the soles of her shoes perfectly dry. Another saw her take the shape of a black hog. And still another claimed that her specter drove his wife to madness. Horses would not cross her path, explained one man, and another reported seeing her attend a satanic revelry.

Susannah Martin was executed on July 19, 1692.

Two centuries after her death she appeared as a witch in Rocks Village of Haverhill. "Susie Martin, also of Rocks," wrote Charles Montgomery

Skinner in his 1896 *Myths and Legends of Our Own Land*, "who was hanged in spite of her devotions in jail, though the rope danced so that it could not be tied, but a crow overhead called for a withe and the law was executed with that."

How did this happen?

That astonishing claim is found in Skinner's essay "Salem and Other Witchcraft," which includes a list of several witches in Haverhill, Amesbury, and Newbury. It also offers the following:

> *Barrow Hill, near Amesbury, was said to be the meeting-place for Indian powwows and witches, and at late hours of the night the light of fires gleamed from its top, while shadowy forms glanced athwart it. Old men say that the lights are still there in winter, though modern doubters declare that they were the aurora borealis. But the belief in witches did not die even when the Salem people came to their senses. In the Merrimac valley the devil found converts for many years after.*

Even today references invoke Barrow Hill in Amesbury as a site of nefarious witchcraft. Cryptozoologist Loren Coleman included it in his list of "Places of High Strangeness within North America."

The only problem is that there is no Barrow Hill in Amesbury and there never was.

Skinner misread "Powow Hill" (now often called Po Hill by residents) as "Barrow Hill." Mistakes of that type occur with some regularity in his work as he culled tales from newspapers across the country, many containing orthographic mistakes. In the same paragraph, for example, he cites "Two Indian servants of the Reverend Mr. Purvis, of Salem, having tried by a spell to discover a witch, were executed as witches themselves."

This is simply wrong. Skinner has in mind Tituba and John Indian, the two slaves of Samuel *Parris* of Salem Village, who in an attempt to assist the afflicted girls made a "witch cake," a biscuit fed to a dog to reveal whether sorcery was at work. Neither was executed.

That unfortunate practice of glaring imprecision spilled onto the presumed witches. Skinner's source was a chapter on witch legends in Rebecca Davis's 1886 *Gleanings from Merrimac Valley*. Davis's story of "Susie Martin" is unequivocally set "about four miles from Rocks Bridge on the river road to Amesbury Ferry"—that is, the historical home of Susannah Martin in Amesbury. In mistakenly identifying "Susie Martin" with Haverhill, Skinner confused himself about her true identity as a victim of the trials.

Davis's own account, however, raises an important issue. She relays the tale that Martin employed incantations to prevent being hanged until a crow gave away the secret. If I have properly tracked it, that motif appears to be borrowed from another tale, "The Ghost of Granny Hogins," published in 1828. It concerns a fictional witch in Boston; the feathered culprit is a parrot. Unfortunately, "tradition says" is all that Davis provides regarding this depiction of Martin's execution, so it remains unclear if it is literary invention or recollection of local lore.

Davis was a personal friend of John Greenleaf Whittier, whose poem "The Witch's Daughter" is set in Amesbury and imagines Susannah's daughter Mabel after her mother's death. It is based, very loosely, on the actual Hannah Martin, Susannah's step-daughter. And as perceptive readers may deduce, it is Whittier who inadvertently supplied the notion that Powow Hill was the site of sorcery. This occurred in a prose piece he published in 1832.

Whittier's fictional account of Powow Hill is also difficult to read. It was composed before his change of heart regarding depictions of Indigenous people. The story literally entails the defeat of malevolent Indian specters by a white man, Malachi, who strikes the ghost of a witch-squaw, Pigwackitiokapog, with his Bible. Whittier's description of Powow Hill is the basis of Skinner's account.

Several times throughout this book I will mention Skinner's tremendous influence on folklore in Massachusetts. In the 1930s the WPA guidebook to the state drew heavily from his work—so heavily, in fact, that its account of Amesbury offers little more than the story of Martin—"a famous Amesbury witch"—and the crow as well as the identification of the nonexistent Barrow Hill as "the scene of witches' routs." Amesbury, the guidebook concluded, "was especially favored by the powers of darkness."

The same devolution of character occurred with Wilmott Redd, a victim from Marblehead. Akin to Martin, the actual woman scorned her accusers' afflicted antics as "a sad condition." She was also an opinionated woman and not afraid to hurl an insult. During her trial, a neighbor testified that when a certain Mrs. Symons accused Redd's servant of theft, Redd defended the accused. In the subsequent verbal altercation Redd wished that Mrs. Symons would suffer not to urinate or defecate. And according to the witness, Mrs. Symons was indeed thereafter pained by numerous digestive problems. An outburst cast in a moment of anger was taken as evidence of witchcraft.

Wilmott Redd was executed on September 22, 1692.

Mammy Red, a folk character based on her, appeared in narratives throughout the 1800s. Samuel Roads Jr. briefly mentioned her in his 1880 history of Marblehead, admittedly conflating the woman with the character. He describes Mammy Red as an old woman, considered a witch, "known to afflict those whom she disliked in various ways," the most appalling of which was wishing a bloody cleaver be found in the cradles of infant children, whereupon the spectral weapon appeared and the child sickened and died. She also could bewitch milk to curdle as it exited the udder or butter to transform into "blue wool."

Four years later "Mammy Redd" appeared in Samuel Drake's *New England Legends and Folklore* as an "old crone." Drake reiterates the spells from Roads, conjectures that the "blue wool" was mold, and adds a folk rhyme from an indeterminate source:

> Old Mammy Redd,
> Of Marblehead,
> Sweet milk could turn
> To mould in churn.

Bewilderingly, Drake also stitches an unattributed passage from Samuel Butler's mock-epic *Hudibras* describing the astrologer Sidrophel. Perhaps Drake assumed readers would catch this comparison. But as written (and especially as read today) the poetic enumeration of wicked powers appears assigned to Mammy Redd.

That was all the permission Skinner needed to run rampant with his description of the purported witch. He included all of Drake's amendments and other supernatural occurrences described by Roads that were in no way connected to Mammy Red in the original text. And then to further muddy the waters, Skinner describes a headless ghost in Amesbury, the sight of which made it "high time to be rid of Mammy Redd."

I admire Skinner and Drake for many reasons, but this is shoddy work. And unfortunately their popularity had far-reaching implications for the reputation of two women who deserved better.

There is another tradition that several of the accused fled from Salem for safer territory. Legends of the "Witch Caves" near the Framingham-Ashland line are an excellent representative of this lore.

Although fully developed narratives are difficult to come by in print, the gist of this still active tale suggests that the accused Sarah Cloyce—a sister to two of the executed, Rebecca Nurse and Mary Esty—escaped from Ipswich prison with the assistance of her husband, Peter. By the aid of friends they made their way through the cold winter, traveling under cover of darkness to avoid authorities on their trail. Other refugees joined them in the haven of the caves, where they could stand watch upon the cliffs for signs of approaching danger. When word arrived that the trials ended, these refugees built houses nearby and established the community known as Salem's End. The caves collapsed over the centuries, bringing a symbolic close to a time of intolerance and ignorance.

It is historically accurate that an accused witch, Sarah Cloyce, found refuge in this area with her husband, Peter. It is also the case that an old tradition holds that she escaped Ipswich prison or a makeshift one. William Barry conveyed such an idea in his 1847 history of Framington. Josiah Temple reiterated the claim in 1887, adding that she was assisted by friends. But neither mention the Witch Caves and Temple directly asserts that she hid near Salem until the spring, when it was safe to travel westward.

More recent research demonstrates that Cloyce remained imprisoned until 1693, when her charges were dropped. She was freed following payment of her prison fees. She and her husband then moved to Boston and eventually to Framingham, where they, along with other families of victims, were granted leases to construct houses on the plantation owned by Thomas Danford, a judge critical of the trials.

Local historians interviewed by the *Boston Globe* in 1992 admitted that many residents believe Cloyce and other refugees hid in the caves, but could find no supporting evidence for the claim. It is very likely that the legend of Cloyce was a family tradition that evolved to incorporate the caves—really a collection of boulders and rocks—sometime in the twentieth century. Given the interest aroused by the tercentenary of the trials and by a 1985 PBS movie *Three Sovereigns for Sarah* (with Vanessa Redgrave as Cloyce), it makes sense that the lore of the Witch Caves grew stronger at this time.

A similar phenomenon occurred at Witch Woods in Beverly. If I have reconstructed the history correctly, Witch Lane has been so called since at least 1805. The name of the adjoining Witch Woods also appeared in the nineteenth century. The earliest traditions, however, postulate that the moniker was earned because of the ease of becoming lost in the dense forest of hemlock and pine. Caroline Howard King argued this explicitly in her memoir from the 1800s, and author James Russell Lowell, who visited in 1854, conveyed the same belief.

In the 1800s the folklore of Witch Woods (and the adjacent Haunted Wood) concerned a ghost "who carried his head under his arm instead of wearing it in its proper place," as King recalled from her youth—and nicknamed him Heady, as only a child's flavorsome sense of the macabre could do. The Woods were also the location of a spectral homestead, a farmhouse that would hail from a distance but disappear as the inquiring visitor neared. King had firsthand experience of this eerie phenomenon and narrated it to Lowell. In her recollections, she called it the Witch Farm, the Witch Homestead Farm, and the Old Homestead Farm. She also mentioned The Homestead, the independent ruins of a once prosperous farm later shunned as haunted.

Lowell included King's narrative in a letter composed in 1854 and published decades later. He mentions the farmhouse "which everyone gets a glimpse of—but no man hath seen twice" and muses, "I think it is the farm of one of the old Salem warlocks." Years later, in 1904, a story (penned by one A. J. R.) circulated in newspapers throughout the country that Lowell had *visited* the Witch Farm, now located on the edge of a forest outside New York City. By that time, it was well established that the farm could be seen only one time by each mortal that cast eyes upon it.

If Lowell hinted at a poetic connection between Witch Woods and the Salem witches, legends became stronger in the decades leading up to the bicentennial of the trials. In 1887 a contentious attempt arose for Beverly Farms (the wealthier portion of the town) to separate from Beverly proper. Legislation was hotly debated at the state house in January 1888. One of the proponents against the division was George Robinson, who had served as governor until only two weeks prior and who became best known as the attorney for Lizzie Borden.

In testimony favoring separation, Augustus Loring pointed out the defined area of the proposed new town and included Witch Woods. He conjectured on the record that it was so named because it provided a hiding place for the accused in Salem. Robinson took the opportunity for a joke about the witches still living in Beverly Farm. The official transcript records peals of laughter by congressmen in response.

A visitor's guide to Salem published in 1895 playfully cited Lowell's warlock. By 1903 an essay in the *Boston Herald* had no compunction asserting that both the woods and the lane were named as a refuge for the accused in 1692. The *Herald* also reported that George Burroughs, one of the executed, passed through before his execution, having been granted permission to say farewell to his family in Gloucester. The "witches"—described as genuine beings—assisted Burroughs in his travels, allowing the speedy journey of a single day. The legend of the farmhouse had been incorporated as well. "There is now to be seen," the article concludes, "at the right season of the year, at sunset, the witch village, which is in a swamp in the woods."

An even more extraordinary claim appeared in 1911. At that time Beverly was a favored vacation site for President William Howard Taft. Hailed in newspapers throughout the United States as the "Summer Capital of the Nation," Beverly's legends became widespread gossip. One nationally distributed story declared that tourists could "hike through the Witch Woods, which the Puritan fathers believed to be infested with blood-thirsty lions."

Blood-thirsty lions?

Porter Sargent's beloved *Handbook of New England* helps shed light on that odd claim. Therein he mentions that early settlers considered a sizeable part of the region bewitched. Sargent cites a passage from William Wood's *New England's Prospect*, a work from 1634. It documents a purported lion in Cape Ann that some thought they heard roar when lost in the woods, the other option being the Devil. Witch Woods was just close enough to fall under that captivating reference.

Lions faded over the twentieth century, but warlocks remained in the lore of Witch Woods. In 1970 a guidebook reported as fact that the woods were a hiding spot in 1692. George Burroughs had been replaced, however, by Giles Corey, the victim of the trials who suffered the indignity of being pressed to death under stones. The change may have been instigated by Corey's general development as a folk hero and specifically his appearance in Arthur Miller's *The Crucible*. And surely storytelling by the students of Endicott College—founded in 1939—nourished these legends. The campus now incorporates Witch Lane and its hiking trails, overtly identifying the area as an "escape route" for the accused.

Legend Tripping

Although Highland Park has no direct connection to the trials and is not adjacent to the attractions within the city, its isolation is precisely what makes the Salem Woods Nature Trail a peaceful and contemplative hike. The 2.3-mile lollipop begins at the free parking lot off Wilson Street. The city of Salem oversees the park and maintains a pamphlet and map at https://www.salem.com/sites/g/files/vyhlif3756/f/uploads/trail.pdf. **Trailhead GPS: N42 30.16 / W70 54.28**

Hikers should ascend Po (Powow) Hill in Amesbury to prove that there is nothing evil afoot. The town of Amesbury (https://www.amesbury ma.gov/home/pages/powow-conservation-area) oversees the site, which includes Batchelder Park at the summit, but some of the most active promotion and conservation improvements are currently being done by the Lake Gardner Improvement Association (http://www.lgia.org/). Both websites post a map; the association's website has additional information on the conservancy. There are several free parking sites to access Po Hill, but the easiest is at Lake Gardner Beach. **Trailhead GPS: N42 51.35 / W70 56.14**

For hikes in Marblehead see the chapter on the Screeching Lady.

The "Witch Caves" in Ashland Town Forest / Cowassock Woods are readily accessible, almost to a fault. They are essentially in the backyard of a few homes on a residential street. The entire woods are, however, well worth exploring and add up to 6 miles of trails. Start at the small free parking lot on Salem End Road. To reach the caves, follow the Red Trail to the Yellow Trail toward the water tower. There are several maps available online from the town and related organizations, but the most clear, concise, and useful is found at the Sudbury Valley Trustees at https://www

.svtweb.org/sites/default/files/Cowassock.pdf. **Trailhead GPS: N42 17.09 / W71 28.17**

The Beverly Commons Conservation Area (https://ecga.org/Property/Beverly-Commons-Conservation-Area) maintains a map of the land associated with Witches' Woods. There is free parking at Greenwood Avenue. **Trailhead GPS: N42 34.07 / W70 49.18** However, Witch Lane is now on the property of Endicott College (as is Caroline Howard King's mansion). The college maintains a series of hiking trails to the north of campus; a pamphlet is available online as of this writing. The trail that ascends Snake Hill near the Sally Milligan Nature Reserve was close to the historical area known as the Haunted Wood in King's journals. **Trailhead GPS: N42 33.43 / W70 51.13**

4

The Witch of Half Way Pond

ELIZABETH WAS AN unorthodox child. Born on Crooked Pond to a father who preferred the solitude of the forest to the chattering company of Barnstable and Yarmouth, she grew up unafraid of the animals and of the darkness. At a young age she charmed a man from England. He built them a house out in the woods that haunted Half Way Pond. There he died under the canopy of branches, leaving his widowed wife mistress of the weald.

Whispers followed Elizabeth, as they always had. Uncivil tongues branded her with a new name for the Devil's pleasure: Liza Towerhill. Tower Hill: the prison in London in whose borough her husband was born. And forever a reminder that she was something foreign to them all.

Her solitary house became a faraway place, a revel ring welcoming all manner of strange things: pigs with the head of cattle, fowl with the head of pigs, cloven-foot rabbits with horns for ears, demonic denizens with their shaggy goat legs, and wolves with women's faces. They came to dance with her in the blue reeds and howl and growl in jubilant chorus with each note of her bewitching song.

Liza Towerhill pranced bare-breasted atop the pond as if it were a pane of glass. She bathed in the aura of moon-white flame. And underneath her feet, all manner of fish and frog and worm and leech circled in rhythm, glowing incandescent, assuming weird shapes with each tattoo of her tapping feet. The trees, too, turned luminous, alight with burning foxfire. And the breathing swamp invited will-o'-the-wisps to come and follow the beat.

No animal could resist her alluring call. She once charmed Mrs. Loring's horse. The poor beast circled the pond in endless rotation with its hapless rider helpless to control the reigns.

Poor Solomon Otis learned the hard way never to tempt a witch. He once bargained to purchase a calf from wily Liza Towerhill, but days later she found someone willing to pay half a crown more. "You will be sorry," she told him, "if you do not pay me the other half crown."

"I am not easily frightened," Otis retorted. A man of more wisdom would have been.

On the day he took the calf into his possession, possession took control of the calf. Their journey home became one of terror. Spectral cattle appeared in the surrounding woods, everywhere, at once, beckoning their cousin to join their ranks. The living calf obliged. Otis watched empty-handed as the herd ran off bellowing and lowing deep into the haunted woods.

Humans, too, were not immune to Towerhill's stygian spells. Joseph Cobb's daughters were found one day bewitched in their room, moving through space without touching the planks of the wooden floor. And sorrowful, anguished Ansel Wood—the man turned nightly into a steed by her whetted wizardry, saddled and ridden to Clam Pudding Pond, where the witches of Plymouth gathered for orgiastic revelry.

The genius of Towerhill's anger was truly transformative. She once attended a party to which she had not been invited in the guise of a baleful black cat. Only a single man, a seventh son of a seventh son, could see through her disguise, and he wisely kept silent for the sake of the ruse. The guests, however, found little in the way of gustatory delights: The butter soured, the tea was bitter, and doughnuts and pies were found stuffed full with a surprise of black sheep's wool.

It was in the shape of a black cat that Liza Towerhill chased Benjamin Goodspeed out to sea. With Ansel Wood spent she took on a new steed, and Goodspeed, soon exhausted, fled to escape her sorcery. But all day, each day, that black cat swam in the wake of the swift ship, eager to take possession of Goodspeed until dawn. Madness would have claimed his soul had a fellow passenger not provided a cure, which the spellbound victim followed with unsparing precision.

Goodspeed loaded his nervous gun with wads torn from his Holy Bible. He shot the cat straight on. White foam churned red with blood. It disappeared into the sea. And miles away, sitting at her spinning loom, Liza Towerhill collapsed, dead, and forever committed her ghost to dance in the swamp and woods surrounding celebrated Half Way Pond.

Careful readers will notice that I did not provide the surname of the purported witch in the tale above. Writing this book is a strange gig. As someone invested in the folklore of Massachusetts, I have no hesitation sharing tales of fantastical characters. But as a professional folklorist who understands the power of storytelling, I am reticent to perpetuate folk narratives that treat actual people as monstrous beings. Such is the case of the "Witch" of Half Way Pond.

There is no doubt that Liza Towerhill the folk character is the genuine article. She is *the* witch of Cape Cod folklore in that her stories were circulated by hundreds if not thousands of people across generations and over a considerable period of time. She is the model for other witch stories on the Cape, one of whom—Goody Hallett—is rapidly replacing her. Denying or ignoring that influence would be an infringement against the historical folklore of the Commonwealth.

But there is a real woman behind the legends who, if accounts are accurate, was greatly pained by those stories and by the implication that she was a witch. It is a balancing act to work through this material. And it is my hope that we divorce the character of Liza Towerhill from the woman who suffered by being associated with her. If we cannot make that distinction as storytellers and audiences, perhaps it is time to let these tales disappear.

The woman upon whom Liza Towerhill is based is Elizabeth Lewis. She was born in Barnstable in 1712 to Benjamin Lewis and Margaret Folland, although it seems that genealogists in the nineteenth century mistook the wrong mother as Hannah Hinckley. Lewis did marry young—age sixteen—a William Blachford, who "by tradition" was an English immigrant from the neighborhood near the Tower of London. They lived at Half Way Pond, a distance from the settled towns. Elizabeth belonged to the Barnstable church and was regarded as a pious woman. She died in 1790.

How is it possible that a respectable woman became the inspiration for a witch?

As is often the case, people talked. And one such person who talked—and recorded scandalous stories of others who did as well—was Amos Otis, a local historian. In 1888 he published a genealogical study of Barnstable families that included several references to the purported witch. But his first foray into the lore of Liza Towerhill came in 1860 when Otis published a lengthy article in the *Barnstable Patriot*. Therein he recalled the tales of Solomon Otis and the spectral cattle, the Cobb daughters, the visitation of Towerhill to a party in the form of a black cat, and Ansel Wood's accusation of her witch-riding him.

But for passing comment about her feline transformation, only the tale of Ansel Wood made it into the 1888 genealogy. In that latter version Otis changed the name of the original location of the witches' orgies from Clam Pudding Pond—a site still found in Plymouth—for the fictitious Plum Pudding Pond. It is safe to assume such alteration was deliberate, an attempt to rectify past transgressions and perhaps to mask real places with a veneer of the chimerical. Indeed, by 1888 Otis was motivated to decry those who believed in tales about witchcraft. Among those he criticized was Ansel Wood, whom Otis deplored as a monomaniac—a nineteenth century term meaning someone exhibiting pathological obsession—for believing his own story of being witch-ridden.

In the 1888 account, Otis ponders the cultural influences that could lead people to scapegoat a devoted woman such as Elizabeth Lewis. He offers several proposals. First, her father's house was in a forest near animals and Indians, both feared by those who lived in the relative safety of the towns. Second, she and her husband followed that pattern of dwelling in the woods with its attendant dangers; and since no harm came to her, Otis theorized, people suspected an unseen force at hand. Third, she was a young woman, merely a teenager, when she set out for a life of demanding labor.

Otis did not acknowledge a fourth possibility, but his genealogy left hints for the perceptive. He mentions that Elizabeth Lewis married William Blachford in November 1728. Their first child, a son, was born in May 1729, merely six months after the union. She was likely pregnant when she married. And if another story is to be believed, her youngest son was an injured deserter during the American Revolution. If that is true, it is not difficult to imagine that the family was shamed through maligned storytelling and that the mother was tarnished for her son's transgressions.

One final element bears notice. Lewis was an independent woman— her husband died around 1855 and left her with several children under age—of compromised socioeconomic means. Otis mentions, for example, that one of her granddaughters married a poor man who died in an almshouse. Too often in the history of colonial New England, women of lower status without husbands were easy targets to be accused of witchcraft or romanticized in folk narratives in league with the Evil One.

Otis was not an uncharitable historian. In his 1860 essay he addressed the ways in which "the reputation she had of being a witch was the cause of much grief and mortification to her and her family." Lewis's children, he added, considered her "persecuted and slandered" and resented the tales. Otis even provided an example in which he accidentally referenced those stories and vexed her grandson Uriah to such a degree that he refused to speak to the historian for two years.

Perhaps as an implicit apology, Otis attempted to chart the folly of the tales he recorded. He proposed that the Cobb sisters suffered from St. Vitus's dance—that is, Sydenham's chorea, a neurological disorder characterized by rapid spasms—and further indicated that the beams in their room were rough-hewn, allowing the girls to grab hold and move about frantically during their fits. He dismissed Ansel Wood's claims by explaining that skeptics asked him to mark the tree where he was tied during a nightly ride. Wood did so and awoke the next day to find the carving in his own bed, suggesting to the modern reader that his fantasies were the result of parasomnia.

And as for Solomon Otis? Amos Otis remarked that Solomon was both a member of the same church as Lewis and a magistrate bound to certain duties of reporting. If there were any truth to the story of the spectral cattle, the historian contended, Solomon Otis would be obliged by the conventions of his day to redress them. That he did not take legal or other action suggests that no such nefarious event took place. And even in the tale, Solomon Otis was solaced by the "thought that he should be able to tell as good a witch story as any of his neighbors."

These hesitations and clarifications demonstrate faithful efforts on the part of Otis to set the record straight. And yet even he gave into the temptation to pass along a cracking tale. In his 1888 genealogy, in a brief footnote Otis recorded that Lydia Ellis, the daughter of "Lizzy Towerhill," was a servant to the illustrious Allyn family.

Towerhill—again called a "reputed witch"—took offense at the mistreatment of her daughter and threatened vengeance. Days later, a black cat appeared at the house, acting strangely and mewing and caterwauling incessantly. Unseen hands turned over "everything in the house"—six fine chairs were utterly smashed—and odd noises continued unabated to keep the family awake at night.

Tales of Liza Towerhill may have slipped into obscurity once local tongues went to their grave, but the preeminent Harvard folklorist George Lyman Kittredge inadvertently added fuel for their continuation. In an article on witchcraft in England first published in 1917, Kittredge marveled at a coincidence of two witch tales on each side of the Atlantic involving the name Blatchford. The American tale was that of Mrs.

Loring's bewitched horse, passed on to him in the late 1880s by an elderly woman who had heard it in her youth directly from Mrs. Loring. In Kittredge's account, however, the witch was solely identified as "Lizzie Blatchford."

Elizabeth Reynard took the tale to new heights in her 1934 *The Narrow Land*. Reynard wove together numerous threads, including Otis's genealogy (she apparently did not have his 1860 article) and Kittredge's work. In her narrative Reynard included the weird animals and eldritch horrors attending to Towerhill while she danced bare-breasted on Half Way Pond—no doubt a salacious description for its time—and cited as her source for that material the unpublished manuscripts of Michael Fitzgerald, whose role in another Cape Cod story, that of Goody Hallett, proved pivotal.

The tale of Benjamin Goodspeed and Towerhill's death was a contribution, Reynard explained, from Mrs. Sylvanus Alexander Hinckley of Hyannis (presumably Ora Adams Hinckley, who died in 1943), but she also recommended an essay published in the *Hyannis Patriot* in 1933.

That essay was composed by Abbie Bodfish, then a teenager. Bodfish heard it from her grandfather, who had heard it from Prissy Bannister, an African American servant of his family, when he was a boy in the 1800s. It is a short essay, notable for its clear exposition of the tale of Ben Goodspeed and the fact that the witch is only referred to as "Tower Hill." Bodfish relayed one other element that has been absent from subsequent stories, namely that Tower Hill's witchery was discovered when "meat put on to cook was mysteriously displaced by sticks and stones," presumably by her sorcerous intervention.

This tale does not end, however, with Liza Towerhill. Half Way Pond was renamed Mary Dunn Pond, and the woman by that name also became subject to witchcraft tales. Over the following century storytellers conflated them.

A remarkable story, "Tale of the Two," was published in the *Yarmouth Register* on October 7, 1896, penned by the paper's editor, Charles Warner Swift. It is difficult to determine if this literary work reflects any substantial folklore concerning Dunn circulating at the time, but the *Barnstable Patriot* praised Swift for incorporating incidents in the lives of "two of Barnstable's most eccentric characters of ye olden times—two Cape Cod celebrities," Mary Dunn and "Estwick," a hermit who lived between Barnstable and Yarmouth.

Smith's tale is high melodrama. It is broken into two parts, the first of which introduces the characters of Estwick and Mary Dunn. Dunn is a fortune-teller living in a hut at the pond that now bears her name. She came to the Cape after being exiled from a Swedish vessel that feared her witchcraft would sink the ship.

Mary Dunn would reveal nothing about herself—"All is mystery" was her reply to any inquiry about her past—but she had companions, especially a dog named Devil, whose wail could frighten the town. Dunn became "a weird and unaccountable being," eking out a living far in the woods. She could call its denizens with a whistle, summoning deer, foxes, rabbits, snakes, and fishes in a bewitching manner akin to Liza Towerhill. Serpents would entwine Dunn's neck and ankles.

Throughout the story Dunn is referred to as "the Indian," but her ancestry turns out to be far more unusual. She is a descendant of a group who arrived before the Indigenous people, when the Cape was still besieged by mythic conflict. One of them, Norod by name, fought "grizzly monsters" on his unicorn—you read that correctly—for weeks on end. Muddy Pond in Yarmouth is the remnant of a lake of blood of the slain. The boulder nearby—so-called Indian Rock—had the imprint of his foot and the hoof of his steed.

Exhausted at the horror of battle, Norod found release when he sunk deep into the earth and entered a protective chamber. The gates to that netherworld would open only for Mary Dunn, and so daily she visited Indian Rock to attend to oracles there. She was warned by her ancestors against revealing their secrets, but as the story progresses, she allows Estwick to enter the prophetic chamber that lies one hundred feet under Mary Dunn Pond. Soon thereafter a demonic being sets fire to her hut and she perishes in the flames.

Residents would have caught the reference. The real Mary Dunn died in 1850 in a house fire. She was born Mary Boston in Yarmouth in 1778 to an African American father and a Native American mother. In 1807 she married Thomas Dunn, an African American man. They occupied a small dwelling, perhaps by squatting, and cared for indigent people of color. Thomas died at sea in the 1830s, and Mary was listed on the pauper rolls in the following decade. Later writers would mistakenly contend that Mary Dunn was an escaped slave from the South who won her freedom through the Underground Railroad.

Dunn fits the pattern of women who are readily represented as witches in the folklore of Massachusetts. In addition, Dunn was a brewer of "yarb beer"—that is, herbal ale, almost certainly alcoholic. And this yarb beer played a role in a tragedy in 1846 when one Henry Chase went missing after seeking her hut. She was arrested on suspicion of his murder, but when his body was found in a shallow pond, she was charged with being an accessory and eventually acquitted. Chase had visited Dunn, imbibed an intoxicating beverage, and drowned when he fell into the water. The sorcery at Half Way Pond may have been found in a bottle.

Legend Tripping

The closest hike to Mary Dunn Pond is an area called the Hyannis Ponds Wildlife Management Area in Barnstable, under the jurisdiction of the Massachusetts Division of Fisheries and Wildlife. This area comprises several hundred acres and forms a rough triangle between Mary Dunn, Israel, and Lamson Ponds. It is just north of the municipal airport. Be aware that this area is not currently being developed for hiking trails. It is used more often for mountain biking, and the various trail names that appear online such as The Back Nine derive from the Cape Cod Chapter of NEMBA (https://www.nemba.org/chapters/ccnemba), which can provide a wealth of information. Wandering through the management area certainly would give a sense of the wilderness associated with Liza Towerhill, but it is best to have a local guide. There is no dedicated parking, but there are some lots and turnoffs on Mary Dunn Road. Visitors should be wary of private property. **Trailhead GPS: N41 40.59 / W70 16.50**

An excellent alternative is to utilize the trails maintained by the Barnstable Land Trust (https://www.blt.org/). Although several hikes are a distance from Mary Dunn Pond, the developing Cape Cod Pathways (a cooperative venture with the town) offers a meandering series of marked trails that provide a sense of walking back into time and leaving organized towns behind. Information and maps are available at the land trust website.

Over the border in Yarmouth there are a few well-traversed hikes near Muddy Pond. The best established is the Nature Trail at the Historical Society of Old Yarmouth in Yarmouth Port (https://www.hsoy.org/), which has information and maps. There is a donation for parking. The hike encompasses 1 mile (solely on the White Trail) to 1.75 miles for those who circle Millers Pond. **Trailhead GPS: N41 42.18 / W70 14.34**

The Dennis Pond Conservation Area also offers a 1-mile hike between Summer and Willow Streets. This is a popular seasonal residential recreational area overseen by the town, which has information and a pamphlet at https://www.yarmouth.ma.us/681/Dennis-Pond. **Trailhead GPS: N41 41.31 / W70 15.21**

5

The "Witches" of Dogtown

I T WAS SPRINGTIME 1745. Exhausted by French attacks upon the British colonies in the Gulf of Maine, William Pepperell organized a military expedition against the proud Fortress at Louisburg perched on Île-Royale. Colonial soldiers from all over Cape Ann volunteered to join the assault. They had suffered enough insult to the British Crown and to their local fishing economy.

On the way to the boats that would carry them far away to Nova Scotia, a few heated young men of Gloucester failed to heed a warning. They stopped at the home of Peg Wesson and insulted the woman rumored to be a witch. She did not take kindly to the insult. She promised swift revenge. The young men laughed at her expense all the way to the docks, wondering how she would have her vengeful way so far across the waves.

The assault upon the fortress was no heroic adventure for the young men. Anything that could misfire or go awry did so for them day after day. After a week of disappointment and extremely close calls, they began to think there might be some truth in Old Peg Wesson's curse. And then there was the crow, the voraciously vocal bird that hovered interminably above them, cawing loudly to distract their aim and to call the enemy's fire. Rumors began to spread about the young men who brought an evil disadvantage to the siege.

It seemed that nothing could distract the single-minded crow. Bullets fired near did not frighten it away. And bullets fired at it always missed their mark.

Finally the young men took some good advice. Away from the prying eyes of the noisy bird, they removed the silver cuff links that adorned their uniforms and fashioned makeshift bullets. Those silver missiles did their violent trick and struck the taunting target. The first hit its leg and the second its heart. The bird, as if surprised by their ingenuity, gasped for a moment and then disappeared into the fog. It left no trophy for the young men to claim, but the cawing ceased and the campaign went on to bring success for the British king and Cape Ann fishermen.

A strange thing happened in Gloucester that day. Peg Wesson was walking down the streets seemingly minding her own affairs when she suddenly stumbled, broke her leg, and collapsed upon the ground. Alarmed citizens rushed to her aid and carried her to her home, but for reasons no one could quite explain, she expired before reaching the door. And stranger still, or so they thought, was the sight of two silver cuff links falling from her dying body, noisily reverberating on the cold ground.

Although Peg Wesson may not be the most sensational witch of Massachusetts folklore, she is one of the most consistent. Her story has been told for two centuries, and the sheer volume of retellings found in print indicates that storytellers and audiences enjoyed hearing of her fate.

Her name changes throughout the tales, so perhaps we might start there: Meg or Peg or Peggy? On the one hand it matters little; they are all nicknames for Margaret, and they all appear with some regularity. On the other hand, it is worth considering that one of the earliest written accounts, Charles Upham's lectures on witchcraft from 1831, identifies the reputed witch as "Old Meg." He does not identify his source and I have not yet been able to uncover it, but Upham was punctilious; it would be surprising if he made an editorial decision to give her that name.

I am being speculative, but if the earliest versions concerned "Old Meg," they might point to other Megs in popular culture at the time, especially Meg Merrilies, the gypsy and presumed witch of Walter Scott's

1815 novel *Guy Mannering*. Scott's novel was wildly successful on both sides of the Atlantic and widely advertised and praised in New England newspapers. Scott's choice for her name was no accident either, for there are numerous other Megs who are witches in the folklore of the British Isles.

I am not arguing that Meg Wesson was a British import. But I pause on account of the role her character plays as an opponent to the Gloucester soldiers who participated in the siege of Louisburg, a French fort on Cape Breton, during King George's War. Her tale became popular after the American Revolution and the War of 1812, yet is set in a time when the New England colonies were loyal subjects to England in every sense of the word. It is also a rarity among witch stories in New England in that it entails international relations rather than the local community. Why would Americans take such interest in a tale about a woman who refused to rally around the British cause?

By today's standards it is difficult to admire the soldiers who incur Peg Wesson's wrath. They are young, impetuous men. They provoke a tempestuous elderly woman and then kill her. Her death is justified in the narrative because of her existence as a witch, but storytellers also reviled her lack of support for the British cause—a deficiency that numerous examples make clear threatened military victory at the siege.

In 1869, for example, an author identified only as W. E. S. passed along a local variant that included a scene of the crow pausing over British heavy artillery at Louisburg. After the bird touched each gun, matches would extinguish inexplicably, powder would flash in the pan, or some other strange occurrence prohibited their firing properly. W. E. S. remarked that although a weird tale, it was believed by many well into the 1800s. It's curious, this one.

Regardless of its potential origin, early tales of Peg Wesson did show the variety one would expect for a vibrant story in the oral tradition. Some mention both her wounded leg and her death, some only her wounded leg, and some only her death. The names of the soldiers change. They are usually left unnamed, but an 1842 essay in the *Boston Transcript* transmits that it was solely John Hardy who uncovered the witch's ruse and dispatched her. In a literary adaptation by Ednah Dow Littlehale Cheney, the team consists of Job and David Stanwood assisted by James Parson, the minister's son. In Sarah Daley's interpretation—one that traveled in newspapers throughout the nation in 1892—they are Martin Sanders, Tom Goodwin, and Job Ayres.

Various reasons arise for the soldiers visiting Peg in the first place. The tale recorded by Upham opens in Louisburg, avoiding the instigating conflict altogether. When the setting in Gloucester appeared in the late 1850s, the reason for her indignation was ambiguous. Later storytellers felt compelled to describe it, so they suggested intoxication on behalf of the young men; a desire to tease or taunt a suspected witch; or inspiration by a pastor's sermon. In Daley's narrative the three men visit to have their fortunes read, but they deceive Peg with lead coins and accordingly enlist her ire.

Peg Wesson was incorporated into other tales. That same article in the *Boston Transcript*, for example, mentions that she was an "ugly old woman" who rode a broomstick at night, bewitched cows, and played similar tricks. In a history of Essex from 1868, Robert Crowell and David Choate readily embraced "Peggy Wesson" as a folk character and invited her into their town. They invoke yarns from Hog—now Choate—Island in which horses were found in the morning with their manes tied in witch knots (that is, tangles), a sure sign Wesson or a friend borrowed the steed overnight to ride instead of a broomstick.

Another travel writer's essay in 1869 added more flavor. This writer, N. G., had as a guide an "old gentleman" from Gloucester who spun stories of witches. Peg Wesson appears as a demanding figure. In one anecdote, a man drives a load of wood past her house. She demands that he surrender the wood. He declines, having labored hard to procure it. The cart then breaks, releasing the logs upon the ground. It breaks again and again each time that he reloads it until at last, exasperated, he abandons the wood at the doorstep of the grinning witch.

That folktale was popular throughout New England and attributed to many witches in the region. Other common motifs were associated with her as well, such as the ruining of butter in a churn. In Cheney's more fanciful literary rendition, Peg Wesson ill effects the butter until a quick-thinking woman touches it with a hot iron, scalding the witch in the process. Wesson later enacts malevolence upon the soldiers: Canteens empty inexplicably; dreadful dreams plague their sleep and cramped bones the hours they are awake. In brief, the panoply of motifs associated with witches becomes ascribed to Wesson over time.

One of the most consequential additions to Wesson's story was her eventual association with Dogtown. The area now known by that name began as the Common Settlement in the late 1600s, inland from Gloucester. Originally supplying wood to the town, it became a site for settlement after deforestation. Numerous reports suggest that families moved there from Gloucester or Annisquam to seek shelter from marauding ships, sometimes depicted as pirates and sometimes as the British.

Those settlements, akin to much of Gloucester, produced men who fought for the American side during the Revolution and the War of 1812. Many also were involved in fishing, the mainstay of the Gloucester economy. As a result of these dangerous activities, too often husbands did not return home, leaving the settlement—at least according to its folkloric origins—the abode of widows and the "yelping curs" that protected their homes, hence the name Dogtown.

The reality is more complicated, of course. Newspapers and related accounts bear witness that by the early 1800s "Dogtown" was a disparaging term, an insult to the majority of residents who were composed of the impoverished, squatters, or people of other compromised means who spent their final days in the almshouse of Gloucester. They were also often widowed or elderly women, African Americans, or people of mixed race. The area was essentially abandoned by 1830, and the houses were in ruin by mid-century. Dogtown was not solely named, in other words, because of its canines; its nomenclature reflects some of the worst impulses of humans to treat others as beneath them.

It should come as no surprise that such a place would readily be conceptualized as the abode of witches. Although many writers assured readers that Peg Wesson's house stood in Gloucester proper and local historian Charles Edward Mann emphatically denied any connection between her and Dogtown, the gravitational pull was simply too strong for storytellers. The account by N. G. links them, for example, and implies that the local guide did as well.

Daley's narrative shifted Wesson's home from a main street in Gloucester to a "wretched cottage" on the outskirts of town—as close to a description of Dogtown as possible without overtly saying so. Later in her story, when the crow is shot in Louisburg, Wesson is discovered in the woods, a stark alteration from earlier narratives that depict her collapsing in town. By 1898 travel writers for the *Boston Herald* were compelled to observe that Wesson lived "near Dogtown, where all later witches and wizards lived." Protests continued against this shift, but in vain.

One complicating factor was the identification of others as the "witches" of Dogtown Common. Unlike Peg Wesson, these were actual women—again, many of them impoverished or outspoken widows—whose reputations were tarnished, increasingly so after they died. Two of them, Tammy Younger and Judy Rhines, have since become infamous regulars, but the names on the list did shift. In 1869, Tammy was identified as the "chief of the witches," a group that included Judy Rhines, Liz Tucker, Bekky Rich, Hetty Rich, and Lyd Muzzy. In the first decades of the twentieth century, Tammy had been elevated to "Queen of the Witches," a number including her aunt Luce George, Judy Rhines, Molly Stevens, and Molly Jacobs.

What made them witches? It is difficult to pin down. Unlike Peg Wesson, their surviving stories are minimal.

In the case of Tammy Younger, the most developed tale imagines her magic bedeviling a young man to surrender a load of pumpkins in the same manner as Wesson seized a load of wood. But that relative lack of stories did not stop later ruminations, such as one appearing in the *Boston Globe* in 1931 which described Younger as a "fearsome hag" who would curse anyone passing her house on the busy road between Gloucester and Annisquam that did not pay her tribute. Mann recorded in his history an anecdote in which the family of a coffin maker refused to keep her casket in their house—a normal practice in the early 1800s—for fear of witchcraft, but no remarkable tale of diabolism accompanies their concerns.

Mann himself wondered if audiences had misapplied the witch label to Tammy Younger. I concur. It appears that the most consistent accusation against her was, as Mann descibed it, "vocal pyrotechnics." A more generous description said she was full of "keen and shrewish wit." Still others explained that no one ever refused to give her what she requested lest they suffer the "vile epithets" or invective she would hurl in denial. She was not a witch in the sense of a sorceress, then, but in the sense of a virago with a venomous tongue.

A tale is told, for example, of Tammy having two long teeth in her upper jaw. She summoned Captain Stanwood to act as a dentist and remove them. But he, "being a joker" as Mann relates, only pulled them partway down so they rested on her upper lip. Stanwood then informed Younger that he could do no more. "The pen refuses to record the torrent of picturesque language," Mann concludes, "which history alleges was poured upon 'Johnny Morgan's' luckless head." Following her outburst, the teeth were hastily removed.

In Mann's estimation, Tammy's aunt Luce George was more deserving of the title insofar as she was believed to have the power to bewitch oxen or topple over carts of wood or perform similar acts of malice. And as for Judy Rhimes, her claim to the weird sisterhood was that people indulged in saying so. The guide who led W. E. S. in 1869, for example, told an anecdote in which he, as a boy, alongside another youthful accomplice, stole a goose from Rhimes, observing the rule that a witch's property could be seized by anyone. When a furious Rhimes—still in her nightdress and armed with a hoe—caught up to the thieves, she yelled, "Now, ye hell-birds! Now I've got ye!"

"No you hain't," retorted one of the boys and struck her so hard in the face with the goose that she fell prostrate on the ground. The boys escaped her clutches and celebrated with a feast the next night.

That is, essentially, the same tale as Peg Wesson. It is a problematic one. An old woman has violence done to her because she is an old woman who will not keep quiet when young men wish to harass her. Treating them as witches removes any ethical responsibility to treat them with respect.

Once enough time had passed, all of the "witches" of Dogtown (and Peg Wesson) were available for literary reinterpretation. The poet Percy MacKaye's widely praised 1921 poem *Dogtown Common*, for example, imagines Judy Rhimes, a witch, falling in love with the local minister. Tammy Younger appears as her aunt. In 1934 Richard Hill Wilkinson published a short story about "Old Shag" Jacobs, borrowing the last name of a Dogtown resident but retelling Peg Wesson's story in detail.

Similarly, travel writers and guidebooks throughout the twentieth century were spellbound by a longing to tempt readers with lurid tales of the witches of Dogtown. These raconteurs routinely invented images for those purposes. A very influential essay by Charles Rosebault, first published in the *New York Times* in 1921, for example, added that all the witches of Dogtown were distinguished by peculiar laughter, "from a penetrating falsetto cackle to a raucous crow-like guffaw." Tammy Younger's cachinnations were akin to the crow, allowing, of course, an implied merger with Peg Wesson's story.

It remains to be seen how their reputations will fair among the raconteurs of the twenty-first century.

Legend Tripping

A hike in Dogtown is not to be missed, but it is imperative to prepare ahead of time. It is very easy to become lost, and it is inadvisable to hike without a map. Dogtown is overseen by the city of Gloucester (https://gloucester-ma.gov/960/Dogtown), but as of this writing there are no maps available online. Maps are available at the Gloucester Office of Tourism. The Essex Heritage National Area website also has excellent information concerning directions, parking, and a brief overview: https://essexheritage.org/attractions/dogtown-dogtown-common-or-dogtown-village.

There is a small free parking lot on Dogtown Road off Cherry Street. There are 3,600 acres in Dogtown and miles of trails. A popular loop around the area easily traverses 8 miles. Many hikers explore the Babson Boulders, stones upon which messages were carved at the direction of Roger Babson, or the cellar holes of the former inhabitants. Maps of various details are posted at individual websites, and local guides are available. The best way to begin is to consult the Friends of Dogtown (https://friendsofdogtown.info/), which has very helpful apps to download along with other interesting information. Be aware of and stay off the MBNA tracks. **Trailhead GPS: N42 38.02 / W70 39.59**

As of this writing the Babson Historical Society (https://babsonassoc.org/resources/) has links to some information and a map of the Babson Boulders. Dogtown lies just to the north of the Babson Museum.

Choate Island is accessible, although only by watercraft. It is part of the Crane Wildlife Refuge on the Crane Estate overseen by the Trustees of Reservations (https://thetrustees.org/place/crane-wildlife-refuge-on-the-crane-estate/), which has a map.

6

The "Witches" of Hadley and Westborough

THIS CHAPTER INTRODUCES two "witches," one celebrated and one unsung. "Witches" is in quotes because they were real women, one accused of witchcraft prior to the Salem Trials and one treated appallingly more than a century later. Neither became full-fledged folk characters, but ample lore surrounds both.

The celebrated "witch" is Mary Webster, the so-called Witch of Hadley. The lamentable story of her accusation and hanging—which she survived—appears in only a few historical documents, the most influential being Sylvester Judd's 1863 history of Hadley. Judd includes the following narrative—not a story per se, but a collection of anecdotes:

The most notable witch in Hampshire County was Mary Webster, the wife of William Webster of Hadley. Her maiden name was Mary Reeve, and they were married in 1670, when he was 53 years old, and she probably some years younger. They became poor, and lived many years in a small house in the middle highway into the meadow, and were sometimes aided by the town. Mary Webster's temper, which was not the most placid, was not improved by poverty and neglect, and she used harsh words when offended. Despised and sometimes ill-treated, she was soured with the world, and rendered spiteful towards some of her neighbors. When they began to call her a witch and to abuse her, she perhaps thought with the "Witch of Edmonton," in the old play, who said, "'Tis all one, to be a witch as to be accounted one." Many stories of the sorceries by which she disturbed the people of Hadley have been lost, but a few traditions have been preserved.

Teams passing to and from the meadow went by her door, and she so bewitched some cattle and horses that they stopped, and ran back, and could not be driven by her house. In such cases, the teamsters used to go into the house and whip or threaten to whip her, and she would then let the teams pass. She once turned over a load of hay near her house, and the driver went in and was about to chastise her, when she turned the load back again. She entered a house, and had such influence upon an infant on the bed or in the cradle, that it was raised to the chamber floor and fell back again, three times, and no visible hand touched it. There is a story that at another house, a hen came down chimney and got scalded in a pot, and it was soon found that Mary Webster was suffering from a scald.

That is essentially the surviving lore of Mary Webster: four incidents, several of which are localized versions of motifs associated with other witches in the 1800s, including the injured familiar, the stuck oxen, and the overturning of a cart. Webster's temper and willingness for profanity falls right in line with other "witches" who populate this book, as does the common circumstance of poverty. Later rumors imagined Webster flying in the air, sometimes on a broomstick, and predicting a flood of the Connecticut River.

If this folklore is unremarkable, Mary Webster is unique in her trial and punishment. Webster was accused of witchcraft in 1683. She was arraigned in Springfield before several judges, including Philip Smith and Peter Tilton of Hadley, and sent to Boston for trial. She was indicted for "not having the fear of God before her eyes, and being instigated by the devil, hath entered into a covenant and had familiarity with him in the shape of a warraneage, and had his imps sucking her, and teats or marks found on her." ("Warraneage" is an Indian word for a fisher, the "black cat" of the woods.)

Unlike Judd's passage above, which is clearly folkloric tales, this is actual court testimony. Webster pleaded not guilty and was acquitted—a remarkable decision considering how matters were stacked against her—and after paying court fees, she returned to Hadley.

In the winter of 1684 Philip Smith fell ill. His sickness led to delirium and an agonizing death. Cotton Mather, the Puritan minister, wrote about Smith's demise as an example of a pious man "murdered with a hideous witchcraft" by a "wretched woman." In Mather's account Smith cried out for divine mercy and uttered suspicions that he had been bewitched. Smith warned his brother that he would appear dead but not actually be so, and admonished his sibling that he too would see strange things—"There shall be a wonder in Hadley!"

Smith apparently identified Webster as his tormentor—much like the spectral evidence used at Salem—which instigated several young men to "give disturbance" to the woman responsible for his calamities. Those youth discovered, Mather continues, that when they were "disturbing" Webster, Smith was able to convalesce—the belief being that she could not project her spirit to antagonize the beloved citizen while her physical form was threatened.

But the attacks upon Smith continued. Mather reports a host of horrors: audible scratchings on his bed while his hands and feet were still, apparitions of fire upon him, something unseen moving under the covers near his body, and his cot shaking violently with no agent to move it. When Smith perished, other signs of witchcraft manifested, including a swollen breast, bruises on his back, and holes drilled into his body as if by an awl. And yet his countenance did not assume the shape of the deceased—recall that he warned he would look dead but still be living—and his body remained warm for three days despite the New England winter. On the third day, a Monday, his face finally carried the look of one who had died, but fresh blood ran down his cheeks and witnesses claimed they heard chairs moving in the empty room the night before.

In some versions of Webster's story, she was seized by a mob after Smith's death in January 1685, but the historical record makes evident that in an attempt to relieve Smith of his pain, a mob broke into her house, dragged her from it, hanged her "until she was near dead," cut her down, rolled and buried her in snow, and abandoned her to the cold. Abruptly the same account remarked that she survived and "the melancholy man died." Mary Webster lived another eleven years, dying in 1696 and leaving behind only a few items, a Bible among them.

The accounts of Webster's trial and hanging are preserved in historical documents. But we are also privy to the source of the four folkloric anecdotes: Rebekah Crow Noble. Noble was born in 1712 and died in 1802. She was from the prosperous Crow family in Hadley, but eventually became impoverished and had to be cared for by the town. In partial return for public support, she became a renowned storyteller. Three important sources identify her as the main weaver of tales about Webster: Judd in 1863, F. D. Huntington in an 1859 address, and an 1868 fictionalized account, "Fishing at the Falls."

The Hadley community's embrace of Noble's anecdotes is even more poignant in light of a literary tale, "Mary Webster, the Witch," composed by Constance du Bois and published in *Demorest's Monthly Magazine* in 1884. In the twenty years that I have been a professor of folklore studies, I have never seen anything like it. It's a wild ride.

It is set in 1684, one year after Philip Smith has died and Mary Webster survived the attempted hanging. Mary Allyn is a young woman living in Hadley with her aunt and uncle Samuel Crowe—as in the family of Rebekah Crow Noble. Mary is the fiancée of Harry Evelyn, a dashing sailor with plans to bring her to Virginia. He is away from Hadley when the story commences and has sent his beloved a letter.

That letter was to be delivered by an Indian servant, Ula. It ends up, however, in the home of Mary Webster, presumably by some trick.

Webster demands that the young woman retrieve the letter from her home. The youth eventually relents and is forced to read the letter to Webster, who longs for entertainment. Webster promises to reciprocate the favor that Mary Allyn showed her.

Mary returns home to find her uncle and aunt with two visitors, Peter Tilton (one of the aforementioned judges) and his wife, Rachel. The topic turns to Webster.

Du Bois weaves each of the four anecdotes into the tale. Rachel Tilton, for example, claims to have scalded the wayward hen that plunged down her chimney, resulting in Webster's grievous injury. Aaron Crow, Mary's cousin, proudly brags how close he and his friends came to killing the witch when they hanged her, an act that Mary decries as barbarous.

The next scene imagines Mary visiting Rachel Tilton to deliver a letter sent by Harry to a guest at her house. That guest is none other than William Goffe, one of the regicides of King Charles I.

The regicides were real men, at least three of whom—Goffe, his father-in-law Edward Whalley, and John Dixwell—fled across the Atlantic when Charles II returned to the throne. Goffe and Whalley spent considerable time around New Haven before retreating to Hadley. (Forgive the promotion, but interested readers can find their tale and great hikes in the Connecticut *Spooky Trails* book.) Local legend suggests they hid at various places throughout Hadley, including the home of the minister John Russell. Whalley died there sometime around 1675. It is not certain when Goffe died, and evidence suggests he fled to Hartford, but there is little chance that he was alive and in Hadley in 1684.

Nevertheless Goffe's time there informs another legendary event often referred to as the Angel of Hadley. During King Philip's War, sometime in 1675 or 1676, hostile Indians attacked the town. All hope seemed lost and morale crushed until as if by a miracle an old man with a white beard and sword appeared, rallied the town militia to defeat the invasion, and then mysteriously vanished. That "angel" was, of course, Goffe.

Returning to du Bois's tale—how she missed "Witches and Angels" for a title mystifies—Mary befriends the aged Goffe. She offers to take him to Virginia so she and Harry might care for his safety. She also learns that it was Goffe who rescued Webster from the snow and nursed her back to life after her hanging, retreating before she became fully conscious and could learn his identity.

Webster was unaware that Goffe had saved her, but she had learned of his concealment in the Tilton home. Seeking vengeance on all who harmed her, Webster reports the matter to two commissioners for the King in the hopes they would arrest Peter Tilton as an accomplice. But Goffe is spirited out of the Tilton home before the first investigation. The commissioners angrily return to Webster. She assures them that Goffe is there—she is so certain, in fact, that she promises they could hang her as a witch if they do not find him on the second attempt, which she would conduct with them.

The commissioners assent. Mary Allyn is tending to Goffe when Webster arrives. The young woman had sought his fatherly advice concerning her cousin, Aaron, who has threatened to accuse *her* of witchcraft if she does not consent to marry him. Now cornered, Goffe implores Mary to save herself. Webster consents to the escape—recall her promise to reciprocate respect—but the young woman refuses to abandon the elderly man. Instead, Mary reveals to Webster that Goffe was her savior the night she was nearly hanged.

Webster has an immediate change of heart and is faced with a dilemma: Either she sacrifices Goffe or she will be hanged. Mary convinces Webster to accept the moral path to protect Goffe. She even agrees to hang beside Webster on the gallows. Goffe agrees to this dire plan only to save the maximum number of lives, knowing that if he were captured, the entire Tilton family and many others in Hadley would be executed as traitors.

Webster accepts her fate. She and Mary turn themselves into the commissioners as liars who deceived the Crown. Nooses are strung. The town gathers to watch the witches hang. Aaron offers to save his cousin if she agrees to marriage, but Mary refuses to betray her true love.

When the townspeople learn that the commissioners only intended to put the scare in an old woman for telling falsehoods, they become a violent mob, demanding bloodshed and two deaths upon the gallows. The town blacksmith prepares the nooses for Webster and Mary's necks.

In the final second before their hangings commence, an arrow pierces the air, striking the blacksmith dead. The crowd panics, fearing another attack by Indians, this time without the protection of their angel. They flee in fear. And so it is that Harry Evelyn and Ula's beloved, Massaomat, rescue Webster and Mary from the clutches of a frantic mob.

I told you it was a wild ride.

Although du Bois's story was praised widely in national periodicals, it never entered or inspired the oral tradition. To the best of my knowledge, no subsequent folklore combines tales of the Witch of Hadley with the Angel of Hadley. But du Bois's tale certainly garnered interest in Webster's fate beyond the local community. By 1937 the WPA guidebook to Massachusetts, for example, included an entry on "witch-baiting" in Hadley and cited Webster's case. In 1946 a radio program broadcast her tale throughout the Pioneer Valley.

In 1985 her story received prominent international attention following the publication of Margaret Atwood's *The Handmaid's Tale*, which the author dedicated to Webster. A decade later Atwood's poem "Half-Hanged Mary" achieved the pinnacle in contemporary narration of her harrowing experience. The poem imagines each slow hour of torment from Webster's perspective and the inextinguishable determination that keeps her alive.

A pivotal line turns on Webster's courage and justifiable anger. She declares that although she was not a witch prior to her ordeal, she has now become one. It is a striking line in splendid poetry, and I mention it for two reasons. The first is to implore readers to find their way to Atwood's poem. The second is to salute the women who have written that line on their heart, including many who have whispered it in solidarity at public lectures I have had the honor to attend, as potent a testimony to the irresistible power of words as one could ever hope to witness.

Webster's notoriety is juxtaposed by the relative obscurity of Ruth Buck, whose story should not be forgotten.

Buck died in 1834 at age ninety-two in the Westborough almshouse, having lived a long life as a pauper—and sometimes as a seamstress—and at the mercy of overseers. As early as 1763 the town attempted to exile her and deter financial responsibilities for her welfare. In 1778 she was forced to make a public confession of adultery for bearing a child out of wedlock, and for the remainder of her life she was treated as an outcast. True to expectations for those frequently labeled a "witch," Buck was well known for an uncertain temper and a ready tongue.

David Fray learned that lesson quickly when he once called out, "Ruth, they say you are a witch," as she ambled past his home.

"If I'm a witch, you are the devil," she retorted without missing a step.

Buck was, fortunately, born too late to be formally accused of witchcraft, but not late enough to escape being rumored as a witch. Numerous tales of the supernatural surround her, many collected by Harriette Merrifield Forbes in her history of Westborough, although Buck's infamy stretched to Grafton and to Hopkinton, where she frequently wandered to find work and to escape vicious rumors and prying eyes.

The stories were typical but no less injurious to the poor woman's reputation: bewitched cattle and bewitched sheep, loads of wood tumbling incessantly from a cart, broken eggs that never made it to market, ruined butter and unrisen bread, and a spinning wheel that refused to spin. If something went awry in the everyday life of the people of Westborough, Ruth Buck was to blame.

A few claims against her were rarer in the litany of bewitchment, including a cow's mysteriously broken leg and candlesticks that were all wicks—Buck's specter apparently ate all the wax. She was also known to possess supernatural hearing, which was a punishment in itself, for she could hear all the insults that children hurled at her under their breath.

In these stories the cures for her witchery were as common as the claims. When the butter would not churn, a hot brick tossed into the mix was just the remedy to scald Ruth Buck and release her grip. So too did an incendiary horseshoe liberate that immobile spinning wheel and deliver Buck a lasting scar to remember for many days. Some say that she wore a handkerchief across her neck to hide the "long purple mark" gifted by a farmer in Grafton, who slit the throat of a sheep she bewitched to free the rest of his flock.

But it was the cap on her head that drew the most attention. Buck never removed it for fear that folks would see her cropped ears, a sure sign of foiled witchcraft. One story claimed that she had troubled a farmer by bewitching his cows and keeping them planted firmly where they stood. In order to break the spell, he sliced off the tops of their bovine ears, taking the tips of Buck's as well. Another tale said her turban remained tight to hide the trimming her ears once suffered when she took the shape of a pig. Either way, that cap on Buck's head never came off, and people continued to talk.

Perhaps someday a different tale of her struggles will appear as well.

Legend Tripping

Thanks especially to the imagery of the woods in du Bois's narrative, there is no difficulty connecting the legend of the Witch and Angel of Hadley with pleasant hikes in the area. The Fort River Division of the Silvio O. Conte National Fish and Wildlife Refuge provides an easy stroll through farmland meadows on boardwalks. It is a 1.2-mile lollipop, readily accessible and welcoming—and the perfect spot for a quick walk to clear one's head after a faculty meeting. Parking is free at the end of the extension from Moody Bridge Road. The Kestrel Land Trust (https://www.kestrel trust.org/) offers a map of the refuge. **Trailhead GPS: N42 20.29 / W72 33.53**

The Land Trust also oversees the Dyer Conservation Area, with free parking near the Porter Phelps Huntington Museum on Route 47. **Trailhead GPS: N42 22.10 / W72 35.06** This hike is 1.5 miles out and back, but it could—and should—be extended by continuing into the Mt. Warner property, overseen by the Trustees of Reservations (https://thetrustees .org/place/mount-warner/), which offers a map. The Salamander Loop Trail runs about 2 miles. Separate free parking is available on Mt. Warner Road. **Trailhead GPS: N42 22.44 / W72 34.39**

The efforts of the Westborough Community Land Trust (https:// westboroughlandtrust.org/) are laudable. They are slowly but steadily developing hiking trails throughout the town. In addition to those in the chapter on Hoccomocco Pond, the best developed sites currently are the Bowman Conservation Area and the adjacent Bowman West. Both offer a hike of roughly 1.5 miles. The Bowman Conservation Area circles Sandra Pond (the Westborough Reservoir), including Minuteman Park. Be aware that both hikes are close to the Pike (that is, the Massachusetts Turnpike) and residential neighborhoods. Parking is free on Bowman Street. The Land Trust website publishes pamphlets and maps. **Trailhead GPS: N42 14.05 / W71 36.32**

Ruth Buck was known to people from Grafton to Hopkinton, which is just the right excuse to visit Upton State Forest (https://www.mass .gov/locations/upton-state-forest), with copious trails to hike and sites to explore ranging from a Civilian Conservation Corp camp to colonial cellar holes to a variety of natural phenomena. The park has an active Friends group (https://friendsofuptonstateforest.org/). **Trailhead GPS: N42 12.31 / W71 36.28**

7

Hannah Screecher and Her Sister

A N ISLAND LIES in the town of Barnstable between Cotuit, North, and West Bays. Long ago it was the lonely home of two sisters, Hannah and Sarah Screecham. One day they quarreled stormily, as siblings often do. Sarah decided to leave her sister and crossed the waters into Mashpee. There she made a new home among the white oak and the green pitch pine surrounding the waters of Witch Pond.

Hannah scratched out a living conspiring with pirates who hid their treasure in the sheltered harbors of the Cape. The crime was perfectly orchestrated. A pirate captain would row ashore with a single member of his crew. Hannah would meet them on the stony beach, watched only by gulls and their kin.

She would kiss the pirate, accept his gift, and signal to the sailor to sneak down a path leading inland from the shore. There he would find a deep pit already dug and waiting. And as soon as the sailor lowered the chest into the earth's sandy maw, there came a sudden shove: Hannah knocked him into the yawning gap and buried him alive as planned.

Her shrill cries then mixed with salty winds and the wail of watchful gulls. The pirate captain returned to his ship, alone, with stories of a strong but unlucky sailor who once belonged to his crew. The ghosts of those sailors still haunt the sites where Hannah's secret led them.

Sarah took up the art of witchcraft. She charmed the woods and claimed them as her own, earning the enmity of the Wampanoag who hunted among those trees. No bullet or arrow could succeed in its task when bewitched by

Sarah's spells. And at dusk each day came the most unusual sight: a great black mare thundering upon the paths paved by the feet of forlorn hunters.

Soon Sarah set lustful attention on a young man from the Mashpee. Fearful of the witch's resentful power, he invited her to his home. When dusk arrived, she disappeared. But the great black horse stood outside. And thinking it a gift from his sorcerous admirer, the young man shod the mare with horseshoes: three of iron and one of silver on the thick left front hoof. He tied the mare to a tree and retired to the warmth of his home.

In the morning the horse was gone, having slipped through a knot no horse could untie. The young man cautiously made his way to Sarah's house under the trees whose branches held together to hide her dwelling from the sun. Inside he discovered what he feared he would see: Sarah, howling in pain, a silver horseshoe nailed deep into her left hand. No one knows what ill fate became the object of Sarah's malefic affection.

One day, when the Wampanoag had suffered enough in the starving woods, a young hunter decided to break the curse. He loaded a single silver bullet into his gun, held his breath, and waited outside Sarah's abode. At dusk he heard her cackle but saw neither woman nor her toothy smile. Instead, there was a deer staring with its stoic black eyes as if to taunt the hunter and his determination.

His quick bullet lodged in the deer's heart.

Wounded, the creature sped away, deep into the white oak and the green pitch pine. He followed—he pursued, he hunted, he tracked—but all of it was in vain. No deer was ever found.

The despondent young hunter cautiously made his way to Sarah's house hidden from the sun. And there he discovered a sight he long desired to see: the old witch, lying dead, a single silver bullet lodged in her heart and lifting the curse upon the woods.

This story of the two weird sisters is now a favored version of the tale, but it is not the oldest, and it is not even the most common in the narrative's genealogy. This version first appeared in Elizabeth Reynard's *The Narrow Land* in 1934. Reynard based her account on a tale shared by Mrs. Frederick (Dorcas Coombs) Gardner, a member of the Mashpee Wampanoag. Subsequent guidebooks borrowed from Reynard and left the indelible impression of two estranged sisters facing different but always grim fates.

It is probable that Gardner merged two disparate stories into a single tale. Sarah Screecham's obviously observes many common motifs of witch tales on the Cape and in Massachusetts as a whole. She has the ability to bewitch animals, lives near a pond away from "civilized" community, is impervious to normal weapons, and dies when her familiar's form is shot by a silver bullet.

The horseshoe is less frequent in Cape Cod witch stories, but not in Massachusetts lore. Clifton Johnson, the distinguished folklorist of the early twentieth century, recorded the routine practice of nailing a horseshoe—always with the curve downward—over a door to keep witches away. And there are ample stories in English folklore in which a witch-woman is shod with a single horseshoe.

This tale is distinctive because some of its characters are Indigenous people. That does not, however, mean that it is exclusively Indigenous lore. As the anthropologist Williams Simmons explains in his analysis of this tale, the Mashpee Wampanoag likely borrowed elements from English storytellers and localized them, just as people do with other folkloric tales across the globe.

Earlier versions of this story found in print are decidedly of white European descent. The earliest that I can find haunts a fictional autobiography penned in 1854 by Anna Matlack Richards, *Memories of a Grandmother by a Lady of Massachusetts*. A single but striking paragraph appears in the fifth chapter—and be forewarned that it contains a brutal description:

> *Across a bay making up from the sea, not far from the old homestead, was a small islet, called Hannah Screecher's Island; where were heard*

dreadful screams during the moonlit nights of summer. It was said that her ghost guarded a buried treasure; that her throat was cut from ear to ear, yet that her cries were loud and distinct. I have felt the blood cease its circulation as those sounds pierced my sense—whether goblin, owl, or Hannah; but to doubt was not my inclination. Nothing gave me more pleasure than to believe in the spirit there; and also in the story told me by a man, who, with others, was once digging for the chest of gold—under an injunction of silence, according to the warning in a dream. Just as it made its appearance, one of the party, overjoyed at the sight spoke, and, presto! It was gone. One of my aunts often rowed me over to the island in summer time, to gather berries and plums during the day; but after sunset no one molested the shade of Hannah Screecher.

This ephemeral passage then peters out, having raised expectations for an explanation that never arrives. Nevertheless it contains clues to its folkloric nature. The most obvious is the name Screecher, cuing readers that she is a folk character, a tortured specter whose screeching frightens the unwary and the living. Less obvious are the location of her disquieting domain and the identity of the murderous villain who cut her throat, although readers in the 1850s would not have to be told his name.

More than twenty years later, in 1877, an editorial appeared in the *Boston Journal* that did not assume readers would possess such knowledge. The essay was signed by "A. L.," a woman of seventy-eight. The *Barnstable Patriot* effortlessly identified her as Adeline Hallett Lovell of Osterville. Lovell repined that a local legend had all but faded away. She offered her recollection to keep it alive. Given her predilection, I think it is appropriate to print her own words in their entirety:

A narrow strip of land divides this island from the Atlantic Ocean. Many years ago, a black, rakish vessel cast anchor a few hours before sunset in its offing, a boat was lowered, loaded and manned, heavy rich robes were placed upon its transom and a lovely woman, escorted by the commander of the ship, was carefully seated upon its cushions. Her pale faced glowed and her eyes beamed with joy as she looked at the green earth and trees before her.

"How well you look, Hannah. I think you have become tired of me and your cabin palace," exclaimed her companion.

"Oh, no," she replied, with averted face, "but I do so long for the solid earth, its flowers and birds; the sea and storms and guns have unnerved me."

"You shall have all you desire," he replied, as he moved away from her side. The boat stranded, and Hannah in the arms of the boatman was carried to the island. The rugs were spread for her rest, and a sweet languor crept over her. Workmen with their implements were directed to a certain spot and commenced excavating the earth.

"Dig deep and wide," said the captain, as he looked anxiously around, marking the trees and stones carefully, "Now, Hannah, I want you to see us bury our treasure. Come with me."

The heavy iron chest of gold and silver rested upon the edge of the vault. Hannah saw it lowered, then upon its top the robes were laid and she saw no more; knew no more; the earth was placed above her; all seemed hurried and confused. The captain and the crew hasted in the twilight to the vessel, sailed away, and soon a lady's wardrobe was thrown from the cabin window, and every vestige destroyed of poor Hannah's presence and captivity. Captain Kidd never returned for his treasure. To this day the faithful Hannah guards it, and moans and shrieks have been heard from that island, which in time was called "Hannah Screecher's Island." Men, boys and women have attested to seeing her ghost when they have approached a certain spot, in pursuit of berries or at wood cutting. Money diggers have left their excavations, which may yet be seen, and a word spoken has proved fatal to securing the treasure. I have conversed with those dwelling opposite the island

67

who believe Hannah Screecher's murder and her guarding the treasure, and who have listened to her plaintive moans in moonlight nights with tender sympathy, instead of dread.

Whether buried alive or dispatched by a merciless cutthroat, Hannah Screecher is a victim of Kidd's treachery and violence in the earliest recorded tales. The only question is whether her ghost cooperates with Kidd's cruel intentions. In some stories her ghost serves as a guardian, scaring off those who would dare to steal treasure from the notorious rogue. In others she screams against every soul alive, including the pirates whose ghastly act turned her into a ghost—or as Frank Stockton once wrote, although "they covered her up, they did not succeed in silencing her spirit." And in still later versions she willingly joins in the macabre game as an honorary member of Kidd's unholy crew.

The real William Kidd was born in Scotland in the mid-1600s and immigrated to New York City. In the 1680s he undertook a career as a privateer for England—that is, essentially, a legal pirate, a mercenary hired by a government to attack and to loot the ships and colonies of rival nations. In 1696 and 1697 Kidd sailed the *Adventure Galley* in an ill-fated journey that nearly resulted in mutiny. He killed one of his own crewmen by striking his skull with a heavy bucket. In 1698 he captured the *Quedagh Merchant* in the Indian Ocean and renamed it the *Adventure Prize*. Soon thereafter and for numerous reasons, England declared Kidd a pirate.

When he learned that he was a wanted man, Kidd decided to return to New York to clear his name. His original patron, the colonial governor Richard Coote, was in Boston at the time. He convinced Kidd to sail there with promises of clemency. On route, Kidd stopped at Gardiner's Island, a small strip just off Long Island, where he buried some acquired riches with permission of the land's proprietor. Presumably, Kidd planned to utilize knowledge of this treasure in negotiations over his fate.

Kidd was arrested upon arrival in Massachusetts. Coote had betrayed him. Kidd spent a year imprisoned in Boston and was then sent to England for trial on charges of piracy and murder. He was found guilty and hanged at the Execution Dock on the Thames River on May 23, 1701. His body was gibbetted for some time—perhaps as long as three years—as a warning to other pirates. And the buried treasure on Gardiner's Island was quickly recovered after his arrest.

In the year of his execution a broadside appeared that romanticized the pirate—called Robert instead of William—as a tragic figure. The folk character of Captain Kidd was born. He appeared in countless tales, passed along in print and by word of mouth. And as these tempting accounts flourished in the nineteenth century, they instigated one of the most opulent traditions of folk narratives and beliefs: that Kidd had buried treasure somewhere other than Gardiner's Island. Treasure hunting for his gold became a popular pastime in the nineteenth century, one that stretched from Florida to the Maritimes.

By the late 1800s folktales of Kidd's treasure followed a predictable pattern. A person of common means discovers the location of the buried wealth, often through preternatural means such as a dream or consultation with a fortune teller. The enticing spot is not necessarily on the coast. All six New England states claim Kidd's treasure, including far inland. Often the hunter is keenly aware that Kidd has cursed his treasure with a prohibition of silence—that is, the slightest noise would cause it to dematerialize and be forever lost. Each story then localizes the elements and competes for the cleverest frustration of the seeker's object of desire.

In many versions of the tale, Kidd shrewdly arranges for hunters to be suddenly frightened—and therefore to shout in fear, robbing themselves of the stolen treasure. Routinely he slays someone, usually a member of his crew or a slave, and tosses the body atop the chest so the haunting ghost would act as a trap. In other tales he recruits spectral animals. New England is replete with horses, dogs, cats, pigs, geese, and serpents in his legion. On rarer occasions Kidd enlists the aid of infernal or demonic beings, including his old friend the Devil himself.

It is very unusual, however, for Kidd's victim to be a woman. The story of Hannah Screecher and her evolving depiction from casualty to accomplice is an important—if morbid—example among an overwhelming treasury of tales.

There is another question lingering about Hannah and her sister: Were they represented as white women?

In Gardner's tale, the complicit Hannah is a villainous figure that conspires with European men who steal from others. The figure of Sarah is even more threatening. She is a malevolent witch whose claims upon the land interfere with the Indigenous people of Mashpee. We do not have incontrovertible evidence, but it is plausible that Gardner's narrative could be understood as protest against white intrusion on ancestral Native land.

Mashpee is a real place, after all—and there is a Witch Pond—and Screecham's Island is no pure fantasy. Today it is called Grand Island, the abode of a posh planned community, but in centuries prior it was Great Oyster Island and reserved for the Wampanoag. White encroachment began in the 1700s, and by the time the first summer houses were erected in the early twentieth century, the Wampanoag had been pushed away.

Reynard, however, considered the Screecham Sisters to be Indian. She may have misunderstood Gardner's subtle intentions, but more recently Mashpee Wampanoag storytellers have reclaimed the Screecham Sisters as integral to their community. Joan Tavares Avant, for example, has published several tales for the *Mashpee Enterprise* in which the sisters appear as "teachers of place and love" who can become hateful when angry, especially if they cannot locate something that rightfully belongs to them.

In one contribution, Avant literally retells Reynard's story. She utilizes direct language from that earlier work and transforms it, taking it back and making it relevant to the worldview of contemporary Mashpee

Wampanoag. Hannah and Sarah become Nokomis Screecham and Sil-vermoon. They remain capable of doing harm and even collaborate with a pirate, Captain Running Bear, to hide his treasure. An unsuspecting sailor ends up dead in a quahog pit, over which strawberries grow.

But there is no witch in Avant's tale that disallows Indigenous people from their hunting ground. Instead, she imagines the sisters scooping up the strawberries to share with mothers throughout Mashpee and to watch the housing project built for the Wampanoag. "Screecham Sisters are here today," Avant concludes. "Look around and you may see them. Remember, they are generations old, our legend tells us. Give them a hug."

Legend Tripping

There is no hiking on Grand Island, including at Noisy Point. Similarly, the Witch Pond Sanctuary in Mashpee, now protected by the Orenda Wildlife Land Trust (https://orendalandtrust.org/wildlife/2012/08/witch-pond-sanctuary/), is wetland. There are some trails in the Jehu Pond Conservation Area, part of the Mashpee National Wildlife Refuge, but are best traversed with a guide and may be closed at times. Another section of the refuge, the South Mashpee Pine Barrens, offers hikes that capture the flora of the legend. **Trailhead GPS: N41 35.12 / W70 29.12** The refuge is under the jurisdiction of the US Fish and Wildlife Service (https://www.fws.gov/refuge/Mashpee/) and has an active Friends association (https://www.friendsofmashpeenationalwildliferefuge.org/). The town of Mashpee also posts updated information (https://www.mashpee ma.gov/conservation).

The surrounding area offers alternatives that readily provide a sense of the area and its legends. Eagle Pond Sanctuary is just north of Grand Island; it abuts the Little River and is overseen by the Barnstable Land Trust (https://www.blt.org/), which maintains a map. The hike around the pond and all adjacent areas is around 3 miles. There are several small parking areas. Be aware that the sanctuary is located within a residential neighborhood. **Trailhead GPS: N41 38.31 / W70 25.37**

There are hiking opportunities on both sides of the Mashpee River. The area is protected by a number of collaborating organizations. Each side of the river offers an out-and-back hike totaling 4 to 5 miles. The best map is available from the Trustees of Reservations (https://thetrustees.org/place/mashpee-river-reservation/), with parking on Quinaquisset Avenue. The hike on the west bank includes the Thorp Trail and Byrnzie Trail (through the John Austin Forest) as well as the Grotzke Grove offshoot. The east bank entails the Mashpee River Woodlands and includes the Long Trail, the Chickadee Trail, the Partridge Berry Trail, and Whitcomb's Landing Trail. Some of these trails are marked, some less so. **Trailhead GPS: N41 37.14 / W70 28.41**

8

The Screeching Lady, the Wizard, and the Pixies

THE FOLLOWING IS another murderous tale bordering on the sadistic. It has appeared numerous times in print, so rather than venture an attempt in my own words, I defer to a classic rendition:

It was said that during the latter part of the seventeenth century a Spanish ship laden with rich merchandise was captured by pirates and brought into the harbor of Marblehead. The crew and every person on board the ill-fated ship had been murdered at the time of the capture, except a beautiful English lady, whom the ruffians brought on shore near what is now called Oakum Bay, and there barbarously murdered her. The few fishermen who inhabited the place were absent, and the women and children who remained could do nothing to prevent the crime. The screams of the victim were loud and dreadful, and her cries of "Lord save me! Mercy! Oh! Lord Jesus, save me!" were distinctly heard. The body was buried where the crime was perpetrated, and for over one hundred and fifty years on the anniversary of that dreadful tragedy the screams of the poor woman were repeated in a voice so shrill and supernatural as to send an indescribable thrill of horror through all who heard them.

That account is taken from *The History and Traditions of Marblehead*, published in 1880 by Samuel Roads Jr. Roads's contribution appeared fifty years after the story arrived in the *Marblehead Register* in April 1830. As would be expected the earlier tale differs slightly, but key elements remain: a captured Spanish vessel, fishermen away at sea, and a slain English lady whose chilling plea ("O mercy, mercy, Lord Jesus Christ save me!") is ruthlessly ignored.

There is, however, a change in the location of the murderous act. In the earlier version the pirates do their dark work inland rather than at Oakum Bay. They carry numerous prisoners, including the English lady, "at the dead of night into a retired glen, and there murdered them." And unlike Roads's story, the ghostly keening does not emanate annually but "at intervals, more or less often, almost every year, in the stillness of a calm starlight or clear moonlight night."

The alteration concerning the timing of the spectral screams is simple to explain as a phenomenon of the oral tradition. If a tale is popular—as this one was—and passed along by numerous people in a community—as this one surely was—then it is susceptible to faulty memories or deliberate choices on the part of raconteurs, unless a date is integral to the narrative. Variety in this case demonstrates that the community adopted the story and told it often.

The change of the criminal setting may also initially seem inconsequential. The peninsula that cradles Marblehead is just about a mile across, so the distance between its coves and inland glens is slight. And given the town's maritime history, the imagery of pirates and their wicked deeds conducted on the shore makes narrative sense. But the notion of a glen—or a valley, as other early accounts describe—may also be a clue as to the origins of this tale. It is remarkably similar to the story of Hannah Screecher on Cape Cod detailed in the previous chapter, and echoes other folktales in which Captain Kidd leads a sacrifice to their doom to haunt his treasure and forever deter gold diggers from their desire.

To be clear, the mere mention of a glen is not proof that the story of the Screeching Lady began as a Kidd treasure tale. Alternatively, it may portend an independent folktale in which a woman of high rank is dispatched by piratical treachery. If that is the case, then Marblehead's Screeching Lady—examples of which are older than those of Hannah Screecher—may be closer to the prototype, with the Cape Cod cousin showing additional merger with Kidd treasure tales. These origins will remain appetizingly speculative until further evidence is found.

There is one other point that might explain why classic Kidd tales did not take root in Marblehead. The town had its own pirate, historical and legendary, in John Quelch. His story is told elsewhere in this book, but it bears mentioning here that Marblehead once boasted "the Pirate House," a small dwelling within a stone's throw of Oakum Bay (today the site is a parking lot). In a separate guidebook penned by Samuel Roads in 1881, the author mentions a prevalent rumor that a pirate lived there. He was warned of approaching investigators and fled, leaving behind silks and other valuables. Although Quelch is not identified as the specific pirate, his biographical details influence the traditions of that house. It is no demand, then, to imagine storytellers wishing to link tales of the pirate's house with tales of piratical action just across the street, including the murder of the Screeching Lady.

A remarkable story from 1839 does just that. It was published as an editorial in the Boston newspaper the *Columbian Centinel* by a writer with the pseudonym of "Nauticus." I suspect that readers' eyes have not seen this version for centuries, so I reprint it here in its entirety:

Early in the 17th Century, when the daring and barbarous depredations of the Buccaneers filled the maritime world with dread and dismay, a descent, attended with deeds of blood and rapine, had been made by the pirates, upon the coast of the Spanish Main, popularly so called, from a swift and well-appointed ship that had long eluded the vigilance of the public cruisers, and booty to an immense amount carried off, together with several prisoners, among whom was a lady of great beauty and accomplishments, and whose father was the governor of the unfortunate city which had been the scene of the cupidity and cruelty of the barbarous invaders. The Buccaneers, after having accomplished the object of their expedition, steered northward till they fell in with the coast of New England; and doubling Cape Cod, sailed toward the head of Massachusetts Bay, at that time very thinly inhabited; and arrived off Marblehead, then the site of only a few fishermen's cottages or huts.

Finding there a good harbor, and apparently a safe retreat, they landed their booty and buried it in the earth, in various places. To increase the security of their deposits, they divided the plunder into several parts; some of which were sent and buried on the neighboring islands, some upon "the Neck," and the residue in various places about where the town now stands.

The male prisoners were treated with great barbarity by their merciless captors, and finally, miserably perished in detail, from the efforts of privations or other cruelties. The lady either fell to the lot of the piratical commander, or was claimed by him as his right. He built a hut, where they for some time dwelt in apparent happiness; the unfortunate captive probably concealing, as best she might, the anguish of her heart, under the semblance of contentment. But whether his jealousy had penetrated the veil which she had adopted to conceal her misery, whether satiety had followed upon possession, or whether both causes combined to ensure the final destruction of the hapless woman, is not known, though both are conjectured.

When such causes of discord exist, the transition from a state of peace and tranquility to one of hatred and revenge, in the breast of such a savage as was the Buccaneer, is appallingly rapid; and the obdurate wretch did not hesitate to imbue his hands in the blood of his resistless victim. On a transcendently bright, clear and calm midnight; the full moon shining in chastened splendor, and the village buried in quiet repose; the tranquility of the fateful hour was suddenly and terrifically broken by long, frequent and agonizing shrieks from the neighboring marsh, or meadow, running through that part of the settlement adjacent to the dwelling of the Buccaneer.

Superstitious terror in some, and a disinclination in others, who guessed the cause, to encounter the formidable pirate, prevented any interference; and shortly, the shrieks subsided into moans; the moans were absorbed in silence; the moon still pursued her uninterrupted career through the azure firmament, and the soul of the unhappy creature was soring aloft to its audit.

For many, many years after this tragical night, at the same hour and same phase of the moon, were repeated to the ears of the horror-stricken neighbors, the soul-harrowing shrieks of "the screeching woman in the marsh!"

This version benefits from literary treatment, so we must be cautious in assuming that its details were readily embraced by everyone in Marblehead, but from the content of the letter it is clear that Nauticus is a resident. Nauticus further offers several fascinating comments on the matter. First is a remark of an octogenarian who, when a girl, had reason to visit a nurse one evening. The nurse hurried the young woman inside, fearful that "the screeching woman had been desperately uneasy and noisy that evening."

Nauticus politely disputes this claim on the grounds that it was not the anniversary for the noise. The implication is that the people of Marblehead—especially those inclined to give the tale some credence—heard the screams routinely. And with a wink to the reader that is as evident today as it was in 1839, Nauticus dismisses those skeptics who think the Screeching Lady is nothing more than "a large sea-fowl called a 'loon,' whose hungry aspirations intimately resemble the human voice in distress."

There is so much more to pursue with this pivotal folk narrative. A version published in 1869 in the *Springfield Republican* by a frequent traveler to Marblehead, for example, claims that the cries are not those of shrieking pain but the frantic woman's final words—that is, on the anniversary of her death, her ghost cries aloud, "Lord Jesus, save me, save me!" to shatter the nocturnal calm.

There is the tale's appearance in a debate over Spiritualism from 1853, where it is used as an example of hallucinations arising under the influence of belief, an argument that mirrors its citation in Charles Wentworth Upham's 1831 study of the Salem Witch Trials. There is its frequent mention in diaries, guidebooks, travelogues, and magazines such as *Harpers*. And there is its invocation in numerous literary works, including John Greenleaf Whittier's "The Murdered Lady," John Osborne Sargent's "The Screeching Lady," and John Berry Bensel's "A Marblehead Legend." And this litany only includes contributions from the 1800s! A rewarding journey awaits the genealogist of this tale.

But the Screeching Lady is not the only acoustic marvel in the folklore of Marblehead. Although there are more occasions in which people mention the telling of stories about Old Dimond than actually tell his stories, enough have survived to confirm his reputation as another significant folk character. Old Dimond—also known as Uncle Dimond—was purportedly a real man, sometimes called Edward and sometimes called John. Tales place him in the 1600s, although historical records suggest he leased land in 1709, and a barber's ledger book had him purchase a wig in 1750.

As a folk character Old Dimond is a wizard possessed of the black arts. The purposes to which he used such sorcery, however, were not always diabolical. According to our same Nauticus, Old Dimond was a fisherman who once pursued his catch on the Grand Banks off Newfoundland. One luckless evening, he ordered his sailors below deck with the stern warnings of a warden. From their prison in the hull the crew suddenly heard "the trampling of innumerable feet and the flapping of thousands of fish upon the deck." Once freed, they returned to find Old Dimond standing alone and satisfied. A vast catch of fish had been split, salted, and stowed away. And they made it safely back to Marblehead in record time, as if the winds were held by an unseen hand.

Later versions of this tale depict the crew overhearing Old Dimond bark orders to beings named "Red Cap" and "Blue Cap"—that is, to the goblins in his employment.

The tale of the goblin master has regrettably slipped away, but even today storytellers imagine his sorcerous ability to interfere with or to harness the pertinacious power of the sea storm. Old Dimond purportedly resided in a dwelling known as the Old Brig, harbored at the foot of Old Burial Hill. In Nauticus's account, one night he sensed that fellow fishermen were in a bad way far off at Sable Island. A devastating storm was intent on driving them to a watery grave.

Prophetic and possessed, Old Dimond marched up the hill and entered the quiet cemetery. He took the helm between two weather-beaten gravestones. His incantations began. And he spoke in a manner that seemed to whisper in the ear of the captain of the vessel threatened so far away. According to the ship's log, at the very moment he uttered those words in the company of gravestones and their ghosts, the schooner fetched past Sable Island and escaped certain doom.

In other stories, sailors report hearing Old Dimond's voice cut through cacophonous gales to guide them to safety—or to shipwreck and ruination should they be imprudent enemies of a wizard who commands the weather. In this manner, Old Dimond's stentorian speech takes on the lore of the raging seas, akin to Harry Main growling in Ipswich, found in another chapter.

Still later rumors hint at more powers of the conjurer. In one tale Old Dimond recovers stolen money for an aged couple and reveals the duplicitous thief. In another he curses a man who has stolen firewood from a widow, magically binding him (much like the legends of witch-riding) to bear a heavy burden upon his back at night. These minor stories add a touch of the mundane—as much as wizardry can be ordinary—in assigning the same suspicious legerdemain of other Massachusetts magicians. They also turn him into a folk hero of sorts, which in many ways denudes Old Dimond of his origins as a cyclonic force, a supernatural being able to control storm and sea because he was a part of them and they a part of him.

Marblehead offers other folkloric gifts. Some, regrettably, have faded away. In his history Roads mentions but does not recount tales of a man chased by a coffin corpse; another man pursued by the Devil holding the reigns of four white horses; and a third man who returns home after long weeks of fishing to his fiancée and watches her disappear before his eyes, as she had died months before while he was being tossed about at sea.

Thankfully there is one tradition that although nearly submerged has held like tenacious seaweed to rock. Nauticus again rescues it for us. On the ferry road leading to Salem, our considerate friend explains, is a rock fragmented into "three sisters," having been cleaved by a bolt of irresistible lightning. Two roads intersect nearby under the shadow of ancient willows.

"It is in a lonely and secluded place," Nauticus opines, and on that account is favored by the "Pixes" as their favorite haunt and den. These "Pixes" are pixies—the fairies of Cornish folklore, whose legends were transplanted across the Atlantic by the town's seafaring settlers. "There are many spots about Marblehead," Nauticus warns, "famous as the resort of these fantastic creations." One must take heed and if subject to the "witcheries of these facetious hobgoblins" have the good sense to turn one's garments inside out in order to break their spell.

If Nauticus's admonition is not enough to convince a wavering reader, perhaps the autobiography of Joseph Story, a Supreme Court justice, would suffice. In 1851 his son published his notes detailing his upbringing in Marblehead. Story confirms that the fishermen and other residents of his town believed in "the Pixies of Devonshire, the Bogels of Scotland, and the Northern Jack o'Lanthorn."

It was not a belief abandoned easily. As late as 1869 the *Springfield Republican* mentioned that the people of Marblehead feared "naughty fairies" and being "pixielated" by them and often turned their jackets inside out whenever they left a well-lit room for the darkness of the outdoors.

Screeching female ghosts, ocean and weather wizards, and mischievous pixies are, of course, the stuff of British folklore. Marblehead had its share because, as a fishing village, it attracted immigrants from western England and the Channel Islands and for many centuries remained relatively isolated. Visiting Bostonians would joke that the boys of Marblehead threw stones at them to keep modern customs away from the town. And in some ways, it is sad that those modern customs prevailed and exiled so many other tales to the bottomless depths before they could be saved by the wizard's call.

But they are not all gone. Indeed, one anecdote appropriately closes out this chapter. In 1821 William Tudor, a Bostonian man of letters, published *Miscellanies*. It contains one of the earliest accounts of the Screeching Lady, culled from an elderly woman in Marblehead. It is the final tale in Tudor's book. And in his final sentence he laments "the account of The Screeching Lady of Marblehead, whose cries and whose story will probably be forgotten by the next generation."

I am writing these lines in January 2021, almost two hundred years later to the day.

Legend Tripping

The purported "beach" site of the Screeching Lady is a small rocky inlet in Marblehead. Similarly, the house associated with Old Dimond lies in a residential neighborhood. The views into the harbor from Fort Sewall, now a public park, and a quick jaunt down Fort Beach are sure to enliven the imagination.

For hikes, imagine the legends in a broader sense. There are several short ones overseen by Marblehead Conservancy Inc. (https://marble headconservancy.org/). Steer Swamp Conservation Area, with 1.6 miles of trails and parking on Beacon or Norman Street, sets the stage for the earlier tales in which the pirates commit their deeds inland. **Trailhead GPS: N42 30.50 / W70 51.05** The 1.5 miles of the Forest River provide another marshy area of equal attraction.

Finally, at just over a mile, the area comprised by Wyman Woods and Lead Mills provides a fine spot to consider the folklore of the Marblehead pixies. The conservancy website has maps and further information. Parking is free but limited in all places. **Trailhead GPS: N42 29.46 / W70 52.41** and **N42 29.51 / W70 53.07**, respectively

9

The Mooncusser's White Horse

LIKE THE DEVIL'S thin finger, the slender bar of Monomoy stretches from Chatham into Nantucket Sound, where it points to watery doom in the patient shoals that wait for careless ships. Today the finger is broken; what was once a bar is now abandoned islands separated from the mainland by a series of uncaring storms.

In the days before the ocean swallowed a measure of Monomoy's sands, it was home to a mysterious horse, a white stallion, owned by a cruel spider of a man whose name no one cared to learn. It was a remarkable beast. It would gallop its way up and down the beach with commanding strength and grace. The fishermen knew it well. They marveled at how it always seemed to be sailing upon the sand.

But the strength of that white stallion served an evil purpose. It was a mooncusser's horse. On foggy, stormy, or starless nights its nameless owner would tie a lantern to its mane and another on its tail. With menacing sway the white stallion pranced at the tip of Monomoy, deceiving foolish and frightened ships that it was a beacon of hope.

Those vessels never made it to the safety of the shore. They snapped in the shoals or broke on the beach. Their cargo washed up to the grasping thin fingers of a waiting spider of a man. And the hungry army of frenzied crustaceans took a feast of flesh home to Crab Bank beneath tumultuous skies.

Again and again the wicked ruse to bring a wrecker wealth cost innocent men their lives.

Then one evening the hurricane came with its disobedient and defiant waves. Rebellious clouds stared at Monomoy like a shark's all-knowing eye. That spider of a man smiled with anticipation at the treasure he and his white horse were sure to steal.

No one disputes that the nameless man and his white stallion rode through the whipping sands. But the treasure of lost ships would never again be plucked by his thin and rapacious fingers. The hurricane had its way: The tides rose, the waters swelled, the winds cut a channel through the forlorn beach. And as if by conspiracy those forces of nature abandoned the wrecker and his white horse, stranding them on a shaking island of sand and surrounded by a heartless sea.

The murmuring moon broke through the clouds to watch an evil man's end. No mortal could survive the onrushing flood. And no wrecker stranded on Monomoy did that night of winds and whipping sands. A calm ocean delivered his broken body two days later at Stage Harbor shore.

No one quite knows what happened to the white stallion that neighed resoundingly across the gathering waves. Some say he panicked. Some say he drowned. And some, who watch the ocean with unwavering eyes, say he embraced the rising tide and still swims beyond the Rip, beckoning sailors when the moon shines to guide them past the patient shoals that wait for careless ships.

The story of the ghostly white horse of Monomoy first appeared in Elizabeth Reynard's *The Narrow Land*, published in 1934. Reynard's notes explain that it was a tale originating in the local oral tradition and immediately borrowed from Charles Kendrick, a resident of Chatham. It was an elaborate example, albeit fantastical, of "mooncussin'."

Mooncussin' is, of course, the pronunciation of "moon-cursing" in the parlance of the Cape. The term comes from the Old World. Richard Head, an Irish author, defined a "moon-curser" in *The Canting Academy*, an exposé of thievery, in 1673. At that time, a "moon-curser" was a link-boy—a young man employed to carry a torch for pedestrians—who would curse the moon for providing light and rendering his work unnecessary. Moon-cursers were especially popular in London, and Head noted that often enough, they would lead the unwary into places where they were easily robbed by accomplices.

The term took on a similar sinister meaning along the coasts of Great Britain and the United States, where "wreckers" purportedly employed false lights to lure unsuspecting ships to certain doom in unsafe or shallow waters. The wreckers would then plunder the ships for loot and share the spoil of bodies with the sharks.

How often such depraved activity succeeded is questionable, but there is no doubt that stories of moon-cursers and wreckers proliferated throughout the nineteenth century. Periodicals routinely carried tales, inadvertently promoting the impression that moon-cursers were more prevalent than they were. These tales became an important aspect of maritime folklore. They were especially popular in the Northeast, and Cape Cod became a magnet for them. To state the obvious, the Cape is defined by its shoreline. Every town in its vicinity touches open water. It is the perfect setting for tales of moon-cursers and their abominable intentions.

The white horse of Monomoy is, then, merely one of many iterations of this theme. And if we dig a little deeper into the singing sands of this story, we will recover our own awaiting treasure of sorts.

This specific tale has an ancestor of a privileged literary influence. In 1835 Nathaniel Hawthorne published "The Mermaid, A Reverie," later rechristened as "The Village Uncle: An Imaginary Retrospect." In its pages the narrator describes an aging and weatherworn Uncle Parker, a teller of yarns, who had lived—and suffered—a life on the demanding sea and all that it entailed. Uncle Parker would regale those who gathered in Mr. Bartlett's store with endless stories of his adventures and misadventures: the campaigns against the French, the taste of liagden fowl in the Grand Banks, the consumption of rum necessary to stay warm in the punishing winters on Sable Island.

One memory always aroused the old salt's ire. "And wrathfully did he shake his fist," Hawthorne's narrator recalls, "as he related how a party of Cape Cod men had robbed him and his companions of their lawful spoil, and sailed away with every keg of old Jamaica, leaving him not a drop to drown his sorrow. Villains they were, and of that wicked brotherhood who are said to tie lanterns to horses' tails, to mislead the mariner along the dangerous shores of the Cape."

Hawthorne did not invent this stirring image. It is far more plausible that he borrowed it from a vibrant oral tradition circulating around maritime cities in Massachusetts, including his own Salem. But Hawthorne's momentous influence would guarantee that the image of villainous wreckers on the Cape would thrive for a century or more.

The notion that wreckers would tie lanterns to the tails of beasts was found on both sides of the Atlantic, especially tales set in Cornwall and Scotland. Horses, donkeys, and cows were the favored accomplice, but on rare occasions even the Devil lent his forked tail for the sinful job. The image may have arisen from what seems to be an actual practice, a practical joke of sorts, in which young men would tie paper lanterns to the tails of kites and fly them in the darkness of night. Sir Isaac Newton was said to have tried the prank and frightened witnesses who thought they were watching comets come crashing to the earth.

The horse, then, makes sense in this tale from Monomoy, but why a *white* horse? There is a clue in the writings of another favored son of Massachusetts, Henry David Thoreau. In *Cape Cod*, he describes walking on the beaches of Nauset. "The white breakers were rushing to the shore," he observed, "the foam ran up the sand. . . . The breakers looked like droves of a thousand wild horses of Neptune, rushing to the shore, with their white manes streaming far behind." The white horses of the god of the sea are an ancient trope, representing the crashing waves.

And finally, why Monomoy? Thoreau again provides a hint when, in describing the "bared and bended arm of Massachusetts," he notes the "elbow, or crazy-bone, at Cape Mallebarre." Malle Barre—the Bad

Bar—the earlier name of Monomoy. It is a legendary place, but not because it is the setting of fantastical tales; it is legendary for its dangerous shoals and unpredictable currents, which have claimed countless ships and far too many lives. Long associated with wrecks, it readily became associated with wreckers.

One of those notorious shoals is Stone Horse, a name that appears in print in the early 1800s. It is far less frequently known as White Horse Shoal, but that too is a clue for this narrative. Stone Horse Shoal is a site where untold ships came to grief as battered, sinking, hopeless wrecks. And in 1970 the intrepid chronicler of maritime folklore, Edward Rowe Snow, confirmed a suspicion to which readers surely are drawn.

Snow heard a tale from Henry Beston, the naturalist whose writings provided impetus to establish the Cape Cod National Shoreline. Beston narrated the story of the Stone Horse—also known as the White Stallion—of Monomoy. It was virtually identical to that version first published by Reynard, except the unnamed mooncusser had now become a wicked master by the name of Spider and employed the horse "for ten years in his nefarious activities." Beston's story testifies to a tradition that brought together an imaginative folktale and a very real site of maritime danger.

This was not the only version of the tale. Eleanor Early captured another one in her 1936 *And This Is Cape Cod!* Although it is not apparent how much is Early's literary adaptation, the added elements instill a sense of haunting ethereality. The horse is no longer a stallion but a mare. (It's a shame storytellers never took up that alteration; the White Mare of Mallebarre has a certain ring to it.)

The mare belonged to a clergyman, but she ate too much cemetery grass and so became a fey horse, familiar with ghosts and with devils. Her eyes glowed with an infernal crimson hue. And she came to relish the dastardly work as much as her diabolical master. "On dark nights he would put one lantern in her mane and tie another to her tail," writes Early, and dutifully the white mare would stalk the beach, "her old body swaying and pitching like a ship on the waves."

The irony is that Monomoy has in reality long been the site of altruistic heroism rather than piratical villainy. Organized lifesavers have operated there for centuries. The Massachusetts Humane Society, for example, established volunteer services soon after the United States became a nation and the formal predecessors of the US Coast Guard arrived in the mid-1800s. Despite these efforts, stories of inhospitable wreckers flourished. An anecdote was told, for example, of a man shipwrecked off Monomoy. He swam to shore where he was met by locals gathered on the beach. "What town is this?" he asked. "Chatham," was the reply, and upon hearing that name the man swam back into the violent sea where his fate held better odds.

To be fair, it was not solely Chatham that maintained an infamous reputation into the twentieth century. In 1938, the *Boston Globe* reported on Truro schoolchildren bringing family relics for an exhibition. Whaling irons, muskets, and leather buckets were among the heirlooms on display. "Nobody," however, "brought the old white horse with a lantern tied to his tail, fabled to have patrolled the outside shore line on dark nights."

A decade earlier, the same paper published an eyebrow-raising anecdote in Frank Sibley's series "Down East." The quip imagined an old sea captain ruminating on human nature. He philosophized that the environment in which one grows up has little influence upon one's nature, except in the case of beavers, people born along the Maine coast, and all the residents of Truro, who "don't know any use for a sock except to fill with wet sand."

"What do they do that for?" asked an innocent bystander.

"They turn an old white horse loose on the path along the bluff," said he, "on a foggy night, with a lantern tied to his tail. Then they go up to Peaked Hill Bar and wait for whatever comes ashore. They take the socks along because some of 'em's liable to be still alive. Any Truro man'll tell you that."

Other tales from this time recorded that Cape Codders, ever industrious, saved the time needed to fill a sock with wet sand and simply employed a brick.

In 1937, Henry Crocker Kittredge published *Mooncussers of Cape Cod.* Akin to Reynard, he denied that any such activities actually took place and that the stories were just that: stories. No one denied that locals salvaged wrecks, but the notion of a culture of murderous robbers was preposterous, no matter how popular the tale among old sailors and young tourists. Jeremiah Digges (the pseudonym of Josef Berger), with his attuned flair for the dramatic, was less convinced in his WPA guide from the same year, *Cape Cod Pilot.* "Those who would ram a clean bill of health for Cape Cod down history's throat," Digges mused, "declare there was never such a crime on the Cape because there is no record of it. That is to say there never was a case of mooncussing because no mooncusser ever was caught."

Digges relays one final fetching story of treachery at Monomoy. It concerns the Devil and Granny Howland, a curious figure of ambiguous origin. In this tale, the two companions play a game to decide who would have the pleasure of claiming the next set of souls lost upon Monomony's shoals. Taking a belaying pin within his fiendish hand, His Satanic Majesty drew a heavy line on the shore.

They would march twenty fathoms and toss the skulls of lost sailors toward the beacon on the beach. Each would throw the best out of three, the closest skull declaring the winner. But when Old Nick was occupied buttoning his coat against the nor'easter that their very meeting had summoned from the abyss, shrewd Granny Howland scooped up a razor clam and hid it under the sand.

The Devil threw first. From out of a ditty bag came a grinning skull. Into its eye socket went his fiery thumb. And down the beach he bowled it. But the skull had a chip, a treacherous souvenir from when a third mate bashed it with a marlinspike, so it bounced off course upon hitting the hard sand. The second throw was no better; despite his practiced skill, the Devil hit a determined piece of driftwood. But the third skull lined up nicely, a quick spit from the target.

"Up stepped Granny," Digges explained, "squinting her good eye and clutching her death's head by the main-hatch." She aimed for the razor clam, and there, with a click, the skull rolled and stopped, closer to the target than any of the Devil's attempts.

"Ah! That's Cap'n Simmons for you!" Granny chuckled. "A born navigator, Nick, keeping a straight course to the last!"

And so it was that Granny Howland won the right to the next shipwreck. She lit a lantern, jumped upon her white horse, and waving the light back and forth sped off down Monomoy to claim her approaching prize.

Regrettably Digges does not provide the source for this tale. It would not be the last time he mentioned Granny Howland, however. She appears again—all too briefly—in his 1941 *In Great Waters: The Story of the Portuguese Fishermen*, where she shares a bed with Old Man Corisco, a demon from the Azores who, akin to her friend the Devil, delights in taking the lives of men upon the ocean deep.

Granny Howland seems to be a local legendary figure associated with New Bedford and Massachusetts whalers. Her name is invoked in passing comments in John Ross Browne's 1846 *Etchings of a Whaling Cruise* and as an expletive in Charles Henry Robbins's 1899 *The Gam: Being a Group of Whaling Stories*. Captain Robbins was a whaler from New Bedford, and Browne, originally from Ireland, wrote at length about sailors from that city, where the Howland family made a fortune in the industry. As a folkloric figure, she was responsible for whipping up in her washtub the winds that made nor'easters and other deadly storms. It is a shame so little of her folklore survived, but I suppose that none of us should rush to salvage it from the bottom of a devilish blue sea.

Legend Tripping

The true drama of Monomoy is nature itself. When many writers collected Monomoy's classic tales in the twentieth century, it was a peninsula. Today, on account of storms and erosion, it is a series of islands. It is well worth the effort to visit North and South Monomoy Islands, but it requires planning for private charter or seasonal ferry. Fortunately, the Morris Island Trail remains accessible. It is located at the Monomoy National Wildlife Refuge, which is under the jurisdiction of the US Fish and Wildlife Service (https://www.fws.gov/refuge/Monomoy/). This roughly 1.5-mile loop includes boardwalks and beach hiking and follows a trail with informative signs. Trail maps and related brochures are available at the refuge website. **Trailhead GPS: N41 39.26 / W69 57.32**

At low tide it is possible to extend the hike and follow a loop around the peninsula of Harding Beach Point, adding roughly another 1.5 miles.

Planning is essential for this visit. The parking lot at the refuge is free but can fill up quickly, and the trail is essentially impossible during high tides. Erosion can rapidly change the nature of the hike or close areas, and the next major storm could render this recommendation outdated.

Opposite Stage Harbor, the hike on Harding's Beach is rewarding and offers views of Monomoy. Follow the dunes trail toward the Stage Harbor Lighthouse (now private property) and return on the sand. **Trailhead GPS: N41 40.08 / W69 59.55**

With proper planning one can also hike Nauset Beach and the privately owned but accessible Pochet Island in Orleans. Although well north of Monomoy, the hike on Nauset Beach when the surf is strong conveys the domain of the white horse. Seasonal parking applies. The bridge to Pochet Island can be inaccessible at times. It is wise to contact local hiking clubs for information. **Trailhead GPS: N41 47.19 / W69 56.12**

Recommended hikes in Truro are found in the chapters on the sea serpent and Provincetown.

10

The Wild Man of Wellfleet

AM BELLAMY'S PIRATE ship the *Whydah* drowned at Wellfleet in a violent storm in April 1717. Two men walked away from the wreck with their sorrowful and shivering lives. One hundred and two washed up on the shore and had their bones buried and blessed in the sand. Only the sharks know what became of the rest, and they rarely share secrets with the warm-blooded beasts that walk with two legs on land.

Each spring and each autumn in the years that followed the wake of that harrowing wreck, a man of very singular and frightful aspect traveled up and down the Cape. His eyes imprisoned fiendish truths, but he walked with dogged purpose. Many thought to follow him to the cliffs, through the dunes, and down the beach, but no one's legs had the courage to do so.

In time he raised a lonely hut, a shelter against the stormy wind. No respectable person called on him there, but the fishermen received him with the kind hospitality of obligation any time he came to their doors. They never learned his name. But they all agreed that if his company grew tiresome and his appetite too ravenous for ale and cider and dried cod, the mere reading of a passage from the Holy Bible would send him on his way to his lonely hut above the singing sands.

The stranger never wanted for lack of money, which as if by sorcery could always be found waiting in the pocket of his belt. Some say he spent his days scouring the beach where the storm scattered the *Whydah*'s crew and their coins. Others suspected a darker secret, a hidden cache of treasure, lurking somewhere in the vicinity of the lonely hut.

The few brave souls who wandered toward his home could never shake the memory of what they heard inside. It was the sounds of a man still alive but tormented in the bowels of hell. His screams, his moans, his blasphemous groans—all pleading to infernal fiends that only he could see, begging to be forgiven for the crimes he committed and the dried thick blood that was still on his hands.

One day the wild man disappeared. Hopeful whispers prayed that he had sailed away.

Then one fisherman broke his secret. He had passed by the lonely hut several nights before and heard his screams in the dark hours howl like the winds. But something was odd even for a nightmare. The fisherman heard the wild man speaking to someone or to something as if desperate to strike a deal.

Finally a few fishermen's legs found the courage to knock at the lonely hut. The wild man lay lifeless and as white as the gift of bloated bodies the *Whydah* once gave to the shore. Gold coins were clutched in his salt-dried fingers, useless trinkets for whatever bargain the dead man had tried to secure that night another secret was born.

I am certain this is not the story most people alive today have heard about the pirate "Black" Sam Bellamy. That privilege belongs to the tragic love story of Bellamy and Maria Hallett, a tale that admittedly has its sea legs, having been circulating for just under a century. Nevertheless the story of the wild man is considerably older and was the inspiration for the dark romance of the Hallett affair.

The facts that feed pirate folklore are always few in number—people operating outside the law do not usually maintain meticulous records of their activities. But most scholars agree that Samuel Bellamy was born in 1689 in Devon, England, and became a member of the Royal Navy. Upon leaving that career he eventually sailed to Massachusetts, purportedly visiting both Eastham and Boston in 1715. He met and befriended

Paulsgrave Williams, scion of an influential family in Newport, Rhode Island.

In 1716 Bellamy and Williams decided to become maritime salvagers and headed to Florida and Cuba, pursuing rumors of the wreckage of a Spanish fleet. They eventually turned pirate and fell in with Benjamin Hornigold, a renowned buccaneer on the sloop *Marianne*. Hornigold's partner was Edward Teach, soon to be known to the world as Blackbeard. But in the summer of 1716, the crew deposed Hornigold and Teach, albeit without bloodshed, and voted Bellamy their new captain. Williams became his second-in-command.

Months later they captured the *Sultana*. Bellamy became its captain and Williams took charge of the *Marianne*. After a three-day chase in the early months of 1717, they seized the *Whydah Galley*, a slave ship commanded by Lawrence Prince. Bellamy transferred to that ship.

The pirates then sailed toward New England. Bellamy and Williams separated, with plans to reconvene at Damariscove Island in Maine. Heading north, Bellamy captured the *Anne Galley*, which he gave to his quartermaster, Richard Nolan. On April 26, 1717, Bellamy overtook the *Mary Anne*, a cargo ship apparently loaded with Madeira wine. At that point, they turned toward the coast of Massachusetts for reasons still debated. The decision would prove disastrous.

A powerful nor'easter tore up the Atlantic. Dense fog heralded the storm and imprisoned Bellamy's ships off Cape Cod. The dangerous shoals near Chatham posed an immediate threat, so Bellamy seized a local ship, the *Fisher*, and coerced its captain, Robert Ingols, to guide them to safety. Ingols was brought aboard the *Whydah*.

As night and inclement weather arrived, the *Anne Galley*, *Mary Anne*, and *Fisher* lost sight of the *Whydah* and its guiding lights. Nolan ordered anchors dropped on the *Anne Galley* and the *Fisher* as devastating waves lashed the ships. His decision saved their lives. The *Mary Anne* suffered greatly but was spotted by lifesavers, who rescued the entire crew, unaware that seven of them were pirates. These men would eventually be arrested, tried, and executed except for one, Thomas South, a carpenter forced into Bellamy's service.

The *Whydah* met an evil fate around the turn of midnight. Desperation soared in the waters of Eastham and Wellfleet. The anchors could not hold against the debilitating winds, and the galley soared toward the shore's immobile cliffs. It struck hard, breaking cannons loose and tossing the crew ruthlessly across the deck. The *Whydah* then snapped into two. Bellamy plunged into the waters never to be seen again.

Most agree that the *Whydah* had approximately 165 bodies that day. Estimates purport that just over one hundred washed ashore and were buried in a mass grave. All agree that only two survived: Thomas Davis—another carpenter intimidated into labor and equally acquitted—and John Julian, an Indigenous person from Cape Cod who was never tried and was likely sold into slavery.

Bellamy's death was not forgotten. He was prominently featured in *A General History of the Pirates*, a 1724 collection of biographies that helped establish their reputations for centuries to follow. Bellamy's entry is riddled with folkloric conjecture but remains a dynamic read. In this account he and Williams, sailing separately, engage in maritime battle against the French between Newfoundland and Nova Scotia. Injuries and damage force them to sail south toward New England. Somewhere between Georges Bank and Nantucket they capture the *Mary Anne* and impel its captain to escort them to Cape Cod.

Bellamy sends several crewmen aboard the *Mary Anne* as a threat against its captain, but they indulge in its cargo and become stormily inebriated. Their compromised consciousness provided the pilot an opportunity to save himself by running aground on Eastham at midnight. The gambit destroyed his ship and killed all aboard except the lucky captain.

Misguided, the *Whydah* followed into the danger. When it struck ground, its crew murdered all prisoners and forced laborers, a deduction culled from the wounds on the mangled bodies found floating in the surf. The narrative omits the nor'easter entirely but still conveys utter destruction, as "not a soul escaped out of her or Williams', who was also lost." No model of consistency, the very next paragraph remarks on seven survivors seized by the inhabitants of Eastham and tried and executed in Boston.

Elements of this story inspired Thomas Hutchinson's 1767 history of Massachusetts. Hutchinson records, for example, that seven of Bellamy's crew were intoxicated upon a vessel—unnamed in his account—which allowed the shrewd pilot to run ashore and surrender the pirates to authorities. The entire crew of the *Whydah* is drowned except "one Englishman and one Indian." Six men are tried and executed for piracy. Hutchinson does not explain the fate of the remaining three survivors, laying the groundwork for folklore to fill in the gap.

Although brief, Hutchinson's account influenced Levi Whitman's 1793 description of Wellfleet. Whitman's pen adds dramatic intrigue, overtly asserting that the captain of a captured snow (a type of vessel) deliberately ran Bellamy's fleet ashore. In this narrative Bellamy promises no harm if the guide sails them safely to Cape Cod Bay. "The captain," Whitman contends, suspects "that the pirate would not keep his promise, and that instead of clearing his ship, as was his pretense, his intentions were to plunder the inhabitants of Provincetown."

Alarmed, the unnamed hero devised a plan of action. "The night being dark, a lantern was hung in the shrouds of the snow," Whitman continues, but instead of guiding the *Whydah* to safety he led Bellamy to crash upon the outer bar; the snow being much smaller, it slipped through that barrier and made it safely to land. A violent storm then arose and pummeled the shipwrecked Bellamy, leaving only two survivors in addition to the pirates who escaped prior to the raging cyclone. Whitman observes that coins from the *Whydah* are still found in his day. "The violence of the seas moves the sands upon the outer bar," he concludes, "so that at times the iron caboose of the ship, at low ebbs, has been seen."

In 1814 Yarmouth-born educator Timothy Alden published *A Collection of American Epitaphs and Inscriptions.* The fourth volume contains an entry on Bellamy, incorporating its predecessors into a distinctive narrative. It also introduces the wild man—"a man of very singular and frightful aspect"—and his struggle with "infernals." Alden does not identify the source for this tale, and the grammar is painfully ambiguous. "Aged people relate that this man frequently spent the night in private houses" could mean that he consulted the elderly directly about an occurrence or that it is a narrative device, part of a fictionalized account.

Regardless of whether Alden recorded a folk narrative or invented it, his tale became the defining story for a century. It appeared in Henry David Thoreau's account of Cape Cod—Thoreau's narrative adds a compelling image of the captain tossing a burning tar-barrel into the water to lure Bellamy to his doom—and was the direct source for Charles Skinner's "The Wild Man of Cape Cod" in *Myths and Legends of Our Own Land.*

At no point in the first two centuries of storytelling about Bellamy is there the slightest mention of a romantic affair with a woman on Cape Cod. Bellamy is exacting and calculatingly villainous. And as folklore, these tales echo a prominent theme in New England, namely the clever Yankee who outwits the Devil, in this case the captain who deceives Bellamy.

Furthermore, the notion of the wild man searching for the *Whydah*'s gold evolved from the ceaseless slew of Kidd treasure tales. Historians of the 1800s overtly noticed the connection, and Edward Hale, minister of the South Congregational Church in Boston, even pondered if Kidd's *Quedah* had been taken back to sea and renamed the *Whidah.* "Twenty years is not a long period of life for a ship built in the East Indies," Hale asserts. "It may be that Kidd's lost treasure-ship is the same vessel which was wrecked, twenty years after, on the back of Cape Cod."

The romance of Bellamy and Hallett threw these earlier folktales off course. Such saccharine tales of unrequited love would have been risible to audiences demanding piratical treachery in the nineteenth century, but they fell on sympathetic eyes and ears in the twentieth.

Michael Fitzgerald provided the intermediary between the two narrative traditions. Fitzgerald was a telegraph cable operator by profession who became superintendent of a major company in New York and then for the French Cable Company's station in Orleans. He retired to East Brewster and turned to a life of writing novels, poetry, and journalism. His *1812: A Tale of Cape Cod* imagines a storyteller, Uncle Jabez, narrating the tale of the wild man.

In Fitzgerald's account the wild man is itinerate. His search for pirate gold, however, occurs near the hut of one Goody Hallett, which was perched between Wellfleet and Eastham. Given her transformation in later tales it is worth reproducing Fitzgerald's description:

> *Goody Hallett lived alone. She was old and most people regarded her as a witch, but this was probably because she kept much to herself. She was expert at the spinning-wheel and ostensibly supported herself by this industry. She never asked charity, though people wondered how so old a woman could earn enough to keep her from want. She courted seclusion, and the situation of her small dwelling far removed from the prying eyes of neighbors, favored this. A tall, thin woman, with dark features strongly telling of Indian blood, her appearance went far to confirm the idea that she rode the broomstick and could work charms. She was not a native of this place. It was said she belonged to a distant part of the Cape, beyond Yarmouth, and she arrived in Eastham soon after the wreck of the "Whidah."*

This Goody Hallett is an amalgam of Liza Towerhill and Mary Dunn—that is, the Witch of Half Way Pond—relocated to the Outer Cape. In Fitzgerald's story she is also first cousin to "Indian Tom," survivor of the *Whydah*—a figure based upon John Julian. He informs her of the treasure that survived the wreck, and after he dies under mysterious circumstances—presumably poison—Hallett moves to its vicinity. The wild man is, of course, the second survivor of the shipwreck, although he is not identified as Tom Davis. Instead, he is a willing—and greedy—member of Bellamy's pirate crew or Bellamy himself.

Elements of Hannah Screecher also bleed into the character of Goody Hallett. Although she and the wild man initially collaborate to divide the spoils, years later Jabez (as a boy) finds her missing from her hovel. The young man overhears a commotion nearby. He peers over the cliffs to the beach below, where the *Whydah*'s dead washed ashore. "Old Goody Hallett was lying on her back," the story continues, "her throat cut from ear to ear." Above her stood the wild man, damning her and claiming for eternity that which belonged to Sam Bellamy.

Bellamy folklore took a profound turn following Elizabeth Reynard's *The Narrow Land*, published in 1934. There one finds Maria Hallett, a fifteen-year-old who falls in love with the handsome Bellamy days before he is to leave with Williams to salvage in southern waters. Bellamy returns her affection and under an apple tree in Eastham promises to return and wed Hallett when he has gathered his fortune.

After Bellamy sails away, Hallett discovers their pregnancy. She gives birth to a boy with black eyes and black hair, the image of his handsome father. Afraid of the consequences, Hallett hides the boy in an accommodating neighbor's barn, where the infant dies after accidentally choking on a piece of straw. The boy's body is discovered and Hallett imprisoned, but she continually escapes and seeks the cliffs, where she pines for Bellamy's sails to return.

The townspeople eventually chase her away as a witch—no one could explain how she escaped jail so often (a later story imagines the Devil bending the bars open for the price of her allegiance)—and in exile Hallett establishes a hut in Wellfleet, ever waiting for her love. The same townspeople whisper that she exchanged her soul with the Devil so that he should bring Bellamy back to her arms.

The Devil provided as he is wont to do—with cruel intention—and cast her shipwrecked lover upon the piratical shore. John Julian and Tom Davis, desperate survivors, find her "nursing a wounded, half-drowned seaman, before whose gaze they quailed." Two days later Paulsgrave Williams appears in the *Marianne*, perhaps to salvage or perhaps "to carry off the wounded man who was hidden in Maria's house."

Tom Davis is acquitted. John Julian never stands trial, having mysteriously disappeared. But he is seen once again, at Hallett's hut, being nursed into a gentle night. She never wants for charity again. The dying Julian reveals the location of the treasure they secured in the aftermath of the wreck.

In the autumn of an unknown year, a tall stranger with black eyes and hair returns to Eastham. His mind is not always clear, but he never lacks for money. That stranger dies in the sultry months of the summer of 1720. A week later, an accommodating neighbor visits Hallett and finds her on the beach below the cliffs, "a gash across her white throat," the suicide weapon still in her grasp.

In her notes Reynard explains that her depiction of Maria Hallett is based on Fitzgerald's novel and oral traditions from Eastham and Orleans. I do not doubt such inspiration, but the story of Maria Hallett is an obvious case of literary license—a quite entertaining one—that was invented in Reynard's book.

In truth, Goody Hallett was never meant to be Bellamy's lover. She was an independent folk character, often called the Witch of Eastham, the Witch of Wellfleet, or the Sea Witch of Billingsgate. Reynard herself included a separate tale about Goody Hallett, a sorceress who lived in a hut in Wellfleet with two familiars, a black cat and a black goat. Goody Hallett was a mooncusser as well, and a skillful one, for she could hang a luring lantern on the tail of a whistling whale. And when she was not at home on land, Hallett was in her other abode, deep in the belly of a whale, where she played dice against the Devil. He strangled her to death one day after she won too many times.

Jeremiah Digges seconded the motion to separate tales of Goody Hallett from Sam Bellamy. In his guidebook from 1937 he overtly distinguished the two traditions, reasonably explaining that they were stitched together simply because of Bellamy's wreck in the waters near the witch's hovel. Two independent folk narratives—a treasure tale connected with Bellamy and a localized version of the Cape Cod witch—collided into a cohesive romance. (Digges mentions an alternative tradition in which an Indigenous woman named Deliah Roach was mistaken as Goody Hallett.)

This clarification arrived too late. Audiences simply adored Reynard's story—and she returned to it in 1951 in her widely praised *The Mutinous Wind*, forever sealing the connection—and ignored the previous two centuries of Bellamy folklore. Raconteurs soon opined that Bellamy opted to return to Cape Cod on the day of his death to fulfill his promise of marriage. And when the *Whydah*'s wreck was discovered in 1984, the swooning story rekindled and flourished as national news.

Admirable curators of local history have recently set out to find the real Maria Hallett. Some will say she was Mary Hallett, an unmarried woman who died in Yarmouth in 1751. Others remain uncertain, charmed by a treasure that cannot be found. I hope we can all agree that the quest itself reveals the intoxicating promise of wild stories.

Legend Tripping

The area known as Goody Hallett's Meadow and the site of the *Whydah* wreck encompasses the stretch of beach, dunes, and cliffs between the Marconi Beach parking lot and the Marconi Station Area, about 1.5 miles. It is part of the Cape Cod National Seashore (https://www.nps .gov/caco/index.htm); seasonal fees apply. It is a stellar out-and-back hike. The parking lot is at the end of Marconi Beach Road; enter the beach and hike north toward the station. The beach hike will pass by the former site of Camp Wellfleet on the dunes. Be aware of erosion, and do not walk on the dunes, which is both dangerous and environmentally unsound. Further information may be found on the CCNS website. **Trailhead GPS: N41 53.27 / W69 57.48**

Plan to visit the Marconi Station Area separately to access two observation decks overlooking the Atlantic and pine for your pirate love. That parking lot is free at the end of Marconi Station Road. To extend the hike, walk the Atlantic White Cedar Swamp Trail, also part of the Cape Cod National Seashore. It is a 1.2-mile loop accessible from the Marconi Station Area, with boardwalks throughout. **Trailhead GPS: N41 54.47 / W69 58.20**

There are other hikes in the area, including a trail known as Fresh Brook Loop, which circles from the Marconi Beach parking lot to the Cape Cod Rail Trail and back. There are no trail markings. It is best to follow a local guide.

To enjoy other great hiking and beaches associated with the wandering wild man, visit the other sites overseen by the Cape Cod National Shoreline in Eastham, including the 1.3-mile Nauset Marsh Trail and its 1.5-mile extension to Coast Guard Beach, the Fort Hill Trail and Red Maple Swamp, and the short Doane Trail to examine the largest glacial erratic on the Cape. **Trailhead GPS: N41 50.16 / W69 58.20**

11

Old Harry Main of Ipswich

HARRY MAIN WAS a dark-souled being whose delight in evil grew over the passage of his life. He was a pirate turned smuggler turned wrecker—a mooncusser, one of those despicable devils who lures trusting souls to sink their ships in the false promise of safe harbor from a storm. All along Plum Island and the Ipswich Bar he sent the unwary to hell, stealing their treasure from broken hulls.

When Harry Main died, eternal justice prevailed. Some say that his restless spirit was sentenced to shovel sand against the rising tides until the end of time. Others say he was given the infernal task to weave ropes from grains of sand. Still others say his ghost haunts the beaches where his crimes and their victims made him infamous forever. All agree that when the squalls rise and the seas rage and the waves lash Ipswich Bar, Old Harry is growling again.

Mortal men can be foolish when the desire for wealth creeps into their dreams. And so it was that a foolish man of Ipswich—his name long since forgotten—dreamed for three nights of Harry Main's treasure. Then, under the blanket of darkness, he found the spot where nocturnal auguries admonished a shovel's hard work. Down the man dug into the soft earth until he stood deep in the pit.

At last his spade hit iron, a bar wrought upon a flat stone. He lifted it up, a satisfied smile upon his face, and heaved its heavy weight out of the hole. He then reached down to wrestle the stone and to take the treasure surely waiting underneath. It was then he realized that he was not alone.

The first green eyes that peered upon him burned with curiosity. But the second, and the third, and all the others—too many to count in quick time—stared squinting as if at imperiled prey. A horde of black cats growled from atop the pit.

"Scat!" ordered the avaricious man to the feline army assembled above. No sooner did the words leave his lips when his heart sank within his chest. He had forgotten the old stories and their deathless moral: Never speak when doing the Devil's work of stealing a pirate's treasure. The cats scurried away, but not for fear of a foolish dreamer.

The pit filled rapidly with icy water, cold enough to kill a man. Fearful that he would drown numb in the searing chill, the man fled the pit. And in its bitter waters he could see the stone and the treasure it surely hid sink deep down into oblivion.

The unlucky man carried home that iron bar as a reminder of the night he almost found Harry Main's buried treasure. And on the nights when Old Harry growled, the man would sometimes touch that souvenir and wonder what would have been if he had only remembered the imperishable wisdom of the stories he once was told.

The legend of Harry Main has entertained the good people of Ipswich— and perhaps frightened its children—for quite some time. And for as long as it has been told, audiences have wondered who Harry Main is and if he ever existed.

A noble attempt was made to identify the person behind the legend in 1905 when local historian Thomas Franklin Waters published *Ipswich in the Massachusetts Bay Colony*. Twice therein Waters points to the sale of land in 1673 by William Roe to two fishermen from the Isle of Shoals, Andrew Diamond and Henry Maine. "Nothing more is known of this Henry Maine," Waters explains, "and his interest was acquired by Diamond."

Despite this flimsy evidence, Waters confidently concludes that Henry Maine is "without doubt the flesh and blood original of the mythical Harry Main."

Water's claim is not impossible—obviously "Harry" substitutes easily for "Henry"—but it raises as many questions as it attempts to solve. Why would the people of Ipswich tell a gruesome tale about a fisherman who barely interacted with their community? If the story of the eternally damned Harry Main is based on the actual Henry Maine, what could their connection be? Waters himself ponders this disconnect, noting in a second volume that Henry Maine was a "reputable citizen so far as we know" undeserving of his "mythical renown as an evil doer."

Recent investigations by local historians underscore that there are remarkably few records concerning Henry Maine's dealings, but one is promising for a folk narrative: It appears that he died by drowning in 1687. Yet many people died by drowning in Ipswich—Joseph Felt, a local clergyman who compiled a town history in 1834, dedicates pages to such untimely deaths—so this fact alone leads only to a dead end. (Please forgive the bad pun.)

Felt mentions, for example, an old man who drowned in 1635 when he set out after being warned of an impending storm, profaning fate and taking along his dog, whom he had taught to steer. But Maine never appears in Felt's book. The absence implies that he was not a man of consequence to the town. And there is not a shred of evidence to suggest an unbroken chain of storytelling about Maine from the 1600s onward. If Henry Maine is not the direct inspiration for the villainous folk character, then who could Harry Main be?

Although we can assume tales were circulating in the oral tradition much earlier, the legends of Harry Main do not appear in print until the mid-1800s. In 1863, for example, the *Boston Journal* published an editorial, "A Day in Ipswich," by a writer identified only as "N. E." N. E. invokes the legend of Harry Main but regrettably offers no details, assuming the reader would know it.

It would take another decade until the tale found a storyteller willing to share its secrets. That year James Appleton Morgan published a poem, "Ipswich Town." It soon became the classic statement of the folklore of Ipswich, aided in its influence when Henry Wadsworth Longfellow included it in a collection of poems in 1878. Morgan's lines have been reprinted untold times to this day. The poem contains this telling stanza:

> I love to think of old Ipswich town;
> Harry Main—you have heard the tale—lived there:
> He blasphemed God—so they put him down
> With an iron shovel, at Ipswich Bar;
> They chained him there for a thousand years,
> As the sea rolls up to shovel it back:
> So when the sea cries, the goodwives say
> "Harry Main growls at his work to day."

Morgan leaves no doubt: The crime for which Main is punished is blasphemy, not piracy or its ilk. But it remains ambiguous, at least here, as to who precisely enacted the punishment.

A story by Earnest Bell one year later sheds some light. "The Wraith of the Winthrop Mansion" appeared in *Appleton's Journal*. In establishing a haunting atmosphere, Bell draws from several Ipswich legends, including that the *Mayflower* visited on route to Plymouth and "was frightened away again by its rough breakers, first having left Harry Main in the surf."

Four years later the novel *For Each Other* reiterated this exceptional idea that the Pilgrims visited Ipswich and decided that while it was too dangerous to land there, it was not too dangerous a place to drop off a blasphemer, Harry Main, and bind him in chains with only an iron shovel to combat the rising tides. (For the curious reader, there was no Harry Main among the passengers of the actual *Mayflower*.)

Morgan's poem is not entirely copasetic with this connection, at least not initially. The first stanza of his poem describes the *Mayflower*'s visit to

Ipswich, but he does not mention Main until his fifth. The three stanzas in between are also dedicated to Ipswich lore. One details witches, another the purported regicides of King Charles I hiding in the town. The third describes a purported contest between the preacher George Whitefield and the Devil lurking in a church steeple. When the Evil One loses and leaps out of town, he leaves his footprint in a stone that is still exhibited today.

Morgan's intention to bond the *Mayflower* and Harry Main came years later. In 1895 he republished "Old Ipswich Town" in *The Magazine of Poetry*. In this version he added another, eighth stanza narrating the legend of Heartbreak Hill, a sorrowful Indian tale. But Morgan made another fascinating edit: He switched the stanzas about Whitefield and Main so that the tale of the punished blasphemer immediately follows in the *Mayflower*'s wake.

James Appleton Morgan was not, incidentally, a native of Ipswich. He was born in Portland, Maine, moved to Wisconsin, studied law at Columbia, married in New Orleans, and was counsel for the Erie Railroad. He retired from the practice of law to follow scholarly pursuits. He was one of the earliest proponents to contend that the works of Shakespeare were composed by committee rather than by a single playwright. Morgan died in 1928 in New York City.

His family, however, had deep roots in Ipswich, including their ancestral home. His grandfather James Appleton was born and spent the final decades of his life on the family farm following a successful career as a politician in Maine. So while it is difficult to ascertain precisely how well acquainted Morgan was with the tales of Ipswich, there is a good chance that his poem conveyed local folklore rather than invented it.

In 1881 Benjamin Hill and Winfield Nevins published a guidebook to the North Shore. Their entry is painfully brief, but it correlates some of Morgan's impressions. "There is a legend," they write, "that one Harry Main, an early settler, was, because of a blasphemous act, chained to this bar with an iron shovel and sentenced to shovel back the sand for a thousand years. So when the sea roars the people say: Harry Main has had hard work today."

An early settler? Perhaps there is a hint of support for Henry Maine in that passing claim. But more importantly, Hill and Nevins do not identify the specific blasphemous act. And although they do not mention the *Mayflower*, they agree that in no way whatsoever was Main's crime one of piracy.

That claim would wait until 1884, the year that Samuel Adams Drake published *A Book of New England Legends and Folklore*. Drake, who lived in Boston at the time, suggests in his account that he had recently toured Ipswich. He was shown the Devil's footprint and various haunted houses. He was also brought down by the river to "the house where Harry Main lived," revealing a new and evolving element of the lore. It is in that context that the notion of mooncussing arises. "It is said that he had been by turns a pirate, a smuggler, and a wrecker," Drake writes of Main, crimes for which his ghost was "doomed to be chained on Ipswich Bar" and "everlastingly to coil a cable of sand there."

It is Drake's account, presumably borrowed from a local storyteller, which secures the image of Harry Main the mooncusser for posterity. Enigmatic references to blasphemy disappear—as does the *Mayflower*—to be replaced with a very specific villainous and piratical activity. And that alteration was appropriate for the late 1800s, when New Englanders were obsessed with tales of pirate treasure. Whoever shared that narrative with Drake was in all likelihood adapting an earlier tradition of Harry Main to one more fashionable for the moment.

In 1896 Main's transformation became permanent. Charles Skinner's widely popular *Myths and Legends of Our Own Land* drew from Drake's account and depicted Harry Main as a wrecker punished in the afterlife. Akin to Drake, Skinner's Main becomes a ghost who frightens people on Plum Island during stormy nights. And Skinner inadvertently made one other element immutable: that the tale of the diabolical cats concerned Main's treasure rather than that of another infamous pirate.

Did Skinner accurately read his predecessor? Here is Drake's original language introducing the tale of the cat-bewitched pit:

> *Harry Main's house—for we must remember that he had one—was ransacked, and every rod of the garden dug up for the money that he was supposed to have buried there; but nothing rewarded the search. Other places, too, have been explored with the same result, in quest of Kidd's hidden treasure.*

Skinner decided that Main owned the loot. But Abbie Farwell Brown, the renowned Massachusetts writer, saw it differently. In an essay on Ipswich published in *New England Magazine* in 1903, she divorces the treasure tale from Main and restores it to Kidd. And honestly, that tale is a perfect example of a Kidd legend, as we have seen numerous times in this book.

Brown and Skinner agree, however, that Main was a wrecker. Undoubtedly he had become so in folk narratives told in the late 1800s, allowing for the conflation and confusion with Kidd in the first place. But there is no question that Main is not a wrecker in earlier narrative traditions. In those, he is a shadowy figure, a blasphemer, sentenced to fight the tides with an iron shovel or to coil ropes of sand.

Those two punishments provide another clue to his identity. In the 1800s numerous stories were told throughout the British Isles and coastal America in which a sinister being is outwitted and made to endlessly coil ropes of sand. That same being appeared in copious folk rhymes sung from Scotland to North Carolina, in which he wields an iron shovel, often to accomplish impossible labor.

That being is, of course, Old Harry himself: the Devil. (Harry, like Nick, is one of the Devil's human-sounding names.)

It is my educated guess that stories of the Infernal One were circulating among Ipswich storytellers of English and Scottish descent and that

Harry Main is a local version of His Satanic Majesty. That would explain why the earliest stories depict him as a blasphemer who is given an occult task. And assuming that Drake is accurate when he reports that worried residents characterized the crashing sound of storms and the howling winds by exclaiming "Old Harry's growling again," we have readily entered superstitious territory long associated with the Devil and seafaring customs.

It appears, furthermore, that those earlier stories simply merged with pirate tales, especially those of Kidd's treasure, in the later 1800s. There are numerous independent tales, for example, that Kidd buried treasure on Plum Island, so such a mixture is expected and tantalizing. It makes for a diabolically rich narrative, one that has tempted storytellers to this day, even those who have no idea of Harry Main's likely origins.

That the house associated with Harry Main the diabolical figure was on the property that once belonged to Henry Maine the fisherman is not purely coincidental. There's a very good chance that storytellers made the connection when they learned of Henry Maine and thereby embedded more local flavor into the tale of an infernal being at work where the waves pummel the shore. But there is no reason to think that Henry Maine was the primary inspiration for Harry Main.

Indeed, with a tinge of historical raillery, Thomas Franklin Waters himself recorded one further piece of evidence that Harry Main was a folk character inspired by the Devil. The house of Jabesh Sweet was constructed on the property once owned by Henry Maine. The Sweet house stood adjacent to the dwelling that visitors identified as the Harry Main house. The Sweet house still stands, now without its companion.

In 1905, Waters explained that the Sweet house was both reputed to be haunted and associated with Harry Main. "Many manifestations of the presence of some uneasy spirit so alarmed the occupants," Waters writes, "that all the ministers of the Town assembled there one day and prayed, and the uncanny doings ceased." Waters does not mention the year in which this purported exorcism of the Sweet house occurred. And he clearly did not believe the rumor to be true.

In an earlier work from 1898, Waters records a similar tale of laying the adjacent Harry Main house. "Tradition is whimsical and fantastic," Waters opines. "It chains poor Harry Main on Ipswich bar, and locates a ghost in his house, recently demolished, which was vanquished by the united efforts of the three ministers then resident here, and effectively cast out. It frightens old Nick out of the meeting house when Whitefield preaches and shows his footprint in the ledge."

Waters is onto something, namely that the tale of an exorcism of a ghost from the purported Harry Main house (a tale that migrated to the Sweet house after the first building was raised) echoes the popular folk story of Whitefield driving the Devil out of Ipswich. The stories of laying the ghost of Harry Main from actual homes repeat the themes of ridding the town of the Evil One.

So just who is Harry Main? Only the Devil knows for sure . . .

Legend Tripping

Although the site of Harry Main's treasure could be hidden anywhere in Ipswich, the site of his eternal damnation is the Ipswich Bar, which is now within Sandy Point State Reservation, a state park (https://www.mass .gov/locations/sandy-point-state-reservation) at the southern tip of Plum Island. There are a few options for hiking, including the very small loop at Bar Head. A longer loop of about 3 miles would start at the Sandy Point public parking and traverse the Ipswich Bar, Ipswich Bluffs, the Stage Island Trail, Bar Head, and some of the beaches. Unfortunately erosion and tidal flooding can cause closures, so it is best to inquire ahead about conditions. Parking fees are seasonal throughout Plum Island. **Trailhead GPS: N42 42.12 / W70 46.32**

Access to Sandy Point State Reservation requires travel down virtually the entire length of Plum Island, starting in Newbury, then through the Rowley section, then into the Ipswich section. The beaches here are well worth exploring. Much of Plum Island is under the jurisdiction of the Parker River National Wildlife Refuge of the US Fish and Wildlife

Service (https://www.fws.gov/refuge/Parker_River/). Among the many opportunities here is the Hellcat Interpretive Trail, a meandering section of 1.4 miles. A new boardwalk was recently installed. As of this writing the pamphlet and map are available at https://www.fws.gov/uploaded Files/HellcatTrailGuide.pdf. **Trailhead GPS: N42 44.28 / W70 47.43**

12

The Treasure of Scraggum Woods

LTHOUGH STORIES OF the sea serpent reign as the most plentiful in Massachusetts folklore, the previous few chapters illustrate that treasure tales are not far behind. In this one, I hope to create a sense of following a weathered map to a very opulent end.

As I noted elsewhere, the quintessential treasure tale in the Commonwealth concerns Captain Kidd. It is an honest jest that it is easier to identify the places where Kidd is *not* said to have buried treasure in the Bay State than to enumerate the places where he did. In hunting for a lesser known one to share, I came across a gem from 1842 in the *Boston Transcript*. It concerns, as the anonymous author writes, "an old woman, whose name I think was Molly Spring."

Molly approaches "one of the well-known men of Gloucester and told him that three nights in succession an old man had come to her in her dreams and confided to her where a pot of money was buried." The man agrees to accompany Molly to the spot the following evening. His muscles are stretched digging for the hidden loot while Molly observes from atop a fence.

"Deeper and deeper grew the hole," the tale continues, "and, at length, his spade struck upon a hard substance, which he doubted not was the desired chest or pot, when he was suddenly arrested by a piercing shriek from Molly. He flew to her assistance and found her lying faint on the ground." When Molly came to her senses, she explained that the very moment her companion reached the chest, the old man of her dreams appeared before her. He "held out his long, skinny arm, and his thin bony fingers" and asked if she would like a pinch of snuff. She screamed in fright from the sudden apparition.

Relieved that Molly was uninjured, the pair returned to the treasure awaiting them in the ground. But it had disappeared forever. Molly's scream had broken the magical prohibition of silence.

On the one hand Molly's narrative is a classic Kidd tale with a dream omen and the loss of the treasure due to an abrupt noise. But it is an interesting variant. It is one of the few in which a woman initiates the treasure hunt. It is also compelling in that the guardian responsible for the breaking of silence is the same figure who beckons to the treasure. It is undeniably an oddity in that the guardian offers snuff to the mortal hunter rather than springs out with malicious intent.

Molly's story points to the "witches" of Dogtown. Tammy Younger, for example, increasingly became associated with pirates—and with sharing in their vices—and a sea captain's snuff box purportedly was discovered in the cellar of her house. Treasure tales anchored there as well. Although no full-fledged legend survives, rumors relay that Cornelius Finson—"Black Neil"—a poor African American and the presumed last resident of Dogtown, lived in the ruined cellars of two widows under the impression they had buried treasure somewhere beneath the ground.

Another tale from 1877 places Kidd's treasure just down the road from Dogtown at the mouth of the Annisquam River. In this brief account, the man who learned its location attempts to inform his grandson of the path, but dies in the process of revealing it. "Scoffers" (so writes the reporter) may ask why the grandfather did not elect to dig up the iron pot himself when in the prime of his life, "but that wouldn't be the conventional way of proceeding in such cases."

On occasion—and regrettably—only a vestige of a storytelling tradition survives. Henry David Thoreau records in his journal on November 5, 1854, that while walking by White Pond two men, John Hosmer and Anthony Wright, hailed him "to come and see where they had dug for money." Thoreau gazed upon a hole six feet square and just as deep. Hosmer explained that people had been digging in the area for over a hundred years. To satisfy Thoreau's inquiry, Hosmer narrated a tale told to him by a Dr. Lee, told to him by "old Mr. Wood"—a delightful example akin to friend-of-a-friend chains in contemporary urban legends.

In the time of Captain Kidd, so went Mr. Wood's story, three pirates arrived at his house with deerskin breeches overflowing with coins. They requested permission to bury this treasure in Mr. Wood's cellar. He refused, fearful of the demands for hiding such a secret. Instead, the helpful host lent his guests some shovels, a lantern, and earthen pots. A woman in the Wood household, however, followed the pirates at a distance "down the next hollow on the south, and saw them go along the meadow-side and turn up this hollow." Self-awareness of the danger that such knowledge could entail suddenly gripped her mind, and appropriately nervous she retreated hastily home. The pirates, in gratitude, returned the shovels and the lantern along with a hat deformed by heavy coins. Mr. Wood initially buried that cache in his cellar but found them useful later in life when misfortune rendered him poor.

If this entry is painfully brief, another recorded by Josiah Temple in 1887 is outrageously so. In a description of Learned Pond in his history of Framingham, Temple provides an account that is too precious to insult by summarizing:

> *Tradition has it, that a chest of gold was sunk near the west shore of this pond by Capt. Kidd, or some other noted pirate, and put under the "charm" by which such treasures were guarded. Several of the early settlers near the pond reported that they had caught sight of the mysterious chest, floating just beneath the surface, but no one had the courage*

and presence of mind to observe the necessary precautions to secure it. These conditions, according to the popular belief of the time, were: the presence of three persons arranged so as to represent the points of a triangle; the three to maintain perfect silence, and not take their eyes from the chest, but move slowly toward it, keeping their exact relative position; and one of them to lay a key or some iron tool upon it, when it would instantly become subject to his control, that is the diabolical spell by which it was held would thus be broken.

The last reputed observer of this chest, so far as is known, was Nathaniel Pratt Jr. (born 1702), who was accustomed to recount the particulars of his exploit, to the amazement of youthful listeners, and to deplore his want of forethought in neglecting to silently lay his jack-knife on the coveted treasure! In his excitement he spoke aloud, and, as he expressed it, "in a minnit the thing squiggled down into the mud out of sight!"

Learned Pond—or adjacent Farm Pond, the treasure's location according to William Barry's earlier history of Framingham—and White Pond are quite a hike for pirates, but they pale in comparison to the efforts necessary to bury treasure in Byfield.

In 2007, Newbury's 375th anniversary celebration included a guided hike to Balancing Rock on Kent Island. An accompanying article by Sabrina Cardin in the *Daily News of Newburyport* summarized the associated legend. "In the late 1700s," Cardin writes, "a lawyer and his friend stole a pirate's treasure and buried it around an oddly positioned boulder nicknamed Balancing Rock, located on an island in the marsh. To remember where the treasure was buried, the thieves carved an 'A' into the side of the rock and planned to return in five years to reclaim their hidden fortune. Legend has it they never returned, but the 'A' is still visible today."

To which Paul Ames, of *Amesie's Automotive Corner*, responds, "bullcrap."

I'm going to break my skepticism as a professional folklorist and inform you that the Byfield treasure is real. It is the YouTube video of Ames's "The Legend of Buried Treasure in Byfield!" His captivating narration of the tale while venturing into the snowy woods is folklore gold. Ames leads viewers to the west of the village of Byfield rather than to the southeast where Kent Island is located.

Although these two narratives differ significantly on the location of the treasure, both are rooted in a story concerning the pirate Roger Hayman. The most complete version of this tale is found in Edward Rowe Snow's 1951 *True Tales of Buried Treasure*. Snow returned to the topic in his 1980 *Sea Disasters and Inland Catastrophes*, where he admits frustration at not being able to put all the pieces together. Before we begin, I would like to state that Snow's instincts and thoroughness never cease to amaze. Although not a professional folklorist by training, he did his homework as well as the best of us: Archival research, detailed interviews, and ethnographic analysis inform all of his work—and his prowess as a storyteller remains unchallenged to this day.

As Snow explains, it required several trips to Newburyport, Byfield, and Georgetown to compile the scattered fragments of the legend into a coherent whole. Many people were only willing to provide information anonymously. Snow credits the two residents willing to go on the record, Orin Arlin and Fred Dudley Pearson, as well as Grace Bixby, the town librarian and historian, and Frederick Green, a critic of the story's historicity.

As pieced together, Roger Hayman had a piratical penchant for raiding British and American ships that traveled near Haiti in the waning decades of the 1700s. He was wounded, however, in a naval battle and returned to England to retire from the buccaneer's career. He also carried home to Liverpool two chests of souvenirs from his once massive loot. But upon reaching the door of his house, Hayman learned that his wife and child had left for the United States. He followed them, still injured, and still carrying a fortune.

Hayman's condition worsened on the ship that ferried him across the Atlantic to New York City. The purser, a man by the name of Hanson, sought the aid of a medical doctor with the last name Griffin. "Don't forget your promise," Hayman whispered to Hanson upon hearing the dire diagnosis of his final days.

Hanson did not forget his promise to deliver the treasure to Hayman's family. He outright ignored it. And he enlisted Griffin's assistance to steal the pirate's treasure as he lay dying in his cabin. Griffin consented and then double-crossed the double-crosser. Conspiring with another passenger, his friend Stearns Compton, Griffin absconded with the loot at the ship's first stop in Newburyport. They headed west to the unassuming village of Byfield. There they stopped at the Pearson Tavern, caught their breath and a fine meal, and in the morning wandered to the Parker River. They buried the treasure and chiseled an "A" into a rock as a beacon for future days.

Griffin and Compton were unaware that a young boy, Howard Noyes, spied on them from a tree. Noyes returned to the spot after the thieves departed. For some reason, however, no search of the earth gave up the treasure, although the letter A remained plain as day to anyone who wishes to see.

Snow's reconstruction includes the discovery by Compton's great-granddaughter of the pact he signed with Griffin. In 1923 she reportedly reached out to the latest owner of the Tavern, Fred Dudley Pearson. She was surprised to learn that town residents were well aware of the treasure's existence thanks to Howard Noyes's revelation when it occurred.

Snow closes with Orin Arlin's recollection of a well digger in 1932, who worked in the area of the rock marked with an A. This laborer disappeared suddenly without completing his task, and was never seen again. Some days later Arlin stopped at a store in Salisbury, where the shop owner showed him the money a well digger had recently used: a handful of silver dollars with the dates from 1794 to 1799.

Snow reports that the *Massachusetts Spy*, a newspaper, recorded the instigating events on three occasions in 1800. An examination reveals an
account by Edward Stevens of a naval battle on the western coast of Haiti
in January of that year. There is no direct mention of Roger Hayman, so
it is my educated guess that Snow's informants introduced a fictional
brigand. And all things considered, Hayman's backstory is of little consequence; the tale just needs a dead pirate to get the treasure on the roads
to Byfield.

There was an alternative tradition in which the treasure came over
on a steamship, perhaps as late as the 1840s. This version was narrated
by Mary Northend to Willard de Lue, the esteemed travel writer for the
Boston Globe in December 1951. And in Northend's story, Edward Joyce's
son, not Howard Noyes, follows the conspirators to the burial location. De
Lue further reports another version in which only one of the accomplices
walks out of the woods alive.

Some of the earliest tales locate the rock with an A close to the
Pearson Tavern. And not all of the stories agree that the men chiseled
an "A" into the rock. In one account collected by de Lue, it is a triangle.
In some tales the treasure was only partially buried there, the remainder
deposited in a hemlock grove to the west of the village, in an area called
Scraggum Woods. In these accounts, a constable discovers the thieves but
never recovers the treasure. These contradictory tales demonstrate vigorous
community storytelling with far-reaching influence, as de Lue interviewed
an Arthur Toneatti of Gloucester, who was actively digging in the woods
in 1951—his seventeenth attempt!

I am not certain quite when the drama shifted to Kent Island, but
it is that name—"Scraggum Woods"—that is the key to the mystery, as
revealed by two essays, one in the *Boston Globe* and one in the *Boston Herald*, both from the first decade of the twentieth century.

"Mystery of Scraggum Woods" appeared in the *Globe* in 1909. It
is genetically related to the stories that Snow and de Lue collected. It
remarks upon the ceaseless activities of hunters in the woods, searching

for treasure buried more than a century prior by "two strange men, poorly dressed," who arrived at the Pearson Tavern in the morning of a midsummer's day.

The duo head to the location of Watts's Mills, today near Main Street not far from the tavern. They pause near a boulder at a section of the Parker—now called the Little River—and bury something small. Howard Noyes, undetected in a tree, observes their activities. The men retrace their steps and head into Scraggum Woods, "crossing a point where the railroad track now lies." In a hemlock bank in the heart of the forest, they dig a deep hole and deposit the bulk of their treasure.

In this version, it is *Noyes* who marks both the boulder and the second burial site. When a constable investigates, the boy leads him to Scraggum Woods, only to discover the mark had disappeared, the implication that it was washed away by natural forces. Noyes takes the constable to the boulder, but nothing is found beneath.

"Who the men were who buried the treasure," this tale concludes, "and where they came from, no one has ever been able to find out, but it is thought that they were pirates who came ashore in a small boat anchored off the Gloucester coast."

One can see the desire to name those men in 1909 be fulfilled with the later tale of Griffin and Compton, but doing so meant sacrificing their character roles as pirates. To maintain that continuity, Roger Hayman was introduced. And while we may never know why Howard Noyes was the name chosen for the shrewd young man who pursued a treasure, I have a suspicion: H. Howard Noyes was a respected citizen and president of the Georgetown Bank. This might be a wink woven into a story about finding a quick fortune.

Our treasure—the narrative treasure, that is—is finally discovered in the *Boston Herald*'s account in 1906. The headline reads "That Pirate Treasure in Scraggum Woods—Will It Ever Be Found?" The *Herald* reports on annual pilgrimages by treasure hunters and counts 153 burrows scarring the woods to date with failed attempts.

The details are in general sympathy with the *Globe*'s story. Two conspirators travel from Newburyport, hide something near a rock behind the Pearson Tavern, and continue into Scraggum Woods, where they bury their treasure. There is no mention of the marked rock. And the stunning reveal is that the two men are crewmembers for the pirate John Quelch—perhaps even Francis King, who escaped the hanging that claimed his captain on Nix's Mate Island in June 1704.

Quelch's tale begins in Marblehead in 1703 when he joined the *Charles*, a privateer ship under command of Daniel Plowman with orders to attack French ships off Canada. Plowman fell ill, however, and died in his cabin—or at least his crew testified to such after throwing his body into the ocean. Quelch was made captain and turned the ship toward Brazil, where they looted Portuguese ships. They returned to Marblehead and, after numerous complaints filed by their sponsors, became wanted men. Forty-six were arrested. Seven were sentenced to death. Six hanged upon the gallows. Quelch hanged, as the story concludes, having warned others to take care of how they bring money into New England.

Rumors grew into legends that Quelch hid treasure somewhere between Marblehead and the Isle of Shoals. And in that part of Essex County, Quelch effectively replaced Kidd as the pirate du jour. The Scraggum Woods story is a splendid example of the Kidd treasure tale evolving over time, long past a point where storytellers know its origins. That is as affluent a store of folklore as one could find searching for riches in Scraggum Woods.

Legend Tripping

White Pond in Concord allows hiking on the southern shore through meandering trails. It is overseen by the town of Concord's Division of Natural Resources, which publishes a pamphlet and map at https://concordma.gov/DocumentCenter/View/2097/White-Pond-Trail-Guide.

As of this writing, however, White Pond is going through some growing pains and active community debate about its use, protection, and accessibility, including parking. Anyone who intends to visit should first inquire with the town about hiking there.

The historical site of the Byfield treasure is found in what is now the Crane Pond Wildlife Management Area, a forest shared between Newbury, West Newbury, Groveland, and Georgetown. It is overseen by the Massachusetts Division of Fisheries and Wildlife (https://www .mass.gov/orgs/division-of-fisheries-and-wildlife). There are miles of trails here, all unmarked. The town of West Newbury Open Space Committee publishes a map (but cautions against entering without a compass) at https://www.wnewbury.org/open-space-committee/pages/ hiking-areas-and-trail-maps.

Hopefully these trails will be developed for hiking in the future, but as of now one should not risk wandering too deep into the forest even with a map. A local guide is indispensable for more rigorous exploration. Be aware that this is a popular area for hunting. The closest entry to Byfield is on Forest Street, where there is room for a vehicle, but again, anyone visiting the area should rely upon local guidance and assistance. **Trailhead GPS: N42 45.31 / W70 57.25**

The Essex National Heritage Area website provides a helpful overview at https://essexheritage.org/attractions/crane-pond-wildlife-management -area.

13

Dungeon Rock

SMALL VESSEL ANCHORED at the mouth of the Saugus River. Four men whose faces had never been seen before took to the waiting shore. They lifted something heavy—so heavy, in fact, that it weighed down their boat as if to smother it in the waters. The four men then lugged that large box deep into the woods that stood to the west of the Iron Works. The vessel was gone the next morning when the people of Lynn came to investigate.

It was later that morning when a blacksmith discovered a letter scribbled from a demanding hand. No name was attached to the request asking for shackles and handcuffs and hatches wrought by his rough hands. Days later he deposited the items in secret, precisely where the letter had ordered. One day later silver coins waited in their place for the silent Iron Works blacksmith.

Months passed quietly and without incident. Then those four faces were suddenly spotted again, arriving unannounced as if by an act of nature. They did not take up residence in Saugus or Lynn. They did not even venture to stare at the marvels accomplished by the sweat at the old Iron Works. Instead they found shelter among the thick pines and the deep woods of hemlock and cedar. There, among craggy rocks, they established a camp for their watchful eyes. In whispers people named it the Pirates Glen, but they were certain not to call upon it and wisely denied that it ever existed.

Word eventually reached the authorities as word of pirates is wont to do. They came quickly, armed, and with the merciless force of the law. Three pirates were taken on the spot, seized for the Crown like another treasure on display, rocking back and forth for all to see on the swinging gallows and gibbets.

The fourth man escaped just in time. On bleeding knees he pushed deeper into the woods far from the Pirates Glen, where a wall of rock stood as sentry to the unfinished business of time. There in a cavern he hid holding his breath, but the footsteps of the authorities never came near, and the tips of their firearms never passed by. It was a sad chance, he thought, that he should hide to save his life in the very cave where he and his mates once stowed away a heavy box of their hidden wealth.

The pirate Thomas Veale and the pirates' treasure survived the manhunt that day. In time he made the cavern a home, ever cautious that rumors would again lead to authorities and their firearms hounding a fugitive hidden deep in the woods. But it was sudden nature, not the law, which the pirate should have feared.

One day in 1658 began calmly, as was commonly the case in the life of the cautious pirate. He awoke in his cavern, spied the treasure, and breathed a sigh of relief for another day. It was at that moment, without warning, the Great Earthquake struck. It shook the ground. It broke the rock. And it sealed Thomas Veale and his heavy treasure deep inside the cave, forever a prison and then a tomb in the darkness of Dungeon Rock.

Originally I considered opening this chapter with a simple declaration:

Dungeon Rock Story here. Everyone knows it.

At least everyone in Massachusetts—if not New England—used to know it. The tale of Thomas Veale was one of the most widely shared folk narratives from the early nineteenth to the late twentieth centuries. It appeared in countless magazines, newspapers, town histories, and guidebooks for those two centuries. It is enjoying renewed excitement thanks to storytellers on the internet—and, of course, to an actual tunnel that can be visited on a hike.

I do not mean to be blasphemous to a beloved tale, but truth be told, this was not a very interesting story to begin with. It is a Kidd treasure tale deprived of supernatural elements, replacing the uncanny with an unfortunate death. In many ways the most noteworthy aspect is that ghost stories surrounding Veale did *not* arise from a folkloristic grave, although it is possible that such lore of hauntings circulated in the oral tradition a century ago.

The earliest recorded version that I can find—and the one always cited as the originating account—is Alonzo Lewis's *History of Lynn*, first published in 1829 with updates throughout the 1800s. Lewis was an admired son of Lynn as an accomplished poet and newspaper editor. In appearing in Lewis's history, the tale of Thomas Veale started life in a luxurious and privileged setting.

Although Lewis does not attribute a source, there is no indication that he was the inventor of this tale. Local historians, reporters, and other citizens treat his version with deference but never identify Lewis as the sole author. And the widespread adoption of names Lewis mentions suggests a broader community investment. Pirates Glen, Pirates Dungeon, and Dungeon Hill, for example, appear on an 1829 map that Lewis prepared for the Massachusetts legislature. It would have been a bold move to christen such locales with nothing more than one's desire, so all of this adds up to suggest that Veale's story circulated as a local variant to the widespread treasure tale.

It may have competed with others for audiences in Lynn. In 1853 Nathan Ames, whose own contribution I soon discuss, mentioned in passing another tradition in which "a beautiful female" was buried by pirates under a hemlock tree, the stump of which was still visible in his day—and dug under regularly. As I explained in the chapter on Hannah Screecher, stories of women as the victim of piratical horror are rare, but Ames's comment may be evidence of a subset that stretched from Cape Cod to

Massachusetts Bay. The fact that this tale lost out to the Veale legend implies the local community wanted to claim a unique contribution or to distance itself from one concerning a murdered woman.

Inevitably the issue of Thomas Veale's existence warrants attention. I am inclined to agree with A. C. Goodell, who in an address in 1869 to the Essex Institute "expressed grave doubts whether any pirate's cave ever existed there, and whether such a man as Thomas Veal ever lived." Goodell argued that there are no records of such a pirate in Massachusetts, a state that kept manifold records about the brigands with whom it dealt harshly. More recent attempts have implied that he might be based on the enigmatic "Captain Veale" who chased John Prentice from New London to Boston in 1685 and who escaped to Cape Ann when authorities took action, but even if that is so, it only underscores that *Thomas* Veale was an imaginary figure and folk character.

Charles Ellms, a Boston publisher, included Lewis's narrative verbatim in his popular collection *The Pirates Own Book* in 1837. No further promotion was necessary to guarantee the Veale legend its celebrity. Indeed, it would require a book of its own to hike through every celebration, imitation, and adaptation of his tale. But there are three important works from the 1800s that had decisive influence on the evolution and belief in the story.

The first is Nathan Ames's 1853 poem *Pirates' Glen and Dungeon Rock*. This is a four-canto epic poem directly inspired, Ames informs readers, by Lewis. It is, however, a wholly literary reinvention of the Veale legend. Veale is literally displaced for another—and Spanish—pirate named Don, the nemesis of a young man named Christopher. Don the pirate abducts Christopher's beloved Arabel, instigating a chase that incorporates the same localities as the earlier legend. Don maintains the upper hand for much of the poem, although eventually Christopher locates and rescues an imprisoned Arabel. Defeated and deserted, Don remains in the cave.

He perishes in the earthquake, but not before a rattlesnake poisons him, a bite guaranteeing final breaths in utter agony.

The poem is melodramatic romance—Don's wife, Clorinda, also dies tragically—and readers should know that it contains a subplot in which a local Indian woman, Ya-Wa-Ta, is enthralled with Christopher. The descriptions of Indigenous people are a product of their time.

The second contribution is James Robinson Newhall's *Lin: Or Jewels of the Third Plantation*, which initially appeared in 1862. An invocation appears in a journal by Obadiah Turner composed in 1658 in the aftermath of the earthquake. This entry provides the astonishing evidence of Veale's existence. Concerning Dungeon Rock, Turner recalls:

> *And it hath been said yet Thomas Veal, a crooked, grizzley and ill look-ing shoemaker did live in ye cave and do his shoemaking there. Some of us did use to purchase his works of him; for tho not neat and comelie to looke upon, yet they were strong and tight; just what we want where there be so many stumps and briars and so much mud and plash at times. On ye splitting of ye rock by ye earthquake as some think ye old man was shut up alive in ye cave; and no great loss to ye world as they will have it; he not beeing thot well of. Some say he was once a pirate robber and did bury treasure hereabout. But it seemeth strange if it be so, yet he should live so poorlie and work so hard. He did often come among us to trade his shoes for provisions, and hath been known, but not often, to have some small pieces of Spanish monie. It hath been fur-ther sayed yet he was one of a number of pirate robbers yet lived hidden in a glen by ye river towardes ye Iron Workes.*

Were it only so! Obadiah Turner was a fictitious character. Newhall created the entire journal—obviously drawing upon sources such as Lewis—but numerous people fell for it. Paranormal investigators still fall for it today, thinking that stories of Veale were passed without pause from the mid-1600s. The Turner hoax demonstrates the power of a good story, but it has been a thorn in the side of many a poor researcher. It also shaped the lore—which percolates even today as a "fact"—that Veale was a pirate-turned-shoemaker who did not want to draw attention so, for some reason, curiously opted to live in a cave rather than in town.

The final adaptation requires explanation. In 1851 newspapers throughout the region noted a stranger petitioning the mayor of Lynn for permission to dig—and to blast—the rock at Pirate's Cave, another name for Dungeon Rock, in pursuit of Veale's treasure. This was not the first time such explosive action was taken there. Lewis, in his 1844 update to the town history, provides a reproving comment about destruction done to the structure in 1834—a result, admittedly, of an enthusiast inspired by the legend he recorded.

In 1851 that stranger was Hiram Marble. And over the next three decades he and his family and their obsession would become well known to Lynn, to Massachusetts, and to the nation. Marble was a Spiritualist, a practitioner in the then emergent belief system that the living could communicate with the dead through a variety of paranormal means such as trances and séances. As Marble's own story unfolded, he detailed encounters with spirit mediums that encouraged his investigation of the treasure. He also claimed that Veale's spirit was among those guiding him to the loot. As Samuel Adams Drake remarked in his collection of New England folklore, the sequel to Veale's legend was more striking than the original by virtue of its reality.

The Marble family dug deep into the earth. The tunnel descends for more than a hundred feet. Hiram passed into the otherworld in 1868, and his son Edwin followed in 1880. The property eventually became the possession of the town and remains a crowning attraction for Lynn Woods. But it has been a tourist destination since excavations commenced, when the Marbles charged for access in order to fund their work—among other moneymaking activities, including selling corn from "Tom Veal's garden."

The third adaptation of the Veale legend is part of this tradition. In 1856 Nanette Snow Emerson published *The History of Dungeon Rock*. Technically she wrote under the nom de plume of Enesee—or transcribed, rather—as Emerson claimed that it was dictated to her by disembodied spirits. While early reviews mistook that assertion as an endearing addition to the romance—in a vein similar to Obadiah Turner's journal—it soon became apparent to the press that Emerson was both a Spiritualist and a firm believer in "the Excavator," Hiram Marble.

The History of Dungeon Rock purports to narrate the genuine biographies of all those involved in the treasure that, Emerson conjectured, Marble would soon liberate—and by doing so, provide evidence for the veracity of Spiritualism. *The History of Dungeon Rock* is a motivated tale, then, not merely one for entertainment. I shall do my best, but this is a tale for which summary does no justice.

The first part introduces William Wallace, a young colonial of English stock who abandons his people, befriends the Indians, and establishes a public house near the ocean. One night during a fearsome storm, Wallace opens his doors to relieve the misery of a group of passengers on a threatened ship. They include a man by the name of Harris, his bride Arabel, and a retinue of sailors, one of whom is named Veale. Harris's crew drags several boxes into the dwelling to protect them from the winds and the water.

The setting then shifts to Italy, where Arabel was born. It is not long after the death of her father. Her mother objects strongly to Arabel's love for the pirate Claud Morillo, but she too soon dies, leaving Arabel alone with her sisters and an uncertain future. After one of her siblings perishes, Arabel elects to leave Italy with her lover, Claud Morillo—who just happens to be the Lord Etheredge and heir to considerable wealth. Incognito as Morillo, he is leader of a pirate band. And when they arrive in the New World, Lord Etheredge takes the name Harris in order to throw authorities off his trail.

Once established, Harris's band oscillates between legitimacy and their old piratical ways. They adopt the area of the Pirates' Glen and

Dungeon Rock where, of course, they hide treasure. Arabel then tragically dies in a manner that deliberately echoes the death of Clorinda in Ames's poem—and recall that Emerson presented this tale as a recounting of actual events—and there is the slightest inkling that her phantom will haunt the cave with eerie laughter to discourage unworthy hunters from claiming its prize.

Following Arabel's death, Harris, Veale, and the remaining crew set off to return to Europe. On route Harris discovers that a young woman assigned to Veale had been left behind. They return to Massachusetts. Veale remains behind with Cathrin this time. Harris and his men are discovered by authorities during the return to their boat.

Separated from the pirate's life, Veale becomes a wrecker—a moon-cusser—and suffers another tragedy when Cathrin dies. Despondent, abandoned, and exiled from everyone, Veale perishes in the dungeon of the cave during the earthquake's thunderous hour.

But Emerson's tale is not complete with the death of Veale. Pages remain to expound failed attempts to reach his treasure in the cave. The first involves a young man with the last name Brown, who lived near Lynn and became convinced that there were riches in Dungeon Pasture. The discovery of a few coins fed his insatiable desire until it reached the point of madness. He would die, years later, a patient at the Ipswich insane asylum.

The town of Lynn was next in its attempt to secure monies for the municipality in perpetuity, but they too—and all too readily—failed. Their successor was Jesse Hutchinson, informed of the proper location by a clairvoyant speaking in a mesmeric state, but he too was found unworthy and ill-prepared for the task. That task, Emerson explained, was at long last in the proper hands of the Excavator, the tireless Hiram Marble. It would only be a matter of time.

It was not the riches he sought, but Marble and his family did find and bequeath a treasure. Their obsession stands as testimony to the endur-ing legacy of folklore. In digging into the rock—always just one shovel behind the elusive gold—they transformed what was a modest variant of the treasure tale into a monument of intrigue, one that called both supporters and detractors, and one that a century and a half later still kindles desire and rewards audiences with its story.

Legend Tripping

Although it is plausible to visit Dungeon Rock relatively quickly, it would be a shame not to spend the entire day in Lynn Woods. There are miles of trails and sites to explore throughout the 2,200-acre park. It is overseen by the city of Lynn (https://www.lynnma.gov/departments/lynnwoods .shtml#gpm1_1). For those who wish to visit Dungeon Rock, it is best to inquire ahead whether the tunnel is open. There is an entrance to Lynn Woods on Great Woods Road, but the closest parking to Dungeon Rock is on Pennybrook Road. Parking is free. **Trailhead GPS: N42 28.37 / W70 59.11**

As of this writing the city posts a map that is not particularly user-friendly but serviceable at http://www.lynnma.gov/cityhall_documents/ maps/misc_maps/Lynn_Woods_2020.pdf.

The old website for the Friends of Lynn Woods also posted a map, but the new website (http://www.lynnwoods.org/) currently does not yet do so. Physical maps are available at the trailhead parking lot. The Essex National Heritage Area website provides a helpful overview at https:// essexheritage.org/attractions/lynn-woods.

14

The Horror of the Bridgewater Triangle

I'M ABOUT TO share with you the secret of the Bridgewater Triangle. Prepare yourself. It's a horror story without comparison. Take a breath, steel your nerves, and read on.

It's a story about a fearsome swamp and a Native American curse.

No, wait. It's a story about Bigfoot.

No, about UFOs. Or satanic cults. Or strange rocks. Or thunderbirds, pterodactyls, animal mutilations, human sacrifice, suicides, murders, a vanishing redheaded hitchhiker, zombies, a mad truck driver, spectral fires, red-eyed dogs, phantom panthers, mystery cats, giant snakes, simian island dwellers, spooky lights, insane asylums, government experiments, ruined factories, haunted cemeteries and college campuses and town halls, and numerous ghosts from the Lady of the Ledge to an incorporeal school-teacher. And Pukwudgies.

The horror of the Bridgewater Triangle is that it is a story that does not know what it wants to be. Like all of us, the Bridgewater Triangle could use a good editor now and then.

For some time I considered not including a chapter on the Bridgewater Triangle. It would not have been in protest of the hot mess of stories associated with it. As a folklorist, I relish hot messes of storytelling; they birth legends and often demonstrate keen investments by raconteurs and audiences.

My concern, rather, is that the Bridgewater Triangle is the folklore that vanity presses invented. There are several people—so-called paranormal investigators and cryptozoologists—motivated to fit all of the items above into a nonsensical geographic boundary, often asserting that a supernatural force binds them together. Media outlets lap it up and routinely interview these "experts," usually at Halloween, with guarantees they will offer outrageous comments. They oblige, discrediting scientific knowledge in the process.

These "researchers" often identify themselves as folklorists despite lacking degrees or formal training in folklore studies. I should be honored that people want to be associated with the fine work folklorists do, but this false representation alarms me. It is the equivalent of people who enjoy recreational drugs calling themselves chemists. I wouldn't recommend buying what they are selling.

The Bridgewater Triangle is a recent phenomenon with unambiguous parentage. Cryptozoologist Loren Coleman invented the term in the 1970s and popularized it in his 1983 *Mysterious America*. Obviously indebted to the Bermuda Triangle, it was initially restricted to Bridgewater, East Bridgewater, and West Bridgewater. Coleman quickly expanded the boundaries to form a triangle within Abington, Freetown, and Rehoboth. This area includes eighteen municipalities and covers, as aficionados are wont to say, about two hundred square miles, including Freetown State Forest. More recent commentators have expanded its reach to include virtually all of Plymouth and Bristol Counties.

In introducing the name, Coleman stressed the cryptozoological over the parapsychological. He compiled—or at least asserted—reports of abnormal animals, especially prevalent around Hockomock Swamp. A few examples of paranormal or heinous criminal activity also punctuated his list as well as unusual phenomena such as Dighton Rock, a boulder with petroglyphs whose nature has long been debated. The narratives that

Coleman assembled are what folklorists call memorates, tales of personal experience with the supernatural.

Joseph DeAndrade, for example, had an incident in 1978. He was walking in the woods near a pond in Bridgewater. A compelling feeling or a disembodied voice told him to pivot. Startled, he queried why and the voice replied, "Turn around and you'll see." When DeAndrade did as instructed, he spied a large and hairy humanoid moving slowly away on the opposite side of the pond. It disappeared before he could discern definable features. A second time, he was camping with two friends in the same area when they heard a roar—"like something from Hell"—but did not see the sonorous beast. To hear him tell these memorates—as he does in the 2013 documentary *The Bridgewater Triangle* or the 2017 episode of *Sasquatch: Out of the Shadows*—is a pleasure; DeAndrade is a compelling narrator.

But memorates are not stories with characters and plot. They are recollections of encounters. And while they may encourage others to report similar experiences, memorates also promote a self-fulfilling belief in the story as it is told again and again. And once a belief is established, it produces another phenomenon: People see what they hope to see. A deer hopping through thick brush becomes any number of supernatural creatures. It is a common optical illusion, one that now permeates storytelling in the preselected context of the Bridgewater Triangle.

This trick of the brain is even more pronounced if the spectator views something uncommon in a familiar context. As evidence of the supernatural qualities of the Triangle, for example, Coleman cites a Norton policeman's report in 1971 of a "tremendous winged creature" in Easton at the edge of Hockomock Swamp. No one needs to doubt that the policeman saw such a creature. But in subsequent narratives by Coleman and others, it becomes identified as a pterodactyl or a thunderbird from Native American folklore. Coleman considers it "the Triangle's own version of Mothman," a strange winged creature spotted in West Virginia in the late 1960s.

I actually agree with that comparison. I would qualify, however, in arguing that the simplest scientific explanation is that both Mothman and the winged creature of the Triangle were likely a sandhill crane, a large bird well known in the American South, just outside its migration or habitation range. But when a storyteller directs the imagination to thunderbirds, pterodactyls, or unknown winged monsters, it is difficult to accept what the eyes actually see.

The overarching idea of the Bridgewater Triangle does not only influence perception. To keep audiences hooked, it requires a constant drip of examples. As a consequence any weird tale within those eighteen towns is smuggled—perhaps smothered—into conformity. Independent folk narrative traditions such as undergraduate stories of haunted campuses are treated as evidence of the Triangle's existence. An urban legend of the Redheaded Hitchhiker on Route 44 in Rehoboth (an interesting local variant of the international Vanishing Hitchhiker tale) becomes subjected to the Triangle's demands. Actual murders such as the ghastly events surrounding the arrest and conviction of Carl Drew and his purported satanic cult in the early 1980s are cast under its shadow.

One so-called paranormal researcher even offered being bit by a tick in Hockomock Swamp as an example of the "unexplained" occurrences that befall the Triangle's victims. Such alien villainy warrants a Lovecraftian response: Who could have imagined such an accursed and tenebrous scavenger reach up from its foetid and charnel clay? Malevolence embodied, indeed!

For people who enjoy stories, this exhausting experiment in making everything come back to the Bridgewater Triangle can wear thin. The rich development of legends concerning the ghosts of various cemeteries becomes less important than personal reports of seeing them. Perhaps this speaks to our cultural moment; there is something tellingly narcissistic in all this. And the Bridgewater Triangle is an apt metaphor for frenetic attention spans in the age of the internet as well as celebrity culture. The Triangle has become famous for being famous.

Nowhere is the desire of seeing what one wants to see on display more acutely than in Coleman's ruminations on the name of Hockomock Swamp. He has staked the reputation of the Bridgewater Triangle on this supposedly eerie site, having established that "Hockomock" is the Algonquian word for the Devil. He found confirmation, he explains, in the WPA guidebook to Massachusetts, where he discovered "the variant name for the swamp, 'Hoccomocco,' as 'evil spirit.'" Let's follow that trail.

Here is the exact line from the WPA guidebook that convinced Coleman: "To the southwest is Hoccomocco Pond, named by the Indians after an evil spirit."

The Hoccomocco in question, however, is in Westborough. As the crow flies it's about forty miles from Hockomock Swamp. Geographically they have nothing to do with one another. As for the notion that Indians named it after an evil spirit, Coleman can be forgiven for his ignorance. He did not understand that the WPA guide was in error and was following a long line of (white) people mistaking "Hoccomocco" for "Hobbomocko," the latter being the name of a deity responsible for illness and health whom European colonialists treated as the Devil.

One such person confused by the distinction was Charles Skinner. His *Myths and Legends of Our Own Land* was the source material for the WPA guidebook, but even Skinner attempted to work it out. In his narrative, "The Hobomak" is the area of land in which there is a pond called "Hochomocko." The WPA author read imprecisely. I do not know why Coleman continued the mistake. But the point remains that Coleman is simply incorrect in assuming that "Hockomock" is an Algonquian word for an evil spirit.

In *American Place Names*, the renowned toponymist George Stewart distinguishes words associated with Hobomak as an evil spirit from those with Hockamock, a word that references hook-shapes. This nomenclature did not fit Coleman's preconceived desire, however, so he simply dismissed it and encouraged others not to trust a professor with a PhD who had published a monumental work of scholarship with Oxford University Press.

In other words, Coleman's claim is pure, unadulterated nonsense. But because it serves the continued investment in the Bridgewater Triangle, it is repeated to this day, and often expanded to suggest that Hockomock Swamp means "the dark place" or "the place where spirits dwell" or "the Devil's place."

The compromised understanding of Indigenous lore does not end there.

Many proponents of the Triangle assert that its multifarious malevolence is the direct result of a curse wrought by Indigenous people in revenge for their loss in King Philip's War, a three-year conflict in the 1670s led by Wampanoag chief Metacom that engulfed all of New England. Others contend that it is a supernatural response to the bloodshed that occurred during the war, a glut of "negative energy" or the opening of an "energy rift" (whatever that is) allowing specters and chthonic beasties into this world. Numerous memorates of Wampanoag ghosts at Anawan Rock, a site of betrayal during the war, support that absurd claim. Still others conjecture that King Philip's War was not the cause but rather a symptom, an indication that the land is evil regardless of who lives upon it.

While it may seem a sympathetic gesture for white storytellers to claim that the land is cursed because of atrocities committed upon Indigenous people, it should not be forgotten that such narrative maneuvering is in the service of maintaining a ridiculous claim that the Triangle is a conduit to otherworldly and inexplicable phenomena. These are just contemporary "Indian tales," stories about Indigenous people that benefit whites, many of which hearken to a colonialist worldview in which the Wampanoag are in league with diabolical forces. It is mind-boggling that claims this irresponsible get into print unchallenged.

The recent introduction of Pukwudgies into the folklore of the Triangle further demonstrates the sheer misunderstanding of cultural traditions. Pukwudgies are supernatural beings akin to fairies or goblins. Readers may be surprised to learn that "Pukwudgie" is not a word with longevity in

Massachusetts. Although the Indigenous people of New England tell tales of Little People, the original Wampanoag term was erased from history. Pukwudgie reached the state through a circuitous route that begins with Henry Rowe Schoolcraft's *Algic Researches*, an 1839 compilation of folk narratives from Indigenous people in Michigan, Wisconsin, Minnesota, and Canada who spoke Central Algonquian languages such as Ojibwe.

Tales of the Puk Wudj Ininee appear in this early work. They are the Little People who inhabit the woods, mountains, and sand dunes on the south shore of Lake Superior. In one story they are responsible for the death of a boastful human hero, Kwasind.

Henry Wadsworth Longfellow based his epic poem *The Song of Hiawatha* on *Algic Researches*. Upon publication in 1855 *Hiawatha* sparked a literary revolution and widespread interest in Great Lakes Native American folklore. It also piqued the interest of a protégé of Schoolcraft, the missionary Granville Sproat, who was stationed on Madeline Island in Lake Superior in the 1830s and 1840s. When the mission closed Sproat returned home to Middleboro, Massachusetts, where he remained for another decade before moving to California. He wrote several poems and essays based on folklore, many of which were published in the town newspaper.

In 1906, Thomas Weston published a history of Middleboro. He included an anonymous "legend" culled from the *Middleboro Gazette* concerning Assawompset Pond. The tale purported to be Wampanoag, but in reality was a retelling of the death of Kwasind at the hand of Pukwudgies relocated to Middleboro. Although I have yet to confirm, I am almost certain that this was a contribution by Sproat to his hometown paper.

What is certain is that ideas about Pukwudgies were imported to Massachusetts, assisted substantially by Longfellow's popularity. They appear, for example, in the work of Winthrop Packard, one of the organizers of the state's Audubon Society. In his 1910 "Bog Bogles," Packard imagines their escapades at Ponkapoag Pond in Canton. They were also featured in a stage performance, a *tableau vivant* called "Longfellow's

Dream," that toured Boston in the late 1800s. John Greenleaf Whittier mentioned them in an essay on fairies in New England.

The Bridgewater Triangle's connection to Pukwudgies is rooted in Elizabeth Reynard's *The Narrow Land*, a collection of folktales from Cape Cod. Reynard included a few retouched stories from Chief Red Shell (Clarence Wixon), a Mashpee Wampanoag, in which Pukwudgies are malicious antagonists to the culture hero Moshup. Chief Red Shell and Chief Wild Horse (Clinton Haynes) were instrumental in reestablishing the Wampanoag tribe and in advancing pan-Indian awareness. As the anthropologist William Simmons discovered, they readily borrowed stories and terms from Ojibwe. Both men had ties to Middleboro and would have been intimately aware of the introduction of Pukwudgies to the state. They elected to use that name in modern Wampanoag storytelling.

Reynard's collection in turn inspired the 1982 children's book *The Good Giants and the Bad Pukwudgies* by acclaimed author Jean Fritz. It is not a model of cultural awareness, to say the least. In 1996 Joseph Citro's *Passing Strange* laid the pipe to connect Pukwudgies to the Triangle, although he specifically mentioned them in reference to the Dover Demon. Within a decade, a handful of paranormal investigators published books and online essays that simply declared the presence of Pukwudgies in Freetown State Forest, especially around Assonet Ledge. Coleman gave his imprimatur of approval to this bewildering gesture, and they have been a major component of Triangle folklore ever since.

I cannot hide my concern for the manner in which Pukwudgies have been placed in service of promoting the Triangle. This demand for association flattens and stunts the development of otherwise compelling tales into rich folklore if left alone.

Bill Russo, for example, had an uncanny encounter with a small hairy being in the autumn of 1990. It was soon after midnight in Raynham. He was walking his dog, Samantha, after returning home from work. Although they usually avoided wandering into the edge of the Hockomock Swamp, that evening Samantha decided to vary the route. Soon they were paralyzed with fear before a creature beckoning "EEE WHA CHEW, KEER"—"We want you, come here." From what Russo could gather the potbellied thing was "in the young stages of old age." Unable to muster the courage to investigate, Russo "slinked away and lost a chance to catalog an entirely new species."

As with DeAndrade, to hear Russo tell his tale is to witness an affable, engaging raconteur, at once unquestionably earnest yet sporting a hint of impishness. Russo narrates the encounter in the aforementioned 2013 documentary and in his own publications. As a memorate this stands resolutely on its own. It is haunting, suggestive, and tantalizing.

Unfortunately, it too has disappeared in the narrative morass that is the Bridgewater Triangle. In his book, Russo explains how he was persuaded by one of the paranormal investigators that "Little Foot"—his nickname for the creature—was both a Pukwudgie and yet another example of the supernatural power of the Triangle. And with that conclusion another opportunity for an interesting independent story was made to fit an arbitrary pattern.

It bears mention that almost all of the paranormal investigators of the Triangle and its Pukwudgies are white men. I raise that in returning to the tales told by Chief Red Shell. For as Simmons notes, the Pukwudgies who kill Moshup's children and sting his body with sharp darts to chase him away from Cape Cod represent European colonialists with their firearms. In a modern Wampanoag storytelling context, the tale of Pukwudgies who do evil was a critique of white people. One wonders what to think of contemporary white men telling tales about Pukwudgies who lurk in an area of land purportedly cursed by Indigenous people because whites seized something that did not belong to them.

The last thing I want to do is rob folks of their fun. But I cannot pretend otherwise: The Bridgewater Triangle is not venerable folklore. It is a collection bin of memorates, anecdotes, and a few localized urban legends, many of which would benefit by liberation from an artificial frame. Worse still, many tales of the Triangle are based on woeful ignorance about the history and traditions of Indigenous people in the area. In other words, it's the folklore of a bunch of misinformed white dudes who have been given one too many public platforms than they deserve. As I wrote earlier, I wouldn't recommend buying what they are selling.

Legend Tripping

The obvious hikes are in Freetown–Fall River State Forest, which is overseen by the Department of Conservation and Recreation (https://www.mass.gov/locations/freetown-fall-river-state-forest), which maintains a map. There are three distinct sections, each with hiking possibilities. The northern section closest to the picnic area and ranger headquarters on Slab Bridge Road is the Massassoit Trail. This used to be popular as an out-and-back trail to Profile Rock, a granite formation shaped like a human face that was identified throughout the decades both as the "Old Man" and as Massassoit, a Wampanoag sachem and father of Metacomet, King Philip. Unfortunately Profile Rock was frequently vandalized by graffiti and litter. In June 2019 it collapsed, leaving an unsafe rock pile. It is not accessible as of this writing.

The second section meanders through the wildlife management area in the southeastern part of the forest. As a loop it utilizes Copicut Road, Clark Field Path, Whitetail Loop, and Grinnell Path. The third section lies in the western area of forest closest to Route 24. This third part utilizes either Ledge Road or Upper Ledge Road to access, well, the Ledge, an old quarry now filled with water. Increasingly in the "research" of paranormal investigators, this site is called Assonet Ledge (Assonet is the village closest to the forest). Most recently, storytellers have begun to narrate clichéd Lovers Leap "Indian tales" about a maiden taking her life here. The view from the top is impressive, although it too is increasingly plagued by graffiti and litter.

Visitors to the forest should be aware that it is a forest. Dedicated and blazed hiking trails are minimal. Much walking consists of the use of bridal paths and unpaved roads, sometimes shared by mountain bikers, motorbikes, and ATVs. It is an active place for seasonal hunting. **Trailhead GPS: N41 46.44 / W71 02.33**

For a closer investigation of the area around Hockomock Swamp and River, check out relevant parts of the southern section of the Bay Circuit Trail and Greenway (https://www.baycircuit.org/). As of this writing this ambitious project is still in development and is shaping up to become an amazing contribution to Massachusetts. It is overseen by the Bay Circuit Alliance with the leadership of the Appalachian Mountain Club. A small section passes through the Hockomock Swamp Wildlife Management Area on the West Bridgewater–Easton line, with free parking on Maple Street. It is just north of "the Nip," Lake Nippenicket, but the trail and greenway deserves your attention far beyond the so-called Bridgewater Triangle. **Trailhead GPS: N41 59.31 / W71 02.35**

15

Dinglehole

I MAGINE IF YOU will a self-proclaimed expert on the folklore of the paranormal broadcasting from a residential neighborhood in the well-mannered town of Millis. In between brazen requests for money, this renowned adventurer promises to enlighten audiences on the Dinglehole, a small pond sprawled between two front yards. Our sagacious explorer of the unknown draws from his prolific store of arcane erudition. He ruminates on the heretical. He speculates on the spectral. And after a word from his sponsors, he shares his faddish savoir faire.

The Dinglehole! That rumored location of a bottomless pit. That place of strange and flickering lights. That hair-raising haunt of a headless apparition. That rendezvous for Satan and his witches, who in their rapacious wickedness change shape into greedy raccoons. The Dinglehole—so named in whispered admonition against the tinkling sounds of "spirit bells," rung by the gnarled hands of hobgoblins that inhabit its surrounding forest of unbending pines.

And then, with one final petition for generous remuneration to line his pockets, our covetous hero is off, but sure to appear again at yet another haunted site with cosmic insights and secrets to sell.

It's captivating drama. And it's made all the more riveting by the simple fact that our celebrated self-proclaimed expert was standing in the wrong town.

If this story were true—who could say?—I might be able to explain how our fearless investigator ended up in a suburban neighborhood about three miles away from where he should be.

The detective work is not difficult. For most contemporary audiences, speculation commences on the pages of Ephraim Orcutt Jameson's 1886 history of Medway. Therein Jameson records that Dinglehole "lies a little to the northeast of the present residence of C. W. Emerson, M.D., and is embraced in Oak Grove Farm." It is "like a large pit, with black, stagnant water of uncertain depth at the bottom," Jameson continues, "a scary place and famous in the legends of the neighborhood on account of the many curious incidents and marvelous adventures which have happened there."

That simple comment, along with the litany of purported supernatural occurrences above—regrettably more a story *about* stories than the stories themselves—formed the basis for a single entry in the 1937 WPA guide-book to Massachusetts. Having previously mentioned the Congregational Church of Christ on the town common (that is Exchange Street / Route 115), the author installs *the* Dinglehole in Millis:

The Dinglehole, northwest of the Center on Union St., is a pit formally filled with water, where Puritans heard the ringing of the bell that summoned the witches to their evil rites and saw on moonlight nights a headless man keeping vigil.

Those two accounts are useful for identifying the location. A simple check of the Massachusetts Historical Commission reveals that Charles Wesley Emerson—the founder of Emerson College—purchased a home in 1885 south of the corner of Ridge and Curve Streets near Richardson's Pond. Oak Grove Farm is indeed northeast of Emerson's house and northwest of the Church of Christ. Jameson is abundantly clear about the location; the WPA not so. But the very next entry in the WPA guidebook recommends driving straight ahead up Route 115 to Bogastow Pond, which would pass Oak Grove Farm.

I say this yet again with admiration: The WPA guidebook to Massachusetts was compiled by well-meaning and hardworking people who often lacked local knowledge and who rarely fact-checked. They scanned town histories searching for tourist sites in order to design automobile drives for travelers to spend money out on the roads. This entry is a prime example of alacritous guesswork instead of research. It consulted only Jameson's account and proffered the additional assumption—narratively satisfying but also incorrect—that its litany of supernatural phenomena originated with the Puritans.

Nearly seventy-five years later, in 2010, the Dinglehole graced an entry on the blog *New England Folklore*. To the blogger's credit he replicated Jameson's list without speculation, confessed that he did not know the Dinglehole's location, and treated the entire affair with humor. The blogger misunderstood the WPA guidebook, however, and thought that "formally filled with water" meant that the pit was filled in.

That minor error caught the attention of readers from Millis, who readily shared affirming anecdotes about the aforementioned small pond in a residential neighborhood just south of Oak Grove Farm. This handful of contributors provided a wealth of information about the integrity of a local tradition. One commentator mentioned, for example, a parent's explanation that the pond was once larger. Another took the opportunity to joke that the previous presence of witches threw light on local political corruption!

Nothing breeds success like success, as the proverb suggests, and that is precisely what has happened to the residential Dinglehole as of late. In 2012 P. T. Crate penned an article, "Questions Still Haunt Millis Dinglehole," for an online newspaper. Crate scoured several sources for information, including the *New England Folklore* blog. Crate uncovered two additional items of note: unconfirmed rumors of the murder of suspected witches and a less spectacular claim that the town built a highway through the Dinglehole. Oriented to the small pond rather than to Oak Grove Farm, Crate presumed the "highway" was the residential street rather than Route 115.

Arguably the most important contribution Crate offers is confirmation from a nonagenarian that children would not venture down the end of the residential street in the 1930s for fear of the Dinglehole. It is only one source, but it suggests that people misunderstood the WPA guidebook's imprecise language or that homeowners embraced the opportunity to claim the Dinglehole as their own, associating it with the small pond. Either way, neighbors passed the rumor on to neighbors in the decades that followed.

It pains me to reveal this—except that I know nothing will stop determined storytellers—but the identification of the small pond as the Dinglehole is based on an error about its original location and composition, a site that the WPA guidebook missed entirely.

Contrary to several recent claims, Jameson was not the first to identify Dinglehole and its location. Jameson's commentary in his history was not even his; it was near verbatim citation of an article published in the Dedham *Village Register* in 1826. Penned by "J. B." this essay, simply entitled "Dinglehole," described it as "a piece of woods" in the area of Bogastow to which "grandams" in the vicinity ascribed legends. These stories circulated in "their early days," J. B. explains, likely the mid- to late 1700s.

Those legends include strange lights, spirit bells rung by hobgoblins—although only "on a dark, misty summer's evening," and a headless apparition who haunted the grounds—not a pit or a pond, but land—and specifically land that "is thought very much to resemble a goose-yoke," that was circled by a road, and through which a Y-shaped path had been recently blazed. Readers are seduced with the hint of a tale:

> *On a dark, moonless night, when the spirits' bell was always most sonorous, strange lights and globes of fire were frequently seen, playing*

about Dinglehole; and the benighted traveler was astonished, and almost petrified by the apparition of a man without a head, who would most unceremoniously lead him round all night in the circular road, without advancing him an inch on his intended journey. It was anciently the custom of the good people in the vicinity of this terrific glen, on approaching it in the night to say their prayers; and it was believed, that, on the pronunciation of certain words, the bell would cease its tinkling, the lights vanish, and the man without a head disappear in the deepest recesses of the wood, and there wait the arrival of a more ignorant, or less pious traveler.

Dinglehole is a glen, not a pit. Indeed, that is precisely what the word "dingle" means in the language of the British Isles and the United States during the 1700s and 1800s: a glen or a hollow, knot, valley, dell, dale, or meadow. In this case, J. B. recorded an apocryphal place-name legend that "dingle" refers to the "dingling" sound of spirit bells, an engaging poetic image that throws off less perspicacious readers.

Jameson, for his part, replicated all of J. B.'s language about the goose-yoke-shaped, circled glen, but for some unknown reason also reported that Dinglehole was "like a pit with black, stagnant water"—"like" being the operative word. Jameson never resolved that confusing contradiction, and people have misread it ever since, including the author of the WPA guidebook entry. (Incidentally, there were wetlands in the middle of Oak Grove Farm, identified as a "bowl" in a 1987 report for the town.)

J. B. recounts another item—again not quite a rich story but a memory of one:

The place is said to have been infested with witches in the shape of 'coons, weasels, and another little odoriferous animal; none of which could be caught, or slain by the ordinary means. One day as a famous modern Nimrod was hunting on this enchanted ground, he espied a large, fat 'coon, sitting with the utmost dignity and composure upon the arm of an old pine tree.

The hunter shot the raccoon point-blank but did not even scratch the creature. He shot a second time to measured failure. Only when he employed a branch of witch hazel as a projectile did the shot succeed in its fatal aim. And, as I suspect readers will have come to expect, at that very moment one Mrs. Murky Mullen, "an elderly, and somewhat unpopular lady in the neighborhood, was badly wounded in the face by some unaccountable accident, which had well-nigh terminated her sublunary state of existence."

This is the shooting of a witch in familiar form, a common motif that permeates Massachusetts folklore (and several chapters of this book). It is yet another localized example with a few intriguing details, including the substitution of witch hazel for silver and inclusion of the motif of an impenetrable wild animal, the best-known example of which comes from Connecticut: the Black Fox of Salmon River.

In J. B.'s original account there is no mention of a satanic rendezvous. Jameson is the originator of that claim, and it is not clear if it represents his own invention or stories circulating in the town between J. B. and his accounts. Jameson's motive for locating Dinglehole at Oak Grove Farm is also unclear. It had only been christened recently to his time when Lansing Millis, the progenitor of the town's name, purchased it. With the little information available, it is difficult to determine if Jameson situated it there by mistake or if he was following a narrative tradition of his time.

Jameson was not a lifelong resident of Millis. He was born in New Hampshire and served as minister in towns throughout that state and Massachusetts before taking up the ministry in Millis in 1871, where he served until 1893. We may simply never know why he saw fit to include reference to Dinglehole as a trysting-place where "Satan met with his disciples" upon a tall pine tree "with its topmost branches strangely woven and twisted together in a fantastic crown" somewhere on Oak Grove Farm.

To recap, J. B. associates Dinglehole with Bogastow. More than a half century later, Jameson links Dinglehole with Millis but is inconsistent in his description. Another half century later the WPA guidebook awards

Millis the nomination in a sparse entry. Millis residents accepted that prize, but led by the WPA's ambiguous language, they moved it from Oak Grove Farm to a small pond in what became a tight-knit neighborhood. That neighborhood tradition answered when a blogger came calling more than another half century later.

So exactly where is Dinglehole?

Bogastow was an area stretching from the southern part of Natick to northern Medway. Dinglehole was a glen located therein, and many accounts recognized its stark beauty. An editorial from 1832, for example, recommended that visitors tour its deep ravines. And in 1897 the Annual Report of the Massachusetts Trustees of Public Reservations gave away the ghost:

> *One new and particularly charming parcel of land is, at this writing, on the point of being transferred to the custody of this Board. Where Charles River forms the boundary between the townships of Medfield and Sherborn there is a place where the narrow stream flows between a bank of woods and a high hemlock knoll, behind which lies a sunny meadow, bordered by more high woods. Locally, the little gorge is known as Rocky Narrows, and the little meadow as the Dingle Hole; but many canoe men from the neighborhood of Boston know the place as the Gate of the Charles. The eastern bank of the river at this point forms a part of the domain surrounding the State Asylum in Medfield, and is thus the property of the Commonwealth.*

The trustees confirm that location one year later in detailing a canoe trip from Natick:

> *Just as one approaches the limits of Medfield, there appears on the Sherborn side of the river a little meadow, known as the "Dingle Hole,"*

framed in by a thickly wooded ridge. Passing this, the river makes a
sudden turn, first to the left and then to the right, flowing between
high ledges crowned with hemlocks. . . . There are many beautiful trees
included in this gift, and a recent clearing a few rods beyond this point
shows how fortunate and timely was the action of Mr. Hemenway.

Take out a map and examine the Charles River as it separates Sherborn from Medfield. You will see Farm Pond and Rocky Narrows, hiking grounds still owned by the Trustees and another gift from Augustus Hemenway. Just south you will find the Medfield Charles River State Reservation. And just above that location you will see the Charles River take a sharp bend in the shape of a goose-yoke, the location of another hiking spot, King Philip's Overlook. That is Dinglehole. It is in Sherborn.

Storytellers may protest, but state reports, newspaper articles, photographic magazine essays, and numerous other records from the same period all agree. Frank Smith's 1897 history of Dover, for example, even identifies Nimrod's Rock in the Dingle Hole Narrows between Sherborn and Dover.

The real mystery, then, is not where Dinglehole lies but rather why Jameson moved it to Oak Grove Farm, a decision that ignited a chain reaction when the WPA guidebook authors did not do their research.

Again, I apologize to the neighborhood in Millis with the small pond, and I assure them that although they are not the original site, their tales are just as interesting and reveal, yet again, how people become invested in a story and part of a legend.

But the story is not quite finished. J. B. gifted one more present, the only formal narrative about Dinglehole. I realize that I am quoting recklessly in this chapter, but the original author tells it best. Having introduced that the "good dames of Bogastow" often gathered in knitting parties to spin yarn into stockings, J. B. spins a yarn as well:

It was on one of these occasions that Mrs. Catherine Cabbage was returning home through Dinglehole, from a winter evening visit. She had a large ball of black yarn, and an unfinished stocking of the same material suspended from her waist, and fastened to her clothes by a pin, when she suddenly heard immediately behind her upon the snow-crust, a noise resembling the step of some wild animal.

She looked round with great trepidation, and saw, close to her heels, a little black creature, which seemed intent on overtaking her, and which, at every new look, seemed to increase in both size and speed. Her walk soon became a trot; next, a run at full speed; but the terrible animal kept nearly the same distance, and continued to increase in size till it became as large as a bear. Mrs. Cabbage was for a time in great tribulation; but being favored by nature with a pair of remarkably long and comely trotters, she soon reached home, almost breathless with terror and fatigue, and just enough in advance of her ravenous enemy, to close and bolt the door upon his Bearship.

After she had recovered in some degree from her terror and confusion, and related with all proper exaggeration the story of her adventures, she examined her waist for her knitting work, and was surprised to find that her stocking and needles were missing, though the ball of yarn still remained appended to her goodly person.

The probability of the case is that the fall of her knitting work in the terrible dingle was the cause of her fright; and the noise of the needles upon the snow-crust was mistaken for the trampling of an animal; and that the tenacity of the yarn which held the stocking continued the pursuit by drawing it after her. In closing the door she probably shut in and broke the yarn, as the innocent cause of her trepidation was discovered next morning upon the door-stone.

If Catherine Cabbage sounds like an opportune name for a folk character populating a children's tale, it appeared precisely that way in *The Youth's Companion* in 1891. In that version the poor woman mistakes the pursuing stocking for a cougar rather than a bear or a supernatural being. Dinglehole does not appear in that retelling, but its message still resounds clear as a bell: Sometimes things are not what they seem. And it's always a good idea to pay attention and to read carefully.

That reminds me! What ever became of our fearless self-proclaimed folklore expert, that cartographer of the unexplained and seeker of all sponsorships mystical and mundane? The last I heard he was lost somewhere in South Dakota, searching for Stonehenge. If you see old Chuck Cabbagehead, tell him I said hello.

Legend Tripping

The original site of Dinglehole remains a place for stellar hiking. It is now known as Rocky Narrows and the Sherborn Town Forest. Rocky Narrows is overseen by the Trustees of Reservations (https://thetrustees.org/place/rocky-narrows/), which publishes a map. The entire area, consisting of several miles of hiking, should be explored, but the most direct hike to Dinglehole begins with free parking on Forest Street. Follow the Red Trail to the Blue Trail, and be sure to visit both Rocky Narrows and King Philip's Overlooks. A path between them winds down toward the Charles River. The loop continues on the Red Trail back to the parking lot, about a 3-mile walk. **Trailhead GPS: N42 13.33 / W71 21.14**

This area is also tended to by the Sherborn Forest and Trails Association (http://www.sherbornforestandtrail.org/) and is part of the Bay Circuit Trails and Greenway (https://www.baycircuit.org/), both of which have additional information.

Oak Grove Farm was eventually developed as a recreational area for the town. It is now known as Oak Grove Playground and includes a baseball diamond and a soccer field. Admittedly, that name is not likely to strike terror into the mind, but anyone who thinks that "a gathering place for Satan and his minions" is a misnomer for such a site clearly has not been around children when they let loose after being indoors too long. **Trailhead GPS: N42 10.52 / W71 21.52**

16

The Dover Demon

AS SOMEONE HONORED to teach at UMass Amherst, I have the great fortune of excellent students. When undergraduates inquire about the folklore of the Commonwealth, there is a very good chance that I am about to be asked my thoughts on the Dover Demon. The same can be said when I speak to students from Connecticut: Inevitably we're going to get to the Melon Heads and Dracula Drive. This is not because they seek confirmation that the Dover Demon exists, but because the topic remains thriving contemporary folklore—a suburban legend, if you will. The internet and entertainment in the guise of educational television have done much to keep this one alive.

Unfortunately the Dover Demon is not a phenomenon of storytelling with characters and plot. It is fundamentally what folklorists call a memorate, a tale of a personal encounter with a supernatural being. Although memorates can evolve into or inspire legends, the Dover Demon is going nowhere in terms of narrative development. One reason has to do with the insufferable demands put upon it by certain people who want to keep open the possibility that the creature is real rather than let it become a folk character or purely fantastical monster.

I'm not quite ready to wear a "Free the Dover Demon" T-shirt to a rally—and I'd prefer the Dover Gremlin, for what it's worth—but in this chapter I work through the material with the optimism that a genuine story will eventually emerge. Before I do, let me come clean on my approach. I often joke—no one laughs, by the way—that there are four general categories of folklore in Massachusetts: (1) the lore of Indigenous people; (2) the lore of European colonialists; (3) the lore of subsequent immigrants; and (4) the utter nonsense that crytozoologists and paranormal investigators invent to keep in business. The Dover Demon is the current state champion of that fourth category.

I am not hiding my disdain for cryptozoologists and paranormal investigators in this book. Perhaps I should do so for the sake of selling merchandise. I have been instructed to comply. One of the dons of nonsense informed me that since I would not kiss his ring, he would not promote my work, which is not the threat he thinks it is. He's actually doing me a favor. I would far rather earn the respect of intelligent readers who both enjoy good stories and value facts than the adoration of fickle, fawning fanboys. But I have an honest job and do not need to grift for a living.

If you are wondering just what a cryptozoologist or a paranormal investigator does, the former "researches" unknown, unusual, or legendary organisms; the latter does the same for dead things—or rather for things that purportedly survive death. Massachusetts is a hotbed for both and has been so for decades. There are numerous groups and individuals who claim expertise in the supernatural, although they generally lack formal training in the hard sciences, social sciences, medical sciences, or forensic sciences. It is very much the way that I claim the status of expert in the abundant consumption of Calabrese vino, hot peppers, and wrapped figs—except that the natural sciences can prove the existence of my hobbies and obsessive interests.

Many of the witnesses involved in the Dover Demon incident, which took place in 1977, are still alive. I have not reached out to them. Although folklorists do conduct interviews, I have read enough to discern that they may be weary of the association and the annual queries at Halloween. And again, the story of the Dover Demon is not really about them. It's about the cryptozoologists who made the beastie into what it is for their own purposes. So I'm going to split the difference here and only use the first names of the informants, including when I cite directly from newspaper reports.

In the late evening on Thursday, April 21, 1977, three teenagers—all age seventeen and all young men—were driving home through the streets of Dover. It was the week of spring break at their high schools. William, the witness to the creature, was at the wheel.

At 10:30 p.m. they were heading northward on Farm Street, a curving two-lane road in a rural setting. William estimated they were driving 40 to 45 mph when they came around a bend nearing Smith Street. Something appeared in the high-beams, standing on a low stone wall. As they drove past the creature, it grabbed onto the rocks with long fingers and turned its head to stare at the moving vehicle.

"I thought it was a dog," William explained in an AP news report, "but when it looked back at me with bright orange eyes, I knew it wasn't a dog."

Shaken, William asked his friends if they had seen anything. They had not. When he described the creature, they insisted that he return to investigate. He resisted—he confessed he was scared—but after continuing for about a mile he complied and turned around on Glen Street. No creature was lurking when they reached the site, and William's companions playfully called out for it to appear to no avail.

When he returned home, William, an accomplished artist, sketched an image of the creature. Within two months that sketch adorned copious newspapers throughout the nation and forever entered contemporary Massachusetts folklore. It is the image of a small humanoid, leaning to the left, with thin arms and legs, hands grasping rocks. Its large oval head has no discernable mouth, nose, or ears but two large and circular eyes that William insisted glowed "like two orange marbles" in the headlights.

Around midnight that same evening, a fifteen-year-old named John was walking northward on Millers Hill Road, which runs parallel to Farm Street. As he proceeded he noticed a small figure approaching him. He called out to it, thinking it might be a friend. The creature scurried off into the woods by a creek; John reported hearing its footsteps on dry leaves. He pursued and looked upon it—as much as he could in the darkness—from what he estimated as fifteen feet away. He noticed two eyes in the middle of its head.

"He was standing on two feet on a rock," John reported, "his feet were molded around a rock, and he was leaning against a tree. It looked like a monkey, with a figure-eight head."

Uneased by the encounter John backed away, hurried from the area, and hitched a ride home. Akin to William he drew a sketch. The being appears similar in both images.

The next evening, Friday, April 22, an eighteen-year-old named Will was escorting fifteen-year-old Abby home, driving west on Springdale Avenue, which terminates on Farm Street. Will was a friend of William's and heard of the encounter the previous evening. As they passed over Trout Brook—Will estimated a speed of about 40 mph—Abby spotted the creature sitting upright or crouched as if on all fours. When she alerted Will he caught a glimpse as well. They agreed that it was a creature with a large head and tan body. Abby described it as hairless, without a nose, mouth, or ears, and no tail. She too described a simian face with round glowing eyes, although green instead of orange. Will estimated the creature was the height of a goat, and Abby thought it the size of a large dog. As with William, Will sped up after driving past the creature.

That is the entirety of reports concerning the Dover Demon. With rare exception, the adults who spoke on behalf of the teenagers testified to their integrity and honesty. Police Chief Carl Sheridan was quoted in the AP report that the only thing that "worries him" was that William was "an outstanding artist and a reliable witness." The worry was not anxiety that a monster was prowling his town, but rather concern about a policeman doing due diligence and not dismissing a claim because it seemed dismissible. In another interview Sheridan said he thought the teenagers did see something.

For the record, I think it is very likely that they saw something as well. And I am willing to venture an educated guess as to what they saw: a great horned owl. They are a common species in Massachusetts, and their natural habitat is woodlands adjacent to marshes and farms—precisely what Dover was in 1977. It is not necessary to match every element of the teenagers' reports—in fact, that very selective but specious reasoning is the game cryptozoologists play when they wish to dismiss reasonable alternatives—but its color, perching behavior, claws, large head, and round glowing eyes fit the description.

Believers will protest that no one would mistake a bird—albeit a bird that most humans do not see in their lifetime despite living among them—for a humanoid. That is true if the prevailing conditions were not designed to fool the brain. Three of the four witnesses were traveling at speeds of at least 40 mph and two of them were driving—that is, they had to direct their attention to the road. Although narrative reconstruction allows for a different sense of time, passing by a stationary figure at that speed only allows seconds for perception. All the encounters occurred in darkness. And in the case of William, his initial report included admission that he had smoked a few puffs of marijuana an hour before.

I do not believe that William or the others hallucinated. But the soundest answer is that they saw a normal creature in its habitat—and note that they, the humans, were the strangers in the environment at that time at night—under compromised perceptions. Their brain played tricks on them. It happens to all of us.

I have seen ample gnomes that turn out to be raccoons less than pleased with my sudden appearance at our garage. As of this writing I have twice jumped in fear of the monster in the pond when I take the trash out late at night, that monster being the beaver slapping its tail as a warning sign. A glimpse of a blue heron ambulating down our road is a strange thing to my eyes but not to its purposes. And the sizeable coyote that momentarily paralyzed my daughter—so she could only utter "wolf" despite knowing what it really was—ducked into the woods before we could confirm either way.

I am happy to be proven wrong about the great horned owl. My colleague Russ Miller, a professional naturalist, suggested that the orange eyeshine could indicate an opossum. He further cautioned against assuming it was the same animal on both nights, which could explain the green eyeshine seen by Abby. And he recommended investigating exotic pet laws in the 1970s to consider whether it could have been an escaped gibbon, a creature that would have been frantically on the move outside its natural habitat.

In other words, had reports of this encounter gone to anyone with a dose of healthy skepticism and awareness of the local ecology, no one today would know the Dover Demon. Instead they found their way to Loren Coleman. Coleman would go on to become—according to his own book—"one of the world's leading investigators of the inexplicable, and an internationally known cryptozoologist." The Dover Demon—an alliterative term he coined—was an early opportunity to launch that curious career.

Indeed, Coleman's presence in the case anchors the AP report about the encounter. "According to Loren Coleman," it concludes, "a local author and investigator of unexplained phenomena, the creature drawn by William is like a creature that attacked a Hopkinsville, KY, farm family in 1955."

This is a pattern—not the only one—followed by numerous pseudo-scientists. Rather than examine the actual natural and plausible conditions, the cryptozoologist catapults to something supernatural but deemed similar and in doing so appears to demonstrate arcane expertise.

That said, in a funny coincidence Coleman and I agree that the Dover Demon is akin to the Hopkinsville case, albeit for radically different reasons. The Kentucky incident involved several people who reported alien beings—later conceptualized as extraterrestrials—attacking a farmhouse during the night. Scientists and skeptics who examined the reports spent little effort in recognizing owls—likely great horned owls—as the culprits.

Regardless of the most likely explanation, with that interjection the story of the Dover Demon became the story of Loren Coleman. Coleman lived in Massachusetts at the time, conducted interviews with the witnesses and others in Dover, and has selectively argued with those who have proposed natural alternatives for the creature such as a moose. (His dedication to scientific inquiry has not, however, dissuaded Coleman from considering a suggestion that the Dover Demon could be a "pygmy mer-being" that crawled out of the Charles River.)

Coleman's gamble worked. As happens all too often, an uncritical press leaped at an opportunity to report the outrageous. Coleman was on his way to celebrity. He has routinely returned to the topic of the Dover Demon, but the beastie received an additional boost with a guest appearance in Joseph Citro's 1996 *Passing Strange: True Tales of New England Hauntings and Horrors*. Citro identifies as a fan of Coleman's work. Unfortunately he also often self-identifies as a folklorist, despite no professional training. *Passing Strange* was, at the time, one of the few collections of folk narratives of the region to include contemporary material such as reports of supernatural encounters.

There is no polite way to say this: In recounting the Dover Demon memorates, Citro speculates recklessly and widens the circle of misinformation. For Citro the Dover Demon is a launching pad to ponder what kind of Little Person—that is, a folkloric being like an imp—it might have been. He invokes the lore of Indigenous people throughout New England as well that of the Cree. He spends some ink on the tradition of fairies in Derry, New Hampshire. Nowhere in those pages does Citro overtly dispute the existence of the Dover Demon; his motivation is to link it to unrelated phenomena in the same manner that Coleman initially sought to connect it to UFOs and aliens.

In 2013 Coleman reproduced his earlier account along with supplementary information for his *Monsters of Massachusetts*. Therein was an additional finding that he had introduced during an interview in the *Boston Globe* for the thirtieth anniversary of the Dover Demon, a passage from Frank Smith's 1914 history of Dover:

> *FARM STREET extends from the Medfield line on the south to Springdale park, on the north, and is the second oldest road in town. . . . In the early time this road went around by the picturesque Polka rock (on the farm of George Battelle) which was called for a man by that name, of whom it is remembered, that amid the superstitions of the age he thought he saw his Satanic Majesty as he was riding on horseback by this secluded spot. The location has long been looked upon as one in which treasures are hid, but why anyone should go so far inland to hide treasures has never been told; however, there has been at times unmistakable evidence of considerable digging in the immediate vicinity of this rock.*

And what feckless speculation followed this observation? One truly profound in its superficiality! Without mentioning a single source, Coleman claims that the colonists of Dover used "Pooka" instead of "Polka"— that is, the name of the small impish beings in the folklore of the British Isles. Armed with this belief that someone saw the Devil at "Pooka Rock" where treasure was buried, Coleman unabashedly informs the *Globe* that the area was long known for unexplained activity. "I think it certainly says something," Coleman declares. "It's almost as if there are certain areas that 'collect' sightings, almost in a magnetic way."

I agree that this certainly says something, but it is probably not what Coleman thinks it says.

For the record, Smith's account is useful to folklorists as yet one more example of Kidd treasure tales brought inland. And although I shudder to think what cryptozoologists will do when they learn the Dover Demon encounter occurred a mere quarter of a mile from the actual location of Dinglehole and its historical rumors of supernatural activity, Smith's comments further help establish that the Gate of the Charles was regarded as an attractive setting for Massachusetts legends from witches to treasure lore.

The nonsense perpetuated by pseudoscientists and their sympathizers would be laughable were it not encouragement of anti-intellectualism and rejection of critical thinking. This case is also an alarming illustration of how often the press simply does not do its job well.

It's also an affront to folklore. The story of the Dover Demon is now the story of how Loren Coleman named the creature and became the protagonist of his own adventure tale by magically uniting non sequiturs and rejecting common sense. As a result, folkloric tales of the creature had no means to be nourished by storytellers in the local community.

A few hints of those tales that could have been revealed themselves—there was some talk of escaped lab animals, for example, and one editorial in the *Globe* feared the creature was a sign of genetic experimentation—but those fantasies were squashed before they could be spun into developed folk narratives. Or take the title for a report in the *North Adams Transcript*: "Gremlins in Dover?" Imagine what rich legends we could have today if tales of gremlins had been allowed to grow organically over several decades.

In other words, in the end, Coleman got his wish: His interference brought him fame, and the creature he imposed on Dover turned out to be a demon.

Legend Tripping

The area of dramatic action concerning the Dover Demon is a lovely spot to hike. It includes two interconnected areas, Chase Woodlands and Peters Reservation, both overseen by the Trustees of Reservations. Chase Woodlands is a 1.5-mile lollipop on the Red Trail; Peters Reservation is a 1.4-mile lollipop on the Blue Trail. Both begin with free parking on Farm

Street. The trustees post a map to both sites at https://thetrustees.org/place/chase-woodlands/. **Trailhead GPS: N42 14.01 / W71 19.23**

Keep an eye on the development of the Charles River Link, which will connect the Bay Circuit Trail and Greenway in Medfield to Boston. The link includes trails in Medfield State Forest, abutting the Charles River, including an area in Dover near the sightings. Information and maps may be found at https://wellesleyma.gov/806/Charles-River-Link-Trail.

Be aware that the Yeti and the Chupacabra often visit this area for a romantic getaway. If you spot them, be courteous, and then start a lucrative career as a cryptozoologist.

17

Rag Rock and Hoccomocco Pond

THE CIDER WAS delectable that evening. As was the ale. And the applejack. And the Medford rum. Husking bees were necessary evils, but they were made easier "keeping spirits up by pouring spirits down." Tom Dunn always followed that sage advice, even when there was no corn to husk.

Ambrosial tastes were aplenty. In addition to exquisite beverages, Tom Dunn had a succulent streak of luck. He alone found a red ear of corn, which by tradition guaranteed a kiss from the soft lips of his choosing. And that night Tom Dunn found as many red ears as he had ample glasses of Medford rum. He left the barn in a fine mood, intoxicated by many flavors.

It's strange how slow molasses can make a drink that hastens poor judgments in the mind, but such was the strength of the Medford rum as Tom Dunn wandered home. He knew enough to shy away from the summit of Rag Rock at night, but that evening and underneath the moon good judgment fell asleep.

As he climbed the hill, Tom Dunn thought he heard the faintest sound of music. He shook his head like a wayward cow, trying to shake away the disorienting sense of drunkenness.

He reached the midnight summit. There in a clearing just beyond the thickets was a fiddle burning like mad. He knew none of the faces gathered in the ring to share a jig or reel, but strangers soon became old friends when Tom Dunn joined the dance.

Soon he spied a lovely young face sitting on a hummock of moss. Her eyes were black and her smile inviting, and with an open hand he asked her to rise and join the dance. Into the circle they went. Together they moved with such fiery ease that the other dancers stopped to stare.

Under the light of the midnight moon, Tom Dunn gazed upon his partner. His eyes saw something they would never wish to see. His partner's face grew long. Her eyes sunk deep into her skull, glowing with feline green. Her teeth grew pointed. Her hands became clawed. And her skin shriveled like the twisted bark of a lifeless tree.

Tom Dunn then knew the rumors were true. Demons lurked on Rag Rock at night.

Fear seized his drunken head, but just enough wits remained to keep him in the ring. Hell's minions would seize him unless he kept moving until the break of dawn. So he settled in as the crowd grinned and toasted the rhythm of an intoxicant dancing with abandon across the floor.

It was at that moment the shrill cramp pierced his calf.

Tom Dunn collapsed upon his back, screaming "God save me!" in his tumble.

He awoke, hours later, alone, under the morning sun atop the summit of Rag Rock. Was it his cry to the Lord that chased the demons away? Or was it the arrival of sobriety? Either way, Tom Dunn attended husking bees again, but never once touched a drop of cider or ale or applejack or even Medford rum.

Compelling as it is, the tale of Tom Dunn is a story with a very simple origin or a mystery with elements yet to be uncovered. It debuted in Parker Lindall Converse's *Legends of Woburn* in 1892. In 1903 it reappeared in Charles Skinner's *American Myths and Legends*, a popular collection of folk narratives. It was honored with inclusion in Benjamin Botkin's *A Treasury of New England Folklore* in 1947 but did not make the second edition. I suspect that I know why. I can find no evidence that the tale preexisted Converse's invention. It appears to be a literary work mistaken as folklore.

In Parker's *Legends* Tom Dunn's story is told as a four-canto poem, "The Midnight Dance." It patently hearkens to the work of John Greenleaf Whittier. And although the expulsion of ghosts, devils, and witches by exclamation of a holy name exists as a motif in folklore, the image of a drunken young man who stumbles upon a witch's dance is straight out of Robert Burns's "Tam o' Shanter." On the other hand, Converse demonstrates an impressive command of Woburn's history and of well-attested New England folk practices, so it cannot be ruled out that this was a local folk narrative which he was the first to record in print.

Incidentally, those earlier narratives include a scene in which Tom Dunn discovers two images of his partner burned onto his jackknife, one lovely and one monstrous. I took the liberty of dropping that heavy-handed conclusion for a more ambiguous tale about alcohol.

Converse's poem employs its moral like a blunt weapon. Tom Dunn survives his encounter with Hecate herself only by calling out to the Christian God who:

> Had so decreed that poor Tom should,
> Through grace divine, and wise gift free,
> Recover, and example be,
> To warn all others to abstain
> From all excess that causes pain;
> Especially to do no evil;
> Nor dance, nor consort with the Devil.

That act of salvation inspires Tom Dunn to become a better person who renounces sin and vices, rejects rum for lemonade, and becomes a model of Christian temperance.

Even if this is Converse's creation to promote certain virtues, it is plausible that actual events on Rag Rock convinced the author such a tale was necessary. In 1873, Hugh Doherty was arrested for the murder of his father at his house on the mountain. Numerous witnesses testified that the crime followed an evening of heavy drinking. One year later William Bouviard accidentally killed John McCourd during a confrontation with other men at a boardinghouse near Rag Rock, another result of an evening of intoxication. The trial judge in both horrific cases was none other than Parker Lindall Converse.

Throughout the 1880s, another motive arose for decrying the vices of the Rag Rock community as a thing of the past. Newspaper advertisements routinely induced readers to relocate to Woburn. The Rag Rock area was depicted as an idyllic location. Similarly, in 1892 the State Park Commission considered developing the area for tourism, a decision that would have immediate economic benefit for the town. Converse's *Legends* played a role in romanticizing and rehabilitating the rough image of that part of Woburn.

A second narrative attached to Rag Rock is deeply disturbing by today's standards, but should not be ignored. It is part of the folklore in Massachusetts, broadly conceptualized, and similar to stories of "witches." In facing these tales we have an opportunity to redress the deeply problematic history of colonialism and its legacy in the Commonwealth.

This tale is also one for which I cannot find precedent except in Converse and later in Skinner. It concerns the Indigenous people of Woburn, called the Aberginian—a misnomer used by other writers who may have misperceived the word "aboriginal" or "Abenaki," and their purported chief Wabanowi, another spurious name that was likely a misunderstanding of "Wabanaki."

Wabanowi has a graceful daughter, Nansema, whose name, Converse suggests, means "she who steals hearts." She lived up to that promise and was sought after by many, eventually falling for Winitihooloo of the Narragansett people of Rhode Island. In seeking permission to marry

Nansema, Winitihooloo explains to Wabanowi that the living forest is showing ominous signs of a long-predicted foe about to attack. He contends the marriage would secure an alliance capable of repelling the approaching evil.

Wabanowi, offended that an outsider would challenge his prowess as a seer, rejects the marriage and dismisses Winitihooloo. "There is no foe approaching," Wabanowi retorts, and if there were, he barks with braggadocio, "Wabanowi and his braves are able to fight their own battles."

That evening a haze gathers atop Mianomo and strange figures dart across its slope. Owls make incessant and prophetic sounds. And in the darkness of night a mysterious female figure appears to Wabanowi and beckons him with a call he cannot resist. This mysterious figure opens a magical door into a cave within Mianomo into which the entranced chief follows.

When Wabanowi awakens, the figure approaches him. She introduces herself as his guardian spirit and explains that she cast him into a deep sleep so he would not suffer the pain of witnessing the prophecy come true. The Great Spirit, she continues, sent European colonialists to take possession of his country and to destroy his people. The guardian spirit then conducts Wabanowi to the summit of Mianomo, where he gazes upon a thriving colonial village. His people and their wigwams are gone.

The one solace remaining for Wabanowi is a safe journey to Rhode Island, where he joins his daughter, who had married Winitihooloo in his long absence. They are members of a remnant tribe that survived King Philip's War. Converse concludes his tale imagining the ghost of Wabanowi appearing on the summit of Rag Rock on the morning nearest the full moon each September to yearn mournfully for what was once his homeland.

Converse offered a second "Indian tale" that made it into Skinner's anthology. This one concerns the chief Wakima and Lake Innitou, now Horn Pond. In this perplexing tale, the Indigenous people—known only as the Aborigines—practice polytheism, including the worship of many lesser gods in "savage rites." In so doing they become vice-ridden and draw the ire of the Great Spirit, who punishes them with disease and unsuccessful hunts and fishing. Mianomo and Towanda (now Horn Pond Mountain) moan nightly in remonstrance, but even that omen fails to drive them from wickedness.

One night Wakima dreams of a spirit upon Lake Innitou, a messenger from Manitou, who commands the tribe cease their incantations and the worship of lesser beings and accept only one supreme god. The Spirit promises abundance if they comply. Wakima experiences this vision for three successive nights, the last of which includes an apparition of a majestic swan appearing in the lake.

Wakima initiates the religion of the Great Spirit. Prosperity returns, the moaning of Mianomo and Towanda cease, and when the entire tribe gathers under the full moon at Innitou, a phantasm of a swan arises from the waters. When it disappears, an island remains as a sign of the Great Spirit's covenant.

There is every reason to believe that Converse was a man who dearly loved Woburn. In addition to his career as a lawyer and judge, he served as selectman, a school board member, an incorporator and vice president of a savings bank, and treasurer of the town's gas light company. He regularly contributed to town newspapers. Converse's desire to make Woburn an esteemed and thriving town is admirable, but his insulting depictions of Indigenous people should not be overlooked.

Converse is capable of producing fine work. In his two-volume collection of Woburn legends, he records a typical treasure tale, stories of numerous haunted houses, and a yarn about a gambling man, Sam Hart, who races against the Devil and wins His Satanic Majesty's infernal horse. He provides invaluable folkloric anecdotes on practices ranging from hunting and the militia to dancing and shoemaking.

Converse even records a fetching ditty about the Devil in pursuit of a sinner, which leads Old Scratch to leap from Step Rock in Saugus— long lost if it ever existed—to Step Rock in North Woburn (possibly once identified as an island in a swamp and now a Superfund site)—to Mianomo to Towanda, where he succeeded in grasping his prey. A rhyme accompanied this legend:

> That Satan came to town one day,
> But could not stay
> Because 'twas winter time;
> Had it been summer,
> Many a bummer,
> Could not got out of his way in time.

Similar stories punctuate New England to explain "footprints" found in rocks. If this is genuine, Converse made a significant collection of folk- lore studies of the area. Unfortunately, all of these positive contributions were eclipsed by his "Indian tales," which are propagated and amplified even today as if they were the lore of Indigenous people rather than appalling lore *about* Indigenous people.

A similar vexing pattern surrounds Hoccomocco Pond in Westborough. Today the pond is a Superfund site identified by the EPA as Hocomonco. From 1924 to 1948 a wood-treatment facility contaminated surface and groundwater with creosote. The 1937 WPA guidebook to Massachusetts did not alert readers to this circumstance but did identify Hoccomocco as a place "named by the Indians after an evil spirit."

As I explained in the chapter on the Bridgewater Triangle, that des- ignation is based on an error with considerable history. As the scholar George Stewart demonstrated, "Hoccomocco" is an Algonquian word for natural phenomena with a hook-shape, such as this pond, which was located in the territory of the Nipmuc people before European colonialization. "Hobbomocko" refers to a deity of shamans often regarded as an evil spirit by Christian colonialists. The two words are frequently confused.

For example, in 1767 the first Christian minister of Westborough, Ebenezer Parkman, identified the pond as Hobbamocka "from some supposed infernal influence, which a man was unhappily under nigh that pond, from morning till the sun sat." White storytellers continued to perpetuate the impression that the Nipmuck regarded the pond as evil and associated with Hobbomocko. And just as Mianomo had its bard in Converse, Hoccomocco Pond had Horace Maynard. Born in Westborough, Maynard lived a distinguished life, serving as a professor at what is now the University of Tennessee, as one of the few congressmen from that state to maintain the cause of the Union and abolition during the American Civil War, as a minister to Turkey under Ulysses Grant, and as postmaster general under Rutherford Hayes.

Before those achievements, Maynard was valedictorian at Amherst College. And it was there, as an undergraduate, that he penned a story for the college's literary magazine in 1838. That tale, "Legend of the Hobomak," enjoyed monumental influence in the Westborough community in the late 1800s as the definitive tale concerning the pond.

Maynard's story concerns the maiden Iano, a typical beautiful Indian sought by countless suitors. She falls in love with Sassacus, the young chief of her tribe, who humbles her proud spirit in a manner recalling the *Taming of the Shrew*. On the night before their wedding, Iano sneaks off to playfully hide from her lover. She takes a canoe onto the Hobomak. There she is seen by Wequoash, a jilted and vengeful suitor, who secretly approaches and drowns her. Wequoash later poisons Sassacus and becomes the new chief of the tribe.

On the anniversary of Iano's death, Wequoash is at the Hobomak and witnesses a ghostly vision of Iano and her canoe. She returns the second year and warns him, "Only once more." On the third anniversary,

Wequoash confesses his crime to the tribe and is taken away on a canoe led by the ghost of Sassacus into a realm of eternal punishment.

There are some later variants—in one version, for example, Sassacus witnesses Iano's drowning but cannot see the human agent behind it and assumes it was an act of the Evil Spirit. Several versions remark that Indigenous people left stones in the pond to mark Iano's grave, much like the "cairn" in the story of Monument Mountain in the Berkshires.

Maynard's tale was anthologized by Skinner in *Myths and Legends of Our Own Land*, but it had become a national sensation prior to that publication. In 1889 Harriette Merrifield Forbes published *The Hundredth Town: Glimpses of Life in Westborough*, which included Maynard's tale. (Duane Hurd published a history of Worcester County that same year and also commended Maynard's work.) In 1893 the *Boston Globe* reworked "Legend of the Hobomak" for inclusion in its Sunday pages. That version spread across the United States. It could be found in newspapers as far away as Hawaii.

Maynard claimed to have heard the legend from an Indian, the last of his tribe in Westborough. In her commentary Forbes nominated Andrew Brown as that source. But her description hints at underlying prejudice. In introducing Brown, she first mentions that he wove baskets and drank up the profits—that is, he was a drunkard—and only thereafter recalls that he served and was injured fighting in the American Revolution. Forbes then shares another anecdote about his intoxication, arguably indulging the stereotype of the Drunken Indian. Neither Forbes—nor Maynard, for that matter—had critical distance from the common opinions of their time concerning the status of Indigenous people. The tale of the Hobomak reflects this impulse among whites in the 1800s.

I suspect that Maynard's attribution to a "last Indian" is merely a literary convention, and a common one for his time. The story's themes echo with other "legends" about Indigenous people invented by whites in the 1800s. Even the names of the characters are taken from other sources. Sassacus was the sachem of the Pequot in Connecticut during the Mystic

Massacre of 1637; Wequoash was an ally to the English in the Pequot War and legendarily converted to Christianity following the massacre. I do not think that this "legend" derives from the oral tradition, then, although it appears to have entered the folklore of white residents following its publication.

I also see no evidence that the Nipmuc named the pond Hobomok. But there might—*might*—be a connection between Hoccomocco Pond and Hobbomocko that people of European descent did not properly understand.

A prominent natural feature now called Boston Hill rises up near Hoccomocco Pond. Many historical and poetic accounts contend that the hill was "serpent-haunted"—that is, the abode of copious snakes, likely rattlesnakes. A traditional jest suggested that the hill was named Boston because it had as many serpents as the city had residents. Snakes—especially venomous ones—were associated with the supernatural being Hobbomocko. It is plausible, then, that there was a hill associated with Hobbomocko adjacent to a hook-shaped pond called Hoccomocco, which readily confused English speakers who took control of that land in its entirety.

In closing, let me again propose that although the "Indian tales" of Rag Rock, Horn Pond, and Hoccomocco Pond are artifacts from a time when prejudice was rampant and accepted as a cultural norm, they should be remembered—not as commendable examples of Massachusetts folklore and certainly not as the narratives told by Indigenous people, but rather as important reminders of the role storytelling had—and continues to have—in shaping worldviews about others. These tales are important examples for critical reflection.

Legend Tripping

Admittedly, these hikes are not sensational—yet. Rag Rock isn't even a hike. It is a small conservation area surrounded by residential streets, made even smaller by the construction of a water tower about a decade ago. **Trailhead GPS: N42 28.59 / W71 09.42**

Horn Pond Conservation Area and Horn Pond Mountain are equally encapsulated. They are included here, however, because of their historical significance and to salute the efforts of dedicated local citizens who are doing astonishing work keeping the area accessible and clean. The associated legends are problematic, but the efforts of contemporary conservationists are admirable.

WREN, the Woburn Residents Environmental Network (http://www .gowren.org/), is one such organization doing important work. As of this writing their website is slightly outdated, but the organization remains active on social media. The city of Woburn Conservation Commission (https://www.woburnma.gov/government/conservation/) also oversees these areas, but does not currently post maps online. WREN posts a basic map for trails on the west side of Horn Pond. **Trailhead GPS: N42 28.01 / W71 09.35**

There are no maps to Horn Pond Mountain (which was developed for skiing in the 1930s), but trails meander throughout. The Nolan Trail is the main path. As with Rag Rock, the views from the summit are impressive. There is also a small glacial pothole atop Horn Pond Mountain, which may give credence to the legend and rhyme that Converse records about the Devil's footprints. **Trailhead GPS: N42 27.46 / W71 09.36**

The hike around Hoccomocco Pond has seen better days, but thanks to the praiseworthy efforts of the Westborough Community Land Trust (https://westboroughlandtrust.org/), it may see them again. The Mill Pond hike, which traverses the George H. Nichols Reservoir, skirts the south shore of Hoccomocco Pond. It is a stone's throw from the MBTA parking lot. **Trailhead GPS: N42 16.07 / W71 38.52**

For additional hikes in the town, see the chapter on the "Witch" of Westborough.

18

Bash Bish Falls

G IVEN THEIR RECENT acclaim as examples of Massachusetts folklore, it would be a glaring omission if I did not share the stories of Bash Bish Falls, Wahconah Falls, the Wizard's Glen, and Monument Mountain. But it is hard to include them.

As I wrote in the introduction, the conundrum of matching stories and hikes was a constant companion in the composition of this book. Nowhere is this division more dramatic than in the Berkshires. Despite incomparable beauty and a profound influence on American literature and arts, the Berkshires cannot boast the same legacy as eastern Massachusetts with respect to folk narratives. In some ways this is not surprising; the towns of the shoreline have a century or more over their western siblings in terms of settlement.

But there is another problem looming over the best-known sites for hiking the folkloric Berkshires: They are magnets for "Indian tales," those stories created by white people of European heritage about Indigenous people, largely passed on to white audiences. Although often purported to be genuine legends told by Indigenous people, they are usually literary romances, inventions of a single author or a few. Many derive from the 1800s, when Indigenous people had been greatly reduced in numbers and effectively removed from the state. During this period romanticized notions of the "noble savage" replaced earlier, colonialist tales of devil-worshipping heathens, but that latter depiction is no less based in stereotyping and exploitation.

These "Indian tales" often complemented rumors of "last Indians"—that is, anecdotes concerning the death of an aged, final living member of a tribe in a given town, whose passing relieves white residents of any responsibilities. To call these tales problematic is an understatement.

Unreflective prejudice against Indigenous people lingered even when writers should have known better. Take the specialized WPA guidebook from 1939, *The Berkshire Hills*. In the latter's entry on Devil's Den, a cavern on Tom Ball Mountain—one that has regrettably suffered recent damage—readers discover that within the den stands "a stone altar fashioned out of curiously arranged boulders; the stones before it are stained as if with sacrificial blood. The visage of Satan appears on a bank nearby. Water, constantly dripping, adds to the weird atmosphere, reinforcing a popular belief that Indians made sacrifices here."

That same year Clay Perry—a resident of Pittsfield, a master storyteller, and a proponent of the sport of spelunking—published *Underground New England*. Perry dedicates three paragraphs to the Devil's Den, "admirably named," he suggests, "for with its dark, yawning opening, the largest cave mouth in New England, so far as explorations have disclosed, and its savage and jumbled interior, it possesses, also, some strangely symbolic natural formations."

Perry describes the altar and the "face of old Satan himself" formed by the dissolving action of water on limestone. He reveals without compunction to the reader that the "bloods stains" are the result of chemical reactions. "Geologically the Devil's Den is fascinating," he concludes, "for its mixture of native rock, and to the imaginative its satanic suggestion is irresistibly chilling." No unconfirmed rumors of Indian sacrifices are made in Perry's account—or necessary.

I do not dispute that the author of the WPA guidebook's entry surmised a local folk belief that Indians sacrificed in the cave. What troubles me is the lack of information conveyed to the tourist. Does that imply human sacrifice or religious worship involving the sacrifice of animals? And why such quick association between Indian sacrifice and Satanic activity?

Perry, a far more skillful raconteur, sees no purpose in that correspondence. He recognizes that there is plenty to stir the imagination with the Devil alone. Both *The Berkshire Hills* and *Underground New England* sought to encourage readers to tour these locations, but the tact adopted by each matters to prepare readers for what to see and how to experience it.

In a previous book on Connecticut folkloric hikes, I opted to tell numerous stories of Lovers Leaps and other "Indian tales" in my own words. I debated doing so at the time, and I have continued to think about it since. In the pages ahead I will share the basic outlines and explain the stories, but I will not narrate them with fond attention. That decision is not meant to censor. Quite the contrary, I think it is extremely important that people know these tales as historical artifacts that influenced and continue to influence public consciousness.

The "legend" of Bash Bish Falls, to hear it today, begins with a Mohican woman who lived in an Indian village near the waterfall that now bears her name. The beautiful Bash Bish was once accused of adultery, a crime punishable by death among her people. Although she protested innocence, her cries fell on deaf ears. The tribe decided to tie her into a canoe and send her over the waterfall to her death.

Bash Bish did not die, at least not in the conventional sense. Before the unjust punishment could be doled out, she broke free of her captors and threw herself off the cliff. As she did so, a thick veil of mist rose up. Butterflies appeared as if out of thin air and surrounded her plummet. Her body was never found, leading those in the tribe to assume she was a witch.

Among those in attendance that horrible day was Bash Bish's infant daughter, White Swan. White Swan grew to be as beautiful as her mother. She became the bride to Whirling Wind, the chieftain's son. But White Swan never produced a child, so Whirling Wind took a second wife into their house that he might have a son and heir.

White Swan languished and began to brood atop the waterfall where her mother had plunged to her death. She began to dream of her mother as well, calling White Swan to join her in an eternal embrace.

One day Whirling Wind came to the precipice to comfort his first wife with a gift of a white butterfly. He arrived too late. White Swan threw herself from the cliff into the pool below. Whirling Wind reached to save White Swan and dropped with her to his doom. His body was recovered and soon buried by the remaining members of the tribe. White Swan's body, like her mother's, was never found.

Perusing the introductions to this story one readily finds claims that it is an Indian legend or even an *ancient* Indian legend. One egregiously misguided "folklore researcher" even specifies that it was a legend shared among the Mohicans. It is none of those things. In fact, that story is not even the oldest version of the tale. It originated in 1972, making it one year younger than I am. Instead, this tale is best described as fakelore—a narrative composed in such a way to appear to be authentic folklore, but one that is not rooted in the cultural traditions it purports to be from.

The tale of Bash Bish originated in Willard Douglas Coxey's 1934 *Ghosts of Old Berkshire* in a story alternatively entitled "The Squaw Witch of Bash-Bish Falls" and "The Spirit Squaw of Bash-Bish Falls." Coxey was an interesting fellow, to say the least. When he died in 1943 at the age of eighty-two, *Billboard* magazine published an obituary. He had spent a career as a public relations agent for various circuses, including Ringling Brothers and Barnum & Bailey, along with theater producers such as William Brady. Coxey retired to the Berkshires to a life of creative writing that included *Ghosts* and his 1931 *Romances of Old Berkshire*.

Ostensibly Coxey based both books—collections of fiction and fictionalized tales—on the folklore of the Berkshires. But in *Romances* he readily admits in the foreword that he intends to take "some latitude with tradition and historical events." His opening sentence in the foreword to *Ghosts* clarifies the veracity of his endeavors. "These tales are true," he opines, "in so far as you believe them true." Coxey then implies the tales were believed by those who came before, but he also remarks that several have never previously been seen—that is, he admits they are his creations.

I cannot stop you from reading Coxey's original tale, and for the sake of understanding the issues at stake, I might recommend that you do so. But be forewarned that you will not likely find it entertaining unless you savor painful stereotyping of Indigenous people as was common practice in the 1930s.

Coxey's story is very different from the one that is currently circulating. In his tale, an Indian by the name of Wi-o-koo-nah, the Wanderer, comes to a colonial town in the Berkshires toward the close of the American Revolution. He is a descendent of the tribe whose remnant still lives at the waterfall, but was taken by the Iroquois in a raid as a youth. Now an old man, he has come to die at the place where he was born.

Wi-o-koo-nah tells the story of White Swan to the white settlers. She was an orphan whose parentage was unknown. She appeared one day in the wigwam of Lo-to-ski-nock, who fostered her. White Swan grew into a beautiful young maiden. She was chosen by the chief Mac-kat-an-a-na-ma-kee (Black Thunder) to be the bride of his only son, Wey-au-we-ya (Whirling Wind). Coxey spends considerable ink describing tribal preparations for the ceremony, including the various activities of the Medicine Man, to bless their union.

Happiness ensues for some time until White Swan cannot conceive a child. Black Thunder instructs Whirling Wind to take a second wife, Au-zhe-bik-a-qua, in order to produce a legitimate heir to the chiefdom. His son obliges the tradition of his tribe. White Swan begins to decline and increasingly spends time at the waterfall. She returns there so often that she is believed to be bewitched.

One day Whirling Wind discovers White Swan teetering on the rocks of the cliff. She calls out to her mother below. "Then, before Wey-au-we-ya's startled eyes," writes Coxey, "there appeared, alternately glistening in the moonlight, and then disappearing in the box of the falls, the white-robed form of a woman." It was the water witch, White's Swan's mother.

White Swan leaps into her mother's arms. Whirling Wind plunges off the cliff after his beloved. Black Thunder's scouts find him dead the next day. White Swan's mortal form was never seen again, but "when a warrior was old and weary, and longed for another life, the White Swan came in the quiet of the night, and smiled on the unhappy one, and bore him in her arms along the spirit trail to the lands of peace."

In Coxey's original tale, Bash Bish is not the name of a supernatural being, and the water witch herself does not appear until eighteen pages into a twenty-one-page story. Indeed, for the next four decades Bash Bish simply does not surface as a character. The story that became popular—and that was sold as an Indian legend—concerned White Swan, the daughter of the water witch residing in the pool at Bash Bish Falls.

Coxey's tale became influential on account of the actions of the Civilian Conservation Corps, a New Deal initiative. Bash Bish Falls became a state park in 1924. The CCC actively began clearing paths to promote tourism, akin to the role played by the WPA guidebooks. The path to Bash Bish Falls was cleared in 1935 to considerable fanfare.

The *Berkshire Eagle*, for example, celebrated the opening of the path by praising its virtues, including that the tourist site was "enriched by Indian legend." The legend, of course, was Coxey's tale, unattributed to him directly. That version remained the dominant story for several decades, appearing routinely in newspapers and guidebooks throughout the Berkshires and occasionally in Boston or New York. A few elements changed on occasion. In one version White Swan committed suicide in protest of her husband taking a new lover, and in another Whirling Wind did not perish, but for the most part the story remains consistent to Coxey's melodramatic romance.

Throughout these decades there was a robust attempt on behalf of the CCC storytellers, the WPA guidebooks, and local newspapers serving the tourism industry to create the impression that White Swan—and sometimes her mother the witch—could be seen in the falls, either in a rock profile or in the cascading water or in the pool. Newspapers published images of this visage and encouraged tourists to visit and see it for themselves. It was, put bluntly, a public relations gimmick. Never quite settling on what part of the waterfall held her image, it eventually fizzled out, although remnants linger today in some versions of the story.

As I mentioned earlier, these "Indian tales" often correlated with "last Indian" stories. The invented tale of White Swan and Whirling Wind is one in which the legitimacy of the tribe ends because Black Thunder's heir never comes to be. Whirling Wind dies without producing issue. In Coxey's tale, Wi-o-koo-nah claims to be a descendent, but he is a powerless one, reliant upon the charity of the white settlers. And he comes to the falls to perish. This tale is a not-so-veiled attempt to romanticize the death and removal of Indigenous people.

1972 saw a new version of the story, the one that is more popular today and summarized above. It appeared in *Haunted New England*, a well-received book by Mary Bolté. She simply retold Coxey's story, changing the elements as she saw fit. And to her credit, she was upfront about doing so. In the preface to her work, Bolté asserts that her tales "are not intended to represent a necessarily authentic version, but only a representative one.... If, in setting them down again on these pages, embellishments have crept in here and there, the author can only claim the traditional right of the storyteller."

That solves any inquiry as to how the second version of the tale arose. It does not, unfortunately, explain why people since then have mistaken Bolté's fictionalized reinterpretation of a previous work of fiction as the genuine folklore of Indigenous people.

The name Bash Bish, incidentally, may not have any association with Indigenous people. In the mid-1800s, inquiries about the name were informed that it was originally named Bash-pish by Swiss immigrants, "pish" or "pisse" a common name for small waterfalls in Switzerland—and for the curious, it does indeed mean a stream that flows, as in urine.

I will not wade into that folk etymology here, but I would raise the point that throughout the 1800s there is a trove of representations of Bash Bish—poems, essays, stories, and travelogues—that celebrate its inspiring nature without any indebtedness to "Indian tales" and their potential prejudice. And while we may salute Coxey and Bolté as well-intended storytellers and not hold them to the expectations of our day, we certainly can consider and debate whether a public relations stunt made to appear like folklore almost a century ago has outlived its utility for the contemporary world.

Legend Tripping

Bash Bish Falls State Park is overseen by the Department of Conservation and Recreation (https://www.mass.gov/locations/bash-bish-falls-state-park), which provides a map for Mt. Washington State Forest. Trails stretch for miles. There is free parking on Falls Road near the site, but the entire area is worth exploration. **Trailhead GPS: N42 06.53 / W73 29.29**

Closest to Bash Bish Falls is the South Taconic Trail, which enters New York. The trailhead for the South Taconic Trail is in Taconic State Park (https://parks.ny.gov/parks/83/details.aspx) across the border and makes for an excellent hike to Bash Bish. Park at Taconic and utilize the map for the north section, providing a hike of 2 miles that gets the heart pumping. **Trailhead GPS: N42 07.15 / W73 31.11**

19

The Wizard's Glen, Wahconah Falls, and Monument Mountain

T HIS CHAPTER FOLLOWS the comments of the previous one regarding certain "Indian tales" that have been become prevalent representatives of folklore in the Berkshires. As with Bash Bish Falls, my intention is not necessarily to criticize those who passed the tale along thinking it was genuine lore, but to right the record for the contemporary reader.

The Berkshire Hills, the specialized WPA guidebook from 1939, is again a fitting place to start. An entry for a site in Dalton opens with a conspicuous claim:

> *Wizard's Glen has a profusion of giant rocks like a huge, crumpled wall. Indian legend calls the pile the Devil's Altar Stone, and here medicine men and tribal wizards are supposed to have offered human sacrifice to Ho-bo-mo-ko [Hobbomocko], Spirit of Evil.*

The guide subsequently provides a brief version of the tale. "Many years ago," it commences, "a local hunter named Chamberlain came to the Glen." He carried the carcass of a deer. A thunderstorm arose suddenly, driving Chamberlain to seek shelter under one of the boulders. He placed the deer under another. A sudden flash of lightning shattered the sky and with it appeared "Satan and his Court," frightful specters. Satan did not look, however, as one would think he would; instead he resembled "the Indian of song and story."

The phantoms were Indians as well and began "a wild chant and dance as two of their number dragged a beautiful maiden"—naked—toward the sacrificial altar. The victim was placed upon the rock and "the Wizard raised his hatchet to strike." The maiden caught sight of Chamberlain and screamed in desperation. Her shriek inspired the hunter to arm himself with the Bible that he always carried with him. As he uttered a passage of Holy Writ, the entire scene disappeared under another crash of thunder. Initially Chamberlain thought he had suffered a nightmare, but when he searched for his venison, it had also dematerialized.

I see no reason to sugarcoat it: This is a racist depiction of Indigenous people.

It is a product of its time, admittedly, and by that I do not solely mean the 1930s. This account is an abbreviation of a much longer tale narrated in 1852 in Godfrey Greylock's—the pseudonym of Joseph Edward Adams Smith—*Taghconic*. "Tradition indeed says," Smith writes in his direct introduction, "before the decay of the native tribes—of whom a scanty remnant were found by the white man in the valley of the Housatonic—this used to be a favorite haunt of the Indian Priests, or Wizards. Here, it was said, they wrought their hellish incantations, and with horrible rites offered up human sacrifices to Ho-bo-mo-ko [Hobbomocko], the Spirit of Evil."

Smith plays loose in his description of "the Devil's altar stone," pontificating that early settlers thought it was stained with blood but that the more educated of his time understood it was dissolved iron ore. His judgment, however, is informative. "For my part," he prefers, "I hold fast to the older and better opinion of those who believed that around this ensanguined shrine a spectral crew of savage wizards nightly reenacted the revolting orgies of the past." If that is not an admission of motive, nothing is. Contemporary storytellers should not turn a blind eye to that comment, nor to Smith's earlier claim that the "red race" had vanished from the land to be replaced by "pious and Godly men."

One could excuse Smith the prejudice of his time; one could also argue that such a comment reflects the opinion of the *narrator* and not of the *author*. Those are fair points, but equal consideration should be given to the acute possibility that Smith's intention here is to demonize—literally—Indigenous people.

The narrator of Smith's tale claims to have heard the story from a ninety-year-old man, who himself heard the story "from an eye witness," presumably John Chamberlain, sometime around 1770. The actual Chamberlain family was present in the Dalton area in the late 1700s, but that fact reveals very little about this tale. It is more telling that the *character* of John Chamberlain was pleased to see that the Devil took the form of an Indigenous person, for the white hero "was no lover of the Indian race."

Only a few distinctions separate Smith's and the WPA's accounts of the Wizard's Glen. Smith's is far more dramatic. Chamberlain is unable to sleep through the storm, and when he gazes out at the altar, he initially sees only Satan, enthroned, awaiting a gala. The first guest to appear is a "wizard," an Indian priest. Smith's description deserves attention for its estimation of Indigenous people:

> *If Chamberlain has not painted him blacker than he deserves, this high priest of Satan was a most villainous looking rascal. His raw-boned and ghastly visage was painted in most bloodthirsty ugliness; scalps, dripping with fresh blood, hung around his body in festoons; on his own scull, by way of scalp lock, burned a lambent blue flame; his distended veins shone through the bright copper-colored skin as if they were filled with molten fire for blood—and, as for his eyes, they glowed with a fiercer light than those of the arch-fiend himself; whence*

Chamberlain maintained that an Indian priest was at least one degree more devilish than the Devil himself.

The Indian specters then materialize, also glowing with blue light and smelling of chthonic sulphur. Finally, the sacrificial maiden appears, who also is an Indian. Throughout the story Smith comments on the dancing done by the tribe, including steps they learned in Hell, and their demonic howling and yelling.

For those who wish to consider this a folkloric tale rather than a purely literary one, there is a significant hurdle. This story is effectively the same as John Greenleaf Whittier's "Powow Hill," published in 1832. It also draws from two of Whittier's other stories—"The Powwaw" and "The Human Sacrifice"—both published in his 1831 *Legends of New England*.

To contextualize, Smith's book was written for tourists, those "summer ramblers on the Berkshire hills." It became the basis for a formal guide-book published in 1875. And although Smith relished recounting local history and commemorating the natural beauty of the Berkshires, he was keenly dedicated to associate the area with the "literary lions" that made their homes or lengthy visits there, including Herman Melville, Nathaniel Hawthorne, Oliver Wendell Holmes, Catherine Sedgwick, and William Cullen Bryant. In other words, Smith was a well-read man. There is no chance he was unaware of Whittier's work and, I think, imitates it here or draws from someone who is aware of it.

While it is the case that folklore exists throughout New England and New York in which the Bible is employed to lay ghosts, the incorporation of that motif into Indian tales is rarer. In addition to Whittier, the classic example is found in Samuel Peters's 1781 *General History of Connecticut*, in which English settlers witnessed devils and Indians rise from the sea, wrapped in flames and howling wildly, until an Episcopal minister, a Mr. Visey, exorcised them by reading from the Bible. Whittier used Peters's account as the basis for "The Powwaw."

I cannot find any examples to date of this tale prior to *Taghconic*, nor is it easy to find versions that come after which are not specific citations of his book. Until I am able to find that additional evidence, I remain of the opinion that is a purely literary invention on Smith's part, written soon after the Stockbridge Mohican had been removed from the area, first to New York and then to Wisconsin. This is certainly not a folkloric story narrated by Indigenous people.

One particular tell that Smith is relying upon Whittier is his choice for the name of the Indian's Spirit of Evil. Hobbomocko is the villainous devil in all three of Whittier's stories. Hobbomocko is, furthermore, the name for a supernatural being associated with the Wampanoag and other coastal Indigenous groups. It is unlikely that name would have been used by the Mohican in the Dalton area in the late 1700s. And finally, the term "Wizard's Glen" itself is anomalous in the folklore of the Indigenous people of New England, but it was a common name for similar eerie places in the literature and folklore of the British Isles throughout the 1800s.

A plausible case could be made that the story of the Wizard's Glen entered into the oral tradition following the publication of Smith's work—and its reinforcement in numerous guidebooks and in Charles Skinner's 1896 popular collection of folktales—rendering it folklore, albeit among whites. That is a legitimate claim, but it does not change the likelihood that the tale was invented in print for the purpose of demonizing Indigenous people.

Smith did record genuine folklore, but he was largely dismissive of it. In a passage that receives very little attention today, for example, he notes an interaction with a man who claims that there "were no firmer believers in supernaturalisms than the people who lived about Onota," including that unnamed informant's grandfather. This grandfather went deer hunting with his dog, and his normally faithful canine companion proved a continual hassle. The hunter believed his dog had been bewitched, so he whipped it and then traveled to the hut of an "old crone"—a suspected witch—and "demanded that she should show him her back, on which he did not doubt he would find the marks of the blows he had inflicted upon his miserable hound." This is, of course, a familiar theme found in this book, of the witch who suffers the physical harm done to her familiar. In this case, the grandfather did not prove the effects of sorcery but was lucky enough to dodge the accused woman's throwing of furniture at him in protest.

Having briefly teased this example of local folklore about witches, Smith launches into another romantic "Indian tale," that of the White Deer of Onota, in which the hunter of a sacred albino deer suffers misfortune. In other words, Smith is simply not a reliable source for folklore; he readily buries actual vibrant traditions in favor of his own creations or those tales he deemed valuable to his agenda.

That admonition brings us to the "Indian legend" of Wahconah Falls. For those interested in a profoundly melodramatic—if not outright affected—but polished narrative, Smith's lengthy tale has no equal. It entails a forbidden romance, although one that surprisingly does not end in tragedy. In the aftermath of the Mystic Massacre of 1637 in which white settlers brutalized entrapped Pequot in Connecticut, a few survivors of that group made their way to the Berkshires led by Miahcomo. Decades later Metacom implored them to join the cause of King Philip's War, but Miahcomo refused.

That decision did not, however, spare him from tensions with the neighboring Mohawks of New York. Miahcomo is summoned to negotiate with the Mohawks and leaves his village for some time. While he is absent, his daughter Wahconah—yet another beautiful Indian maiden—visits the forest. There she discovers Nessacus, a warrior who had fought for King Philip's cause but who had since fled the English victory. Wahconah welcomes him to her father's village. They fall in love.

Miahcomo returned with his delegation and with Yonnongah, a Mohawk to whom Wahconah had been pledged to marry. She objected and asked her father's permission to wed Nessacus instead.

Miahcomo deferred to the Great Spirit to decide which of the two men should have his daughter. In doing so he sought the counsel of the tribe's shaman, Tashmu, unaware that the priest favored Yonnongah. Tashmu pretended to consult with the Great Spirit in the Wizard's Glen, but instead devised a clandestine scheme: An empty canoe would be released in the river that feeds the falls, and Wahconah would be given to the man at whose feet it lands. Unbeknownst to Miahcomo, Tashmu rearranged the rocks in the stream to guarantee the canoe would land before Yonnongah.

When the canoe failed to do so and delivered Wahconah instead to the arms of her beloved—a sure sign of the intervention of the Great Spirit—Tashmu disappeared. He sought out John Talcott, one of the English settlers who led a contingency of allied Indians against King Philip. Tashmu is captured, returned to the tribe, and punished—presumably by execution—but it is too late; Talcott is on the path to destroy them, believing the lies that Tashmu plied about Miahcomo and his people. In response to this threat, Nessacus summoned the Indians of the area and "led them to a home in the West."

As this story continued to be told, especially in the twentieth century, it increasingly transformed into a love story with Wahconah as the primary figure and protagonist. Skinner's *Myths and Legends*, for example, reworked the tale to emphasize romantic elements and Wahconah's emotional trial. That emphasis continues to this day.

Although understandable, the shift to Wahconah's inner turmoil misses—perhaps even absolves—several important themes in Smith's original version. Notable among them is yet another incarnation of a malicious "Indian wizard" whose evil manifests at the Glen. More poignant is the conclusion of this story in which Nessacus leads the Indians away from the Berkshires. This is a "last Indian" tale applied to an entire community. And in Smith's tale the Indians who leave the region are happy for doing so. Wahconah loses her home but gains a joy "sweet as the perfume which a western gale might bring from a far-off prairie."

In other words, this tale is a white person's fantasy that the Stockbridge Indians benefitted by being removed from the area to Wisconsin. Smith even attributes it to an unnamed "young Indian of the civilized Stockbridge tribe, who had come from his exile in the Far West, to be educated at an Eastern college." It is not impossible that such a Stockbridge Indian existed, returned east, and passed along this tale, but it does strike a tone of being convenient to the point of dubiousness, especially given the happy ending which Smith purports.

There is some evidence that this tale was Smith's literary invention. In 1899, the Berkshire Historical and Scientific Society published an article by Dalton resident Ella S. Brown entitled "Wahconah Falls—Their History and Traditions." Brown briefly mentions three legends associated with the falls. The first is Smith's, which she praises for its composition and influence.

"But the simple, unwritten legends possess a certain charm and interest," Brown counters. "They have come down to us through several generations and seem to bring with them a glimpse of the wild unrestrained life of the Red Man." While she is in error about the lore belonging to Indigenous people, the greater point is that Brown distinguishes between Smith's literary entertainment and folk narratives circulating in the oral tradition.

The two tales she records both contain the common theme of a Lover's Leap suicide. In one of them, two men of the same tribe seek a maiden's hand. They compete to leap the furthest over the banks at the head of the waterfall. The man unwanted by the maiden clears to the other side. Her beloved fails, however, landing instead in the middle of the stream. Rather than accept her fate, the maiden embraces her chosen one and they throw themselves off the waterfall to their entwined doom, she calling out *his* name, Wahconah. In the second tale, Wahconah is the maiden's name. She falls in love with a member of the hostile tribe at Pontoosuc and takes her life at the falls when her father, the chief, forbids the union.

Although not strictly an imitation, Smith's literary inclinations followed a path set out decades earlier by William Cullen Bryant. Bryant's poem "Monument Mountain" blazed the trail in narrating "a sad tradition of unhappy love." Although a summary insults the poetic language, the gist of the tale concerns an unnamed Indian maiden who falls in love with her cousin. The love is deemed incestuous and forbidden, and the Indian maiden begins to pine away. She frequents the forests and the high rocks of the mountain "to weep where no eye saw her."

Sick of living, the Indian maiden confesses to an old playmate:

> All night I weep in darkness, and the more
> Glares on me, as upon a thing accursed,
> That has no business on the earth. I hate
> The pastimes and the pleasant tolls that once
> I loved; the cheerful voices of my friends
> Have an unnatural horror in mine ear.
> In dreams my mother, from the land of souls,
> Calls me and chides me. All that look on me
> Do seem to know my shame; I cannot bear
> Their eyes; I cannot from my heart root out
> The love that wrings it so, and I must die.

Soon thereafter she throws herself from a steep precipice and perishes. Bryant closes with mention of her grave—a sort of cairn—built up as Indians pile another stone each time they pass, and hence:

> The mountain where the hapless maiden died
> Is called the Mountain of the Monument.

A Mohican stone monument did stand near Monument Mountain in the ancient trail systems. It was vandalized and destroyed some-time between the late 1700s and early 1800s. When Smith visited the mountain, for example, it was nowhere to be found, and his guide disputed both its existence and the tale of the Indian maiden. But Bryant's poem eventually proved so popular—and a lure for tourists—that businessmen from Great Barrington reconstructed one in the 1880s.

As the anthropologist Lucianne Lavin explains, Indigenous people were hesitant to identify the significance of such monuments and often provided conflicting explanations to white settlers. In this specific case, if Indigenous people rather than whites were the source for this story—a point that is far from settled fact, they may have proffered the tale about a maiden in order to protect the monument's true meaning.

The colonization of the monument (as well as the mountain) is undeniable in an alternative tale published in 1902, "Strange Legend of an Indian Maiden." In this grisly version, a beautiful squaw marries into a hostile tribe but is captured by her relatives and sentenced to death. She is unable to summon the courage to commit suicide by leaping from the precipice, so she is bound and thrown to her doom. In her descent she catches on a pine tree, where she hangs for two days and two nights, mocked incessantly by her tribe. On the second night a thunderstorm approaches. Lightning strikes the branch and the maiden, set aflame, launches into the air. Her body is never recovered. The tribe elects to erect a monument of stones in honor of the Great Spirit's action that night.

I do not wish to be repetitive about the considerable problems of treating "Indian tales" as the folklore of Indigenous people, but I also wish these stories were not repeated with the frequency they manifested for nearly two centuries. In laying their genealogy bare for the reader, I hope it will provoke a long overdue discussion about this "folklore" and whether it should continue.

Legend Tripping

Wahconah Falls State Park is overseen by the Department of Conservation and Recreation (https://www.mass.gov/locations/wahconah-falls-state-park). As of this writing the DCR does not provide a map, but the falls are easy to access. There is free parking on Wahconah Falls Road in Dalton where the trailhead begins. The trail, which is often overgrown, extends for about a half mile to the falls, so this is not a strenuous hike by any means. **Trailhead GPS: N42 29.21 / W73 06.54**

The Wizard's Glen area is also in Dalton. The best way to explore is to park on Gulf Road, where one can pick up the Appalachian Trail. The boulders in that area compose the Wizard's Glen. Many of them are now painted or covered in graffiti. **Trailhead GPS: N42 28.54 / W73 10.41**

While in the Dalton and Pittsfield area, a hike at The Boulders is certainly worth the effort. This property is overseen by the Berkshire Natural Resources Council (https://www.bnrc.org/trails-and-maps/the-boulders/), which maintains a pamphlet and map. There are six miles of trails within this conservation area, where the remnants of glacial activity are sure to fire the imagination. Use the same parking lot for the Wizard's Glen at the AT trail. The entry to The Boulders is on the other side of the street.

Monument Mountain in Great Barrington is overseen by the Trustees of Reservations (https://thetrustees.org/place/monument-mountain/), which offers a map. Parking is free for this 3-mile loop that includes Squaw Peak. Be sure to take the side trail to Devil's Pulpit for an astonishing view. **Trailhead GPS: N42 14.35 / W73 20.07**

20

Hobbomocko and Moshup

THIS CHAPTER ADDRESSES several stories of Indigenous people in Massachusetts, materials that would be called, in the language of our day, complex. They would be conspicuous by their absence, especially since many entail renowned hikes, but their inclusion raises a host of ethical issues given their long-standing exploitation by people of European descent. Historically, many of these tales were filtered through white—and often deliberately colonialist—perspectives, with authors motivated to demonize, romanticize, and otherwise delegitimize Indigenous people in the Commonwealth. Fortunately, over the past century Native American voices have increasingly corrected the colonial record.

For additional commentary about Hobbomocko and Moshup, I strongly recommend readers search out reputable storytellers and scholars, especially those with tribal membership and related affiliations. Readers should also be aware that significant misinformation and problematic tales continue to be propagated, included by those who in their enthusiasm for folklore fail to fully recognize the underlying history of prejudice and racism at stake.

It would be the understatement of this book to call the supernatural being known as Hobbomocko a complicated figure. He was an absolute befuddlement to European colonialists, who misunderstood him from the start—literally. The earliest written reference to Hobbomocko appears in 1624, in which Edward Winslow, a *Mayflower* passenger and governor of Plymouth Colony, summarizes his identity by asserting "this as far as we can conceive is the Devil." In the limiting dualism of good versus evil that characterized Puritan Christianity, ambiguous beings of the Indigenous cosmology were almost always reduced to the side of evil, but Hobbomocko was singled out.

Hobbomocko is connected to what is best termed "shamanism" in English—that is, with the practices of the *powwow* (the name for a spiritual expert) and the *pniese* (the name for an elite warrior with ties to the spirit world). Hobbomocko is associated with divination, dreams, visions, and analogous uncanny but significant experiences. His domain is also that of curing and of disease. While that may strike readers as contradictory, there are ample comparative examples throughout other polytheistic religions in which the same being is responsible for both illness and health.

In a similar vein, Hobbomocko was considered both a fearsome, terrifying power and one who could provide tremendous benefits to those who proved worthy. A man who became a *pniese*, for example, did so through ordeal, a rigorous initiation rite that may have included self-inflicted pain and ingestion of hallucinogens. Winslow simply dismissed those practices as the preparation to become acceptable to the Devil. But from the perspective of the Indigenous people of Massachusetts, the successful accomplishment of such a rite bestowed supernatural favor—for example, invulnerability to arrows or bullets—and influence with the sachem, the leader of the tribe.

Perhaps not surprisingly, Hobbomocko is often linked to liminal spaces such as swamps or dark woods, as well as to the night and its attendant dangers. And although they may reflect European influences, early colonial references also suggest that the Indigenous people associated Hobbomocko with the color black, with the chilling northeast wind, and with certain animals, especially snakes. (A man who dreamed of a serpent, for example, was a candidate to become a *powwow*.)

Hobbomocko is, furthermore, a being who could transform into other shapes, including humans, animals, monstrous creatures, and inanimate forms. Finally, he has some correspondence with disembodied spirits and the dead through his influence over disease and healing. Accordingly, Hobbomocko is often affiliated with a figure (or beings) called Cheepi, a name conveying the sense of both a "spirit" and a "specter."

It will not tax the reader to guess how such a figure as Hobbomocko was received by the Puritans' paranoid imagination. Winslow, in outright calling him the Devil, was in many ways being charitable. Early colonialists saw in Hobbomocko and those who performed rites in his honor immoral practitioners of diabolism and witchcraft and by extension a threat to themselves, the moral people elected by the Christian God to possess the land of the New World. Indeed, throughout those early texts Hobbomocko is often glossed as the Evil One, a term that reveals more about Puritan worldview than it accurately conveys Indigenous cultural understandings.

It may well be true that precolonial Indigenous people recognized the potential for harm and even wickedness in Hobbomocko and his associates, including the restless spirits of the dead and dangerous animals such as venomous snakes. But under the increasing influence of Christianity, his multivalent and ambivalent personality was reduced and rejected by colonialists and converts alike. Within a century of European arrival, Hobbomocko was regarded simply as "the Indian Devil" and dismissed in written records as a font of sorcery.

That reductive stereotyping continued uninterrupted into the 1800s. With the Indigenous people of the state decimated, removed, or converted to Christianity, the name Hobbomocko became a generic term for an "angry Indian god" or "the Spirit of Evil" in the literary fancies of nineteenth-century white writers. Several examples of that deliberate misrepresentation have appeared throughout this book. Even authors otherwise praised for their generosity and sympathy such as John Greenleaf Whittier routinely employed Hobbomocko as a stock character of pure malevolence in stories envisioning the hellacious villainy of Indians.

With all of this in mind, let us turn to Sugarloaf Mountain in Deerfield and the homeland site of the Pocumtuck people, who were violently removed by European colonialists and exiled to New York and Canada. In 1871 Phinehas Field published a Native story—really a summary—that he entitled "The Great Beaver":

> *Whose pond flowed over the whole basin north of Mt. Tom, made havoc among the fish and when these failed he would come ashore and devour Indians. A pow-wow was held and Hobmock raised, who came to their relief. With a great stake in hand, he waded the river until he found the beaver, and so hotly chased him that he sought to escape by digging into the ground. Hobmock saw his plan and his whereabouts, and with his great stake jammed the beaver's head off. The earth over the beaver's head we call Sugarloaf, his body lies just north of it.*

Later writers followed suit, contending that Hobbomocko came to defend the Pocumtuck from a monstrous and carnivorous beaver. When he strikes the creature in the neck and kills the beast, it petrifies, forming the mountain range that casts a shadow upon the Connecticut River. The outline of the Great Beaver can still be seen today with its head comprising Sugarloaf and its body and tail descending to Greenfield.

Immediately prior to the Great Beaver story, Field recounts another "Indian Tradition" regarding an area between Sunderland and Leverett where an evil spirit dwelled. Akin to the Great Beaver, this monster had devoured many Indians, so they raise Hobbomocko seeking protection. He chases the evil spirit "to the mountains," where it pivots to dive into the Connecticut River. Hobbomocko strikes down his opponent as it leaps in the air. The beast then "sank into the earth on the plain that lies north of the brook and west of the road. . . . The place where this monster disappeared showed a depression in the ground some six or eight inches deep, in shape somewhat like a man with outstretched limbs. No weeds or grass were known to grow in that spot until the Indians had left the region."

Field concludes his narrative recalling that his father was shown a "white oak tree, touched by the toe of the man-eater in his descent, on which there never afterward grew a straight limb." He does not mention whether the person who revealed the tree was of European or Pocumtuck heritage.

In 1910, Edward Pearson Pressey retold the Great Beaver tale in his history of Montague. Pressey follows Field closely but overtly identifies Hobbomocko as "a benevolent spirit giant." He also recounts the story of the second monster, now named Wittum the demon, and locates the mountain lair mentioned by Field as Mt. Toby. The name "Wittum" appears in no other historical accounts from the region. I can only speculate, but it may be a surviving or borrowed term related to other Algonquian cannibal monsters, such as the windigo among the Ojibwe. Frustratingly, Pressey does not name his sources.

How are we to understand these stories of Hobbomocko, which depict him as a benefactor of his people?

I am not the only one to find them unusual, especially because they treat Hobbomocko as a culture hero and earth-shaper, two roles for which there are no comparable accounts among the coastal tribes where he was a significant figure. While it is plausible that these tales represent positive aspects of Hobbomocko's nature, there is no indication that Field or Pressey consulted with Indigenous people for these stories.

I will not bore you with all the scholarly discussion, but there is a reasonable chance that what is happening here is a misplaced name. Field or his informant very likely inserted the name Hobbomocko, following a common practice among white literati in Massachusetts throughout the 1800s—and long after the Indigenous people of the Deerfield area had effectively been removed.

I am suggesting—recognizing full well that additional evidence may prove me wrong—that these tales, when narrated by the Pocumtuck, may have named a different protector against the cannibal monster and the man-eating Great Beaver, a name that was erased by colonialism. The supernatural being in this story far more resembles Gluscap or Odzihozo, culture heroes of the tribes of northern New England, than a coastal sha-man's deity.

A third tale collected by Field supports the idea that the name Hob-bomocko was a common substitute when white storytellers took over narration. This story was simply entitled "Indian Legend." It references Rattlesnake Den in Northfield, an outcropping near an area known as Cold Spring, which was in the domain of a group of Abenaki called the Squakheags:

> *An evil spirit has his abode deep down in the ground in this place, and these fissures are his breathing holes. Long ago, he foamed and bellowed so, in his deep cavern, that he shook the whole mountain, and large rocks were thrown into the air. This monster has been quiet, so I am informed, since I first knew his dwelling-place.*

Field does not give a name to this evil spirit, but four years later Josiah Howard Temple and George Sheldon, in their history of Northfield, offered the following:

> *Brush Mountain, which in their language would be called Mish-om-assek—from its being the resort of a numerous colony of rattlesnakes—was held in superstitious veneration by the Squakheags. They believed that Hobamock, the evil Spirit, dwelt inside the mountain, and that the fissures in the rocks about Cold Spring, where the snakes denned, were the holes through which he sent forth his hot breath and melted the snow, and made any one faint who dared to inhale the poisonous air. They had a tradition that he once in anger bellowed forth from this hiding-place and shook the earth! Partly from dread of the evil Spirit, and partly from fear of the rattlesnakes, the Indians shunned the Gulf, and the adjacent mountain sides.*

On the one hand, this account is consistent with depictions of Hobbomocko and his association with snakes, and his later identification as an evil spirit. On the other hand, Temple and Sheldon directly cite an Abenaki term for Brush Mountain—*Mish-om-assek*—but fail to clarify whether "Hobamock" similarly comes from their language or if they, the two white authors, employed that name because they had no alternative. I think it is the latter, and I think Field equally plugged in that name following a tradition practiced by whites in the 1800s. Field's substitution created one of the few sympathetic renderings of Hobbomocko, which is laudable, but he may have done so because he did not have the name of the original being to share.

A host of parallel problems arise concerning many of the stories of Moshup the giant and his wife, Squant. Moshup is a culture hero and earth-shaper among many coastal tribes, especially the Wampanoag of Aquinnah and Mashpee. The paramount tales of Moshup, passed on in various forms for centuries, entail his activities establishing the landscape around Martha's Vineyard. Traditionally his home is on the southwestern side of the island, formerly known as Gay Head, with its striking cliffs and beaches.

There Moshup would cook whales. Traditional stories have been preserved explaining how the colors of the sand display the remains of those feasts and the blood, grease, and char of Moshup's favorite food. The barrenness of Aquinnah has likewise been attributed to his uprooting trees for the roasting pits.

A considerable group of stories turns on Moshup's attempt to erect a bridge of stones between the Vineyard and Elizabeth Islands (or between Nonamesset and the mainland). His efforts are thwarted during construction, usually when he plants his foot upon a crab that does not hesitate to pinch him. Writhing in pain Moshup drops the boulders, creating the dangerous submerged rocks and shoals that lurk between Aquinnah and

Cuttyhunk Island. In some tales he flings the insulting crab out to Nantucket, establishing their prodigious prevalence there. In others he tosses the offender far out into the ocean, where it transforms into Nomans Land.

Other Native stories assert that Moshup separated Nomans Land from Martha's Vineyard by digging a ditch in the sand with his toe, which later flooded with the rising tide. Still others reveal that Moshup created Nantucket by emptying the ashes of his pipe out into the sea. In these tales, the fog that surrounds the islands is taken as a sign of his enjoying another smoke.

Many Native stories, both historical and contemporary, depict Moshup as a benevolent figure who teaches agriculture and lodge building. In some he becomes a mooncusser and shares the spoils gained from English shipwrecks with the tribes on the islands. In another important set of tales, Moshup hunts a gigantic bird that, akin to the Great Beaver or Wittum, abducts his people—often children—and eats them.

As with Hobbomocko, Moshup is not a being of simple caricature. Many Native stories address his anger, including eruptive occasions that involve his own children and his wife. In a cycle with numerous variants, for example, he abandons his children on Nomans Land, but upon seeing their generosity toward each other as the deadly waters rise, transforms them into fishes or whales or porpoises.

His spouse, Squant, is another captivating figure, sometimes depicted as a powerful being responsible for the howling winds and other activities of the awakened sea, and sometimes as Granny Squannit, the leader of the Little People who both teaches traditional healing practices and corrects the misbehaving or the disrespectful—again, often children—through frightening supernatural means.

Demonization and cultural appropriation of Moshup and Squant occurred during European colonization of coastal Massachusetts. The Elizabeth Islands, the Vineyard, and Mashpee were among the earliest sites for conversion to Christianity. Moshup was often treated as a diabolical being during that process. The name "the Devil's Bridge" for the unfinished walkway to Cuttyhunk—admittedly a title that also invokes the obvious dangers to ships—reflects that cultural shift, as does "the Devil's Den," a craterlike depression atop the cliffs at Aquinnah. Squant similarly appeared as a Euro-American stylized witch in tales passed on by white raconteurs.

Some of the most culturally deleterious tales feature an English minister such as Richard Bourne besting a being identified as the Christian Devil but who is described in terms that match up with Moshup, right down to his dropping of stones throughout Cape Cod in defeat. And in still other stories, Moshup realizes that he no longer belongs in the human world. William Baylies, for example, in a 1793 description of Aquinnah proffers that "When the Christian religion took place in the island, Moshup told them, as light had come among them, and he belonged to the kingdom of darkness, he must take his leave; which, of their great sorrow, he accordingly did; and has never been heard of since."

Ignoring the obviously self-serving aspects of such narratives, there is something important to consider in tales of Moshup's retreat. I mentioned briefly in the chapter on the Bridgewater Triangle that several "paranormal experts" have recently begun to tell a tale of Pukwudgies who slay Moshup's children and drive him away with sharp darts or kill him. That story initially appeared in Elizabeth Reynard's 1934 collection *The Narrow Land* and was based on a narrative shared by Chief Red Shell, a Wampanoag activist. Apparently neither Reynard's audiences nor recent white storytellers seem to grasp that it is a story in which the attacking monstrous beings are loosely-veiled substitutes for European colonialists.

In a related way, the tale of the Great Beaver may have had different purposes depending on the reasons and contexts for its narration. If it were passed on by Pocumtuck to white audiences, it may have been intended as a story concerning English encroachment—and a warning of sorts that the monster would not succeed in its insatiable hunger to seize their land and take their lives. Comparable tales told about Moshup and his pursuit and victory over the cannibal bird that takes hostages and kills children imply resistance to European domination, a point made all the more poignant in light of a trope in Native stories that imagines the white sails of colonial ships as the wings of gigantic birds.

Legend Tripping

Mount Sugarloaf State Reservation is overseen by the Department of Conservation and Recreation (https://www.mass.gov/locations/mount-sugarloaf-state-reservation), which offers pamphlets and maps. Free parking is available in the lot on Sugarloaf Street. Follow the Pocumtuck Ridge Trail up to the summit of South Sugarloaf and its observation deck. At this point there are countless options, including a simple return to the parking lot. But hikers should at a minimum follow the Pocumtuck Ridge Trail north for just a bit until it intersects with the Old Mountain Trail and then return to the parking lot. Another option is to press forward on the Pocumtuck Ridge Trail to the summit of North Sugarloaf and then retrace back to the parking lot, a hike of about 4.5 miles. This hike can be extended by exploring the additional meandering trails. **Trailhead GPS: N42 28.04 / W72 35.42**

True splendor awaits the hiker who tackles all 15 miles of the Pocumtuck Ridge Trail, which spans the entire length from Sugarloaf into Greenfield, but this is best accomplished with a local guide, as the paths often break up.

Much of Mt. Toby State Forest is managed by the Department of Natural Resources Conservation at UMass Amherst (https://eco.umass.edu/facilities/our-forest-properties/mt-toby/), which offers a map. Although the entire area deserves attention, including a waterfall and caves and other summits, a fine loop can be made starting with free parking on Reservation Road just off Route 63. This route follows Cranberry Pond Trail to Tower Road (a carriage road once used for the hotel at the summit long ago destroyed) to its merger with the Robert Frost Trail that leads to the summit of Mt. Toby. The RFT descends from the summit down to Reservation Road and parking. **Trailhead GPS: N42 30.12 / W72 31.31**

Brush Mountain has gone through several transitions over the past two decades. It used to link up with the adjacent Crag Mountain as part of the Metacomet-Monadnock Trail, but private property has closed that trail. Please respect the homeowners. Currently the Brush Mountain Conservation Area is under the jurisdiction of the town of Northfield's Open Space Committee (https://www.northfieldma.gov/open-space-committee), which has a map. Free parking is on Gulf Road for the 1.5-mile out-and-back hike up to the summit. **Trailhead GPS: N42 39.28 / W72 25.19**

Having traveled to Martha's Vineyard, there are short hikes available at the western point. The Martha's Vineyard Land Bank Commission (http://www.mvlandbank.com/index.shtml) maintains the Aquinnah Headlands Preserve, including a map. The North Head overlooks the cliffs; the South Head winds down below the cliffs to Moshup Beach (Aquinnah Public Beach). The Aquinnah Wampanoag own and protect the cliffs. Planning is obviously required to reach this site with respect to travel, fees, and transportation. **Trailhead GPS: N41 20.49 / W70 50.10**

Another remarkable view on the Vineyard of lands associated with Moshup is found at Menemsha Hills, overseen by the Trustees of Reservations (https://thetrustees.org/place/menemsha-hills/), which offers a map to the 3 miles of trails on the property. **Trailhead GPS: N41 21.53 / W70 44.33**

21

The Ghost of Mount Greylock

TO TELL OR not to tell? The folklorist's dilemma.

Some chapters of this book do not begin with a legend narrated in my own words in order that I not perpetuate a deeply problematic story. The tale that anchors this chapter—that of the Old Coot, the Ghost of Mount Greylock—is not in that category in any way. This one is a sheer delight, brimming with possibility and amusement.

But it is a sheer delight *in the making*. As I write these lines, the legend of the Old Coot is emerging from hibernation. It has found a few storytellers to help shape its future—Michael Whalen, a park interpreter at Mount Greylock State Reservation, for example. And it is, hopefully, being told around countless campfires and hiking trails and maybe a beer or two. So out of respect for those voices and for a story still being birthed, I am not going to interfere with a version of my own. I will, of course, share several stories that others have told.

But be forewarned, dear reader: Narrative dangers—or in our parlance, spoilers—lie ahead! In the pages that follow I explain how this emerging legend has come to be in a manner that some might argue robs it of its ethereal magnetism.

I am of the opinion that if a story has legs—if it is well crafted and speaks to a moment in time—then its plot can be known beforehand without compromising the audience's enjoyment. (Case in point: Ahab goes down with the whale.) In a similar way, I do not believe that legends are bereft of their value if the history of their composition comes to light. And if they are so easily ruined, they probably were never meaningful in the first place. So read on if you dare.

In 1939, commercial skiing was nascent on Mount Greylock. Formal ski clubs and lodges were only a few years old. Trails were still being cut, many by the Civilian Conservation Corps, to employ young men during the Great Depression. The CCC cut the Thunderbolt Trail in 1934 and had a hand in the creation of the later Bellows Pipe Trail. Travel writers did their part as well. The specialized WPA guidebook, *The Berkshire Hills*, was published that same year and praised the mountain as some of the best skiing in the county. A great deal rode on the hopes that tourists would come, spend money, and stimulate the economy. In an attempt to attract visitors, organizations held competitive races.

Into that wintry mix entered a fascinating phantom: a specter haunting the mountain slopes.

"Ghost on the Thunderbolt." So read the title of the first record of the specter in the pages of the *North Adams Transcript* on January 19, 1939. A mere two weeks before the Massachusetts Downhill championship, rumors of the toothless and bearded ghost of the "Old Coot" caught the eyes of attentive readers.

The Old Coot's real name was William Saunders. He came to the Berkshires, the report informed readers, "while he was still in the prime of his life, taking with him a twenty-year-old wife and two young children, and bought a large tract of land on the northern outskirts in what is now the city of North Adams." He soon earned the Yankee pride of owning one of the finest farms in the area.

Then a fateful call: The US Civil War had begun. William Saunders was no militant, but as an unknown quoted source remarked, "he'd be durned if he wanted any of them there whip-lashing slave owners taking over his land." And so in 1861, Saunders kissed his wife, Belle, farewell and headed to the Deep South to defend his home in the Berkshires.

"Nothing is known, unfortunately," continues the story in the *Transcript*, "of those years of Saunders' life other than he undoubtedly saw action on at least one battlefield, for he was seriously wounded and hospitalized."

Saunders never communicated with Belle while he was away. She waited dutifully for a year, but convinced that he had been killed, she searched for another husband and father to her children. She found that man in Milton Cliffords, a laborer Saunders hired to assist in his absence from his farm.

It is not clear when Saunders returned—whether during the war or thereafter—but when he returned, he was unrecognizable. The impressive figure of a youth returned emaciated and worn by the ravages of combat and pain.

Saunders's hopes lifted with each step he took closer to his farm and his beloved family. No one quite knows the reaction he had upon seeing that another man was husband to his wife and owner of his farm; he kept those inner thoughts locked stoically within. Instead of returning home, Saunders took the pittance of a soldier's pension and purchased a place to build a cabin. That cabin just happened to be on the very spot of the final dip of the Thunderbolt Trail.

Saunders lived there as a hermit, except in spring and autumn, when he secured enough work to purchase supplies for another lonely year. Some say—as unbelievable as it may seem—that he even found occasional labor on Milton Clifford's farm and ate at the same table as his wife and children without revealing who he was.

One day—the exact date is lost to time—a group of hunters stumbled upon his shack in the bitter cold of early February. They found Saunders dead inside, his discharge papers kept safe so the truth of who the Old Coot was could finally be known.

Whatever fate Saunders earned in the world beyond this one, he would never come to know. His ghost remained, appearing every late

January for two weeks, an eternal remembrance of the final days when bitter cold took his life. "So if Old Coot's ghost runs true to form," the article concludes, "he'll be on the Thunderbolt within the next few weeks for the intrepid 'Bolt skiers to see. It is hoped that they'll not scare him away!"

If you are a skeptic, you might be thinking this tale seems a bit suspicious. If you are a perceptive skeptic, you might even be thinking it sounds remarkably akin to the public relations operation that invented the "legend" of Bash Bish Falls to encourage tourists to see the ghost of White Swan. Had you read the original story in 1939, you might have noticed it appeared in the *Transcript* next to a column about the discovery of the sea serpent's skeleton in Provincetown.

Your skepticism would, however, be challenged by an article published one week later in the *Transcript*, "Ghost of Thunderbolt Photographed." There, for all the world to see—on page six, dedicated to the Massachusetts Downhill Championship—was incontrovertible evidence of existence beyond the grave: a photograph of Old Coot Saunders, his back turned to the camera as he shuffled away, having shuffled off his mortal coil countless decades ago.

The accompanying article explained how the photograph was achieved. The *Transcript*'s photographer led an expedition of "ghost raisers" to investigate the matter—a pressing one, indeed, with the championship hoping to attract throngs of interested spectators. They spent three days combing every inch of the woods and the CCC trails. And then, in the early morning just before dawn on the fourth day of their exhausting labor, all of the ghost raisers went off "to do whatever ghost raisers do when they want to raise a ghost." I'm not precisely certain what that entailed in 1939, but perhaps like ghost-hunting celebrities today they called an agent, claimed expertise they did not have, and set off to publish in vanity presses.

Only the photographer remained, wrapped in his sleeping bag.

An old man appeared to him suddenly. "He was dressed in a worn and ragged Civil War uniform," the article explains, "which seemed to afford little protection to his skinny shanks."

The old man uttered two words to the incredulous photographer: "Ski heil!"

The photographer scrambled for his camera to snap an image of the gaunt face that hovered above him, harmless but amazing in its spectral ways. But by the time the shutter was prepared, the Old Coot was off into the woods, racing at an unnatural speed, and disappeared into thin air. Fortunately, a single photograph of his fleeing form found its way into readers' engrossed hands.

Unfortunately, as Howard Lanfair reported in his "Down the Ski Trail" column in March, the races at Mount Greylock did not bring the tourist crowds that the organizers hoped for.

That photographer—P. Randolph "Randy" Trabold—would admit in 1972 that he was "embarrassed" at how many people believed that image—simple trick photography—was a genuine photo of a ghost.

To state what might not be obvious to contemporary readers, the Old Coot story echoed with other aspects of popular culture from 1939. I have already mentioned the WPA guidebook to the Berkshires. That year also saw the release of *Gone with the Wind*, albeit in December, but following the raging success of the 1936 novel. Saunders's tale was not based on that story but culled similar themes. And although it has dropped out of subsequent narrations following the horrors of the Second World War, "Ski Heil" was a jest parodying the signature greeting of the Nazi party in Germany at the time.

Trabold and the editors who created the tale of the Old Coot did so winking at shared public knowledge. More than eighty years later, contemporary audiences increasingly treat this story as a paranormal experience because they miss those inside jokes. There is, nevertheless, no disputing the origins of this "legend": It was concocted by the *Transcript* in order to attract tourists to a fledgling ski resort.

Saunders's story may have died out had a local woman not inquired about it in 1965. Trabold was still employed by the *Transcript* and saw firsthand how it could be revived. In 1971 he and reporter Charlie Hoye spun another yarn. This time Trabold claimed he had finally found the negative, mysteriously missing since 1939, which inspired him to inquire if the Old Coot still haunted the mountain.

This "discovery" occurred in March, so the original element of a restricted January haunting simply dropped out. Trabold and Hoye reported seeing something in the woods that disappeared before they could snap another picture. They theorized that the Old Coot was wise to their cameras and did not want a second photo taken. But as they trudged back to West Road, the wind whispered to them: "Bye, Randy, bye, Randy."

News of the Old Coot worked like a charm to stimulate conversation again, and within a few months the Boy Scouts were making organized sojourns on the mountain to search for the ghost.

For anyone who refuses to believe that this was an attempted viral marketing campaign before the internet—to borrow an image from the *Transcript*'s perceptive journalist Joe Durwin writing in 2009, I submit a collaborating editorial. Entitled "Old Coot, Ghost of Greylock," it was written by Maynard Leahey on August 4, 1978. In its opening lines Leahey laments that "the trouble with promoting the Old Coot as a tourist attraction in these parts is that the not exactly famous ghost of the Bellows Pipe trail hasn't been seen in 40 years."

In Leahey's estimation, too many people had visited the mountain—hikers, skiers, and automobile drivers—for too long without any sightings. But Leahey also considered that with just the right promotion people could be inspired to want to believe, much in the same manner that a few sightings of the Loch Ness Monster could fuel rabid interest. He proposed, not without tongue in cheek, that if locals wanted to ignite tourist interest, they should establish the Order of the Old Coots, an elite group who had encountered Saunders and were willing to tell stories about their experience.

Two such attempts were made in 1979 and 1988. In the first, a writer and a photographer for the *Transcript*, Rodney Doherty and Richard Lodge, captured the second image of the Old Coot, who had "telepathically" called the spirit-sensitive Lodge. (They were just as surprised as anyone that the ghost summoned them on Halloween.) Doherty and Lodge retooled the story for a new generation. The ghost was now Bill Saunders, and he simply became a heartbroken hermit upon returning home to find his love with another man. His frozen body was found by hunters "almost 100 years ago"—that's 1879—and when they discovered it, a spectral shadow darted into the woods. They assured readers that his ghost had been seen regularly for a century. And in a nice callback, when they spotted the Old Coot, the wind whispered "Randy" in their ears.

In 1988 the *Transcript* informed readers that "ace reporter" Jane Kaufman had rushed to the scene when hikers during that year's organized Ramble spotted the ghost, floating above the ground and fulfilling "a century-old legend." Kaufman caught a glimpse of the specter but was unable to snap a photo. Promisingly, another spirit-sensitive reporter, Anne Levesque, was sent out to investigate. Readers were encouraged to return in two weeks, when Levesque would reveal her discoveries. And just by coincidence, her article would be filed on Halloween.

Levesque's report from October 31, 1988, forever changed human understanding. It proved paranormal investigators correct and put scientific skeptics to shame. Levesque did not only spy the Old Coot; she interviewed him.

"You know I don't like my picture taken," Saunders explained in a deep voice that sounded like it was played at half speed. "Why do you keep bothering me? I'm not running for office."

"But Mr. Coot," Levesque pleaded, "my managing editor will kill me if I don't get your picture!"

"And what's wrong with being dead?" he inquired in reply.

Levesque was a polished journalist and she knew that ghosts, just like ghost hunters, were motivated by one thing: flattery. So she explained to Saunders that he had become famous. And as he learned of his celebrity, his spectral body began to glow with pride. He consented to one final photograph, to be published in the *Transcript* that Halloween day. But Saunders made clear he would allow no other images and did so in a determined tone, echoing George H. W. Bush at the recent Republican National Convention.

"Read my lips," Saunders demurred. "No more pictures!"

And with that the Old Coot was gone.

Leahey's editorial and the 1988 story have faded from public consciousness, but the 1979 account has thrived. For obvious reasons, the two accounts which reveal the Old Coot to be a hoax meant to drum up interest and perhaps dupe the gullible, had to be minimized for the tale to appear legitimate and for it to be available for further entertainments.

That decision succeeded. By the mid-1990s—the period of the *X-Files* in their prime—the story combined elements from both the 1939 and the 1979 accounts. A decade later tales of the Old Coot were a regular feature for storytellers leading hikes on the mountain. And by 2013, paranormal investigators were hawking their wares, treating the Old Coot as if he was a real ghost—or whatever sold their books and secured them gigs. Even a well-meaning scholar mistook the Old Coot's story as a long-standing legend rather than a public relations campaign that required a few decades to take off.

Signs are positive, however, that the Old Coot is starting to become folklore in the sense of a shared narrative, circulating in the oral tradition, and evolving as it passes from storyteller to storyteller. In Michael Whalen's 2015 version—told on the mountain at a campfire—Bill Saunder's wife is named Emma rather than Belle. He finds numerous odd jobs when he returns from the war. He dies when a relentless storm blows down the door of his cabin and freezes him. The hunters who find him are attracted to his cabin by a mysterious candle that does not obey the laws of science. They later bring a constable to the hut, only to discover that Saunder's body is missing. As the hunters flee in fright, the constable looks around to see a vaporous shape assume the form of a raven and fly away.

With a little luck, the Old Coot will escape the extinction of other folktales once attached to Greylock. Most of them concerned Tories or counterfeiters or others hiding wealth—including Captain Kidd. And perhaps those tales might return from the dead someday. In 1896, Charles Skinner summarized them thusly:

> In Massachusetts, the Heart of Greylock is the name given to the crater-like recess, a thousand feet deep, in the tallest of the Berkshire peaks, but it was formerly best known as Money Hole, and the stream that courses through it as Money Brook, for a gang of counterfeiters worked in that recess, and there some spurious coinage may still be concealed. The stream is also known as Spectre Brook, for late wandering hunters and scouting soldiers, seeing the forgers moving to and fro about their furnaces, took them for ghosts.

Only time will tell.

There is one final element of the legend of the Old Coot worth celebrating. In 1971, following his update, Trabold was summoned to one of the toughest crowds anyone could face: the third graders of Mrs. Kalkowski's class at Mark Hopkins School in North Adams. The children asked penetrating questions and wrote brief essays to express their opinions about the ghost's existence. Consensus held that the tale was enjoyable but that it did not prove the reality of the supernatural. "They simply don't believe," Trabold concludes with gleeful admiration, "that photos always tell the truth."

People who appreciate a good story *and* critical thinking? Maybe we have a ghost of a chance after all.

Legend Tripping

Mount Greylock State Reservation is overseen by the Department of Conservation and Recreation (https://www.mass.gov/locations/mount -greylock-state-reservation), which provides a map and numerous suggestions for hiking. To access the area associated with the Old Coot by the Bellows Pipe and Thunderbolt Trails, there are two solid options. The first is to park for free on Gould Road in Adams and ascend the Bellows Pipe Trail. Hikers can simply lollipop from Bellows Pipe Trail to Thunderbolt Trail and return, about 2.5 miles; that is the area where much of the early activity was reported. It would be a shame to miss a greater journey, however; so hikers can continue up Bellows Pipe Trail and at the lean-to take the side trail east to the summit of Ragged Mountain and then return or head west at the lean-to and connect with the Appalachian Trail to visit Greylock's summit. **Trailhead GPS: N42 37.38 / W73 08.42**

Another option is to park at the free lot on Notch Road in North Adams close to Reservoir Road. The northern section of Bellows Pipe Trail begins there. It's about 3 miles to the lean-to, where hikers can continue south to the Thunderbolt Trail, then circle back via the southern portion of Bellows Pipe Trail closer to Gould Road. Upon returning to the lean-to, it makes sense to head west to the AT, see the summit, and then follow the AT north to Bernard Farm Trail, which returns to the parking lot on Notch Road. This is a demanding hike of at least 10 miles. **Trailhead GPS: N42 40.28 / W73 08.29**

For additional hiking, notice the Money Brook Trail on the west side of the Hopper. This used to be the site of the folklore of counterfeiters and their kin in the earlier twentieth century.

22

Popcorn Snow of Petersham

A SA SNOW OF Petersham was an eccentric man. His penchant for popcorn was harmless enough—except for the farmhands who had to adopt his strict diet of popcorn and milk in order to work on his prosperous farm. But he nursed an obsession, forever wondering how he would leave this world and what would happen to his body when he did.

He lost his first wife not long after they had moved to Petersham. Their daughter, Minerva, followed her mother to the grave, one year later on November 15, 1845. He buried them in a small plot across a brook not far from their prosperous farm. There his wife and daughter remained for two decades as the eccentric Popcorn Snow became a very wealthy man.

In time another woman became his second wife. She was a patient woman. She had to be, living with Popcorn Snow. And he tested that patience on the day that he announced he would dig a tomb in a nearby hill to wait patiently for his bones. Soon the hole was cut and the stones were laid. And then the eccentric Popcorn Snow moved his first wife and child from the cemetery across the brook. He placed them in the tomb with the strength of his own hands. That was in the year 1868.

That same year Popcorn Snow traveled to the undertaker and the coffin maker to discuss the day he would join their company. And while being measured for a casket, a metal coffin caught his eye. He ordered one to size and with a very specific design: a glass square where his face would rest as if his corpse could look out on the world.

When the casket was ready, Popcorn Snow welcomed it into his home like a guest. There it waited four long years until the cold winter of 1872, when the metal coffin went to work with the same mettle as his loyal farmhands.

The eccentric man had struck a deal with a friendly neighbor from Petersham, a man whose name has been lost to the passing of endless time. This man vowed to check Snow's body each day for a week to make sure his life was extinct. Dutifully the neighbor entered the tomb and stared upon the casket. There was no breath on the glass, no sign of life on the first day or the second or the third.

On the fourth a wintry storm covered Popcorn Snow's tomb with white snow. And his living wife released the neighbor from his week of obligation. "If he wasn't dead when they placed him in the coffin," she shrewdly surmised, "he's frozen to death by now."

Popcorn Snow's widow never joined her husband inside that quiet tomb; they buried her underneath a simple, humble gravestone. And so the eccentric man was to spend eternity in his metal casket with the bones of his first wife and child gently atop his own.

But death, like life, can be a strange thing. And sometimes spirits are not ready to rest patiently for all eternity.

At least that's what the neighbors said when an eccentric specter left his tomb each midnight on the fifteenth of November. Residents were sure to stay away from the road near his house that night.

Word spread, as it will do, of a haunted tomb of a wealthy man in an unwatched hill in Petersham. The rumor reached two daring men belonging to the city of Boston, both fond of gambling at unique games of chance. One bet the other that he couldn't spend a midnight in the dark tomb of Popcorn Snow. Ten dollars was the wager, no meager prize in that day. The second man accepted, rode to Petersham, and entered the eccentric's tomb.

The cool silence echoed there among the metal casket and the wooden box of a woman's bones. The man was grateful he had no light. He had no desire to see Popcorn Snow staring from behind the glass. He had heard the rumors and feared they were true that no decay had befallen the corpse—that Snow's hair was as rich as the day he died and his clothes none worse for their age. Had the gambling man been a morbid type and rummaged through the box of bones, he would have found one missing skull and one skull missing all its teeth, the feat of foul thieves who came showing no respect for the dead.

No, he was just a betting man, so all he brought into the tomb was a bottle of whiskey from Connecticut rye to place upon the casket, a sign that his courage had carried him inside. The midnight hour came and he breathed a sigh of relief. But then, quite suddenly, he heard the shaken stamping and snorting of his steed. His horse had inexplicably lost its patience waiting for a gambling man from Boston who took too many chances. It ran away down the road charging at full speed. Who untied the poor creature, no one would ever know.

When the gambling man caught up with his horse, they were a mile from the eccentric's tomb. He was as shaken as the stallion for a reason he could not explain. He did not return until the morning light in the company of his wagering companion.

There, inside the dark tomb, was the bottle of whiskey from Connecticut rye. But the bottle was broken, smashed to bits, thrown by an unseen and impatient hand. And when his friend offered ten times the amount to try another midnight with the eccentric Popcorn Snow, the gambling man refused to comply. Winning a wager was not worth the cost of never sleeping well again.

The tale of Popcorn Snow's ghost is lesser known in Massachusetts folklore, but it has all the elements to thrive in the future. I was reticent to tell it in my own words for concern of interfering with local storytellers who may well be sharing it in the oral tradition, but the account above is very close to an original source, so I hope this will have the effect of expanding this lore in waiting.

Popcorn Snow's story has not been entirely neglected by contemporary writers. Local historian J. R. Greene has done a yeoman's job preserving the tale. Asa Snow was also a source of inspiration for a character in Maryanne O'Hara's widely praised 2012 novel *Cascade*. And his tale occasionally appears in travel writing.

Asa Snow is no longer buried in the vault that he cut into the hillside near his farm in Petersham. Today he lies in repose with his two wives and children in Quabbin Park Cemetery in Ware. This cemetery was established as the resting place for exhumed remains of more than 7,600 residents in the towns that were disincorporated to create the Quabbin Reservoir in the 1930s. Although Petersham still exists, Snow's house and burial site were over the border in Dana, one of the flooded towns.

The actual man, Asa Snow, was born on Cape Cod in 1797. He eventually moved to the Dana-Petersham area and became financially successful. He was also a man who suffered grief. In 1844, newspapers carried word of his first wife's suicide by hanging. Another from 1857 details an itinerant peddler staying the night at his home. The guest was missing in the morning, having robbed Snow's treasure of clothes.

Newspapers throughout the region noted his death in November 1872. Those same papers followed his will at probate—a considerable sum of $6,000—and final administration made for his widow, Eunice, by 1876. When he died, initial reports tersely declared that he was an old man found dead on his doorstep. Later ones added that he was "a very eccentric man" who had kept a coffin ready in his house for a few years. Still another merely identified him as an active member of the Baptist church, the third of that congregation to die in as many months.

Little was seen of Snow in print thereafter until 1912, when periodicals reported that the selectmen of Petersham had granted Charles Eddy permission to close Snow's tomb "so people morbidly curious will no longer be able to see the bones of a man who has been dead over 40 years." The *Springfield Republican* was one of the newspapers that carried this unremarkable notice.

Two weeks later, a rival paper, the *Springfield Union*, published a lengthy story—"Lonesome Road Offers Weirdly Unusual Sight"— stretched across two pages that detailed all of the lore recounted above. That essay introduced his nickname, Popcorn Snow, and his purported diet and commitment to vegetarianism. It also indicated that his death came from a heart attack induced by carrying a dressed pig across his farm. Incorrectly identifying his worth at only $3,000 upon his death, the *Union* article fostered the impression he had buried an excess of wealth in the woods near his home—a budding treasure tale, no doubt.

In specifying the fate of his wife's and child's skulls, the essay admonished an unnamed Springfield man for wearing a charm consisting of a tooth taken from Snow's tomb. It also mentioned his ghostly annual walk to his first wife's grave. The explanation for it is obscure, but I think it was meant to imply that the specter visited the site of his *daughter's* grave—November 15 being the anniversary of her death—in a profound and eternal act of carrying the grief he had carried each year to her grave while alive.

Two photographs, one of the exterior and one of the interior of the vault, accompany the *Union* article, as does an equally vague tale of two recent photographers who snuck into the tomb, bordered up the door, and lit flashlights in order to snap an image. One of the flashlights blazed up and caused the tomb to fill with smoke. The men panicked to find the exit—and a breath of air—in the darkness, a darting crawl that resulted with them touching human bones in the scramble. This incident seemed like it would be connected to a ghost tale, but it went nowhere into that legend.

The *Union's* account is the primary source for subsequent tales of Snow, so it raises the question of whether this was simply yellow journalism, a purely editorial invention of a tale with no basis in the oral tradition of the local community. The *Union* invokes "some of the old residents of

Petersham, who remember Mr. Snow"—recall that in 1912 he had been dead forty years—but it does not name them. It is difficult to determine, then, if this is a record of folklore that followed his death.

There is another complicating factor in this genealogy. In 1948 Mabel Cook Coolidge published a history of Petersham. She mentions Asa Snow several times in passing, but they are all within dull contexts. No words recount his purported eccentricities, but Coolidge shares ample chatty stories about numerous other figures in the community, including two named eccentrics, Hermit Allen and Quaker Brewer. She also records with swift precision the traditions for naming places such as Devil's Den, Rum Rock, Tom's Swamp, and Pirateville. The absence of tales about Popcorn Snow in her book raises the question of whether they were shared among its residents.

It is safe to assume that Snow kept a coffin for years. It also appears that his tomb became accessible and occasionally visited by the curious. Incidentally, metal coffins were available in the 1860s, and were markers of wealth. It is possible that the original folklore gathering around Snow was going to develop into a common one throughout New England at the time, that of a wealthy eccentric who lived like a hermit and who hid his treasure rather than spend it.

Tales of Snow eventually began to develop again in the twentieth century. In 1992, for example, the *Boston Globe* reported on stories shared by members of the Swift Valley Historical Society. In these accounts an additional anecdote purported that he was buried on a bed of popcorn inside his metal casket. This version also postulates that his ghost walked the woods in protest of vandals who desecrated his tomb and disfigured his corpse.

Today tales tend to emphasize his fear of being buried alive, but an earlier account helps to define the motives more clearly. This story, entitled "Strange Tale of Asa Snow, Embalming Wizard," appeared in the *Boston Herald* on August 10, 1924. It is a complete reinvention of Asa Snow's legacy. He is not the wistfully eccentric Popcorn Snow—that nickname never occurs—but rather the Hermit of Nichewaug (a village of Petersham), a recluse with mysterious plans to cheat the decay that follows death. In this tale Snow fashions a coffin entirely on his own, enlisting the aid of an undertaker, an unknown man, and the town tinsmith Collins Andrews.

Snow designs a casket with a glass cover. Three years after his death the iron lock of his tomb rusts and townspeople sneak in to see if his plan succeeded. To their horror, his body defied nature. It was perfectly preserved and untouched by time—akin to that of Lenin, as the article announced. When word spread of his miraculous defiance, it attracted the worst instincts of the human species. People would break into the tomb to play cards upon his casket and to hold wild orgies—their words, not mine—in the gloomy vault, employing his coffin as a table, with Snow's "inscrutable countenance beneath."

No one could unlock the secrets of his eternal preservation. Scores of people tried, so the story claims, including "men of letters and scientific persons," but Snow eluded them all. That is, until he faced a power greater than time, decay, and the conquering worm: the recklessness of youth.

One day Snow's mystery was solved by a young boy being as thoughtless as young boys can be. The irreverent youngster used the glass coffin as a target for his air rifle and shattered it with a dead shot. Once exposed to air the corpse immediately crumbled into dust before the youth's eyes, revealing the secret at last. Asa Snow had been preserved not by embalming or by magic but by collaborating with intelligent men. They hermetically sealed his coffin, taking a week's time to pump out the air and create a vacuum. Upon this discovery, the selectmen ordered that the tomb forever be closed.

There is very little chance that this tale was circulating in the local community in the 1920s. It has all the hallmarks of yellow journalism and of editorial distance from the family involved. It also shows the slightest hint of influence from a tale in Charles Skinner's *American Myths and Legends*,

"The Walking Corpse of Malden." For the record, Asa and Eunice Snow produced two children, one of whom lived in Amherst and the other in East Brookfield. They had numerous grandchildren who thrived throughout the entire region.

It would not have been unusual, however, for Asa Snow to become a hermit had raconteurs continued to develop him as a folk character. Tales of eccentric hermits were widespread in New England in the late 1800s and early 1900s. In the 1920s, for example, storytellers in that region of Massachusetts were still swapping yarns about John Smith, the Hermit of Erving Castle.

John Smith was a lonely hermit who became a beloved celebrity. His castle, a cave—or in actuality, a series of ledges—became a surprising tourist sensation in the late 1800s. With apologies for the shameless self-promotion, I tell his story in detail in *Wicked Weird & Wily Yankees*, but the gist is that Smith claimed to be from Scotland, where the loss of his first love drove him near to madness. He adopted the hermit's life and eventually fled to the United States in 1866. He made his way into the wilderness of Erving, where he discovered the cave and erected a rudimentary home for himself, his many cats, and his books of poetry.

Smith was discovered in 1867 but not evicted. To the contrary, he was readily embraced, initially by the Erving community and then by countless tourists—some reports recorded up to fifteen thousand visitors a year—as well as historical societies and other local institutions that invited him to narrate the tale of his sufferings and hermitage. In 1868 a pamphlet was produced to encourage tourists to visit him and his cave; in 1871 Smith published his own account, *The Hermit of Erving Castle*. In 1900 he was buried in the Erving Center Cemetery. The tombstone of his favorite cat, Toby, was moved next to his remains.

Smith's exploits echoed for decades throughout the region. Snow's movement into legend, on the other hand, was abruptly halted when the construction of the Quabbin Reservoir resulted in the destruction of his tomb. Now we may never know if he was destined to become Popcorn

Snow the eccentric or Asa Snow the Hermit of Nichewaug or some combination thereof.

Then again, death, like life, can be a strange thing. Perhaps his stories are not yet done. And the cellar hole of his house still remains, patiently waiting for storytellers to shape a legend or two.

Legend Tripping

The Quabbin Reservoir is administered by the Department of Conservation and Recreation's Office of Watershed Management (https://www .mass.gov/locations/quabbin-reservoir), which publishes pamphlets, maps, and additional information for the miles of trails. The area associated with Popcorn Snow really needs no map. Free parking is available at Gate 40 on Route 32A in Petersham (technically the village of Nichewaug). Snow's house and tomb were at the intersection of 32A with the trail, the former Dana-Petersham Road. Hike down, minimally, to the Dana Common about 1.5 miles near Pottapaug Pond. Return to the parking lot or continue to the Quabbin itself and explore the beauty. **Trailhead GPS: N42 26.27 / W72 12.32**

Hermit's Castle is in Erving. An enjoyable hike starts with free parking off Mountain Road, by the access road just south of Fourmile Brook. The New England Trail (the new name of the Metacomet-Monadnock Trail) winds south to Hermit Mountain. The NET will intersect there with the blue-blazed Hermit's Castle Trail. Follow that trail, enjoy the home of John Smith, and then intersect with the NET again, looping back and returning to parking or explore more of the area. As described, this hike stretches for about 5 miles. **Trailhead GPS: N42 37.37 / W72 25.04**

Unfortunately, there are no readily accessible maps online, but the website for the NET does post information including printable sections for its entire map. Its entry for the Hermit's Castle (also known as Erving Castle by locals) is on a page called Erving Ledges–Hermit Mountain at https://newenglandtrail.org/hike/erving-ledges-hermit-mountain/.

Be aware that the NET hike moves northward, so it recommends a lollipop that begins closer to Millers River and the Northfield Mountain Reservoir and not the parking space on Mountain Road.

23

The Haunts of Boston Harbor: Part One

N O OTHER AMERICAN bay," boasted Moses Sweetser about Boston Harbor in 1895, "has such a wealth of history, tradition, and poetry. None on the North Atlantic coast surpasses it in natural beauty." It is a touching sentiment from an author who had embraced all the virtues of his beloved Boston. And in true Bostonian fashion, Sweetser concluded his paean to the Hub by taking a swipe at New York City. "Here is the yachting headquarters of the Western World, for though New York has richer yachtsmen and more costly boats," he observed, Boston Harbor "has a vastly greater number, and very many more men who find delight in blue-water sailing."

This chapter and the following one deviate slightly insofar as they recommend islands, which require additional preparation to visit in season and which do not offer lengthy hikes. (The Legend Tripping section for both is found in the sibling chapter.) It is also true that several islands with the richest folklore are not accessible as of this writing. It would be criminal negligence, however, to ignore these important stories. And if one of the joys of hiking is to escape the throngs of civilization for a restorative breath, the efforts to visit the islands of Boston Harbor handsomely reward the hiker.

In 1819 Frederick William Augustus Steuben Brown published *A Valedictory Poem*. It was addressed, as the title continues, to the *Inhabitants of*

Rainsford's, George's, Gallop's, Light House, and Deer Islands, in Boston Harbor. In his "Tribute of Respect" to Deer Island, Brown drops a provocative clue of a folkloric tradition concerning a headless ghost:

> Here superstition often tells,
> Of ghost, that's heard to screech,
> And utter dismal piercing yells,
> At midnight on the beach.
>
> For oft I've heard the story told,
> How ghost, without a head;
> Here guards some thousand pounds in gold,
> By some strange fancy led.

It is a shame that additional records of this legend did not survive or otherwise remain hidden. One wonders if this headless phantom belonged to the Kidd cycle and whether the screeching ghost connected to the Hannah Screecher variant, or if it was an independent tale unique to the area. Sweetser leaves a similar tantalizing entry invoking a teakettle filled with silver coins, buried in Winthrop by a slave who died before revealing its location.

Compensation for these all-too-brief comments is found in James Lloyd Homer's 1848 *Nahant and Other Places on the North Shore.* As one of the longest and most detailed narratives of a treasure tale hunt, it is an incredible find. I reproduce it here in its entirety except for some modernization of spacing and punctuation:

> *There is an amusing story, all about money digging, which is related with considerable gravity by some of the good people who reside at Deer Island and at Point Shirley. Shall I tell it to you as it was told to me? Very well, here goes!*

There is a place on Deer Island, at the extreme South East point of it, called Money Head Bluff. In 1824 a party of individuals from Boston, headed by Capt. Crooker, proceeded to this spot to dig for money, a large quantity of which was supposed to have been buried there during the revolutionary war. Capt. Kidd had nothing to do with that lot. Crooker's party consisted of Capt. William Tewksbury and Mr. Brown, of the island, and Messrs. Tuttle, Green, Boynton, and Henry, of Boston, besides two boys who belonged on the island. It will thus be seen that this party was composed of six men and two boys, all of whom were "armed and equipped according to law."

They were headed by Crooker, who carried in his hands two sounding-rods; and, at his request, the party—who were urgently admonished by him not to say a word—marched in single file from the house Capt. Tewskbury to the bluff: how they must have looked, ha!

Having proceeded about half the distance, it was discovered that the party had no Bible, to "keep the evil spirit off." Mr. Brown, who now keeps the telegraphic station on Central wharf, was sent back to obtain one, and the party awaited his return in solemn silence. Not being able to find a Bible, Mrs. Tewksbury thoughtlessly sent a spelling-book; and as soon as Mr. Brown (who had a waggish disposition at the time—as he probably has now) returned with his precious charge, the party moved on, to the old willow tree under which—as Solomon Swap would say—they were make their "eternal fortunes."

Capt. Crooker, before commencing operations, addressed the party, enjoining upon them the most profound silence. He stated that, if any one spoke while the digging was going on, the expedition would inevitably be disastrous, and the consequences fatal to some of them, as the evil spirit would rise up and blast them with his vaporous breath, if he did not unceremoniously carry them away.

He proceeded to draw a circle of about twenty feet, over which he passed his sounding-rods several times. Opening the spelling-book—which he thought was the sacred volume—with great solemnity, placing it on the ground, and taking off his hat, he said, in an emphatic tone of voice, "THIS IS THE PLACE."

He then commenced digging—the party all the time standing mute. "Either stand in the circle, or sit on the grass, gentlemen—just as you please; but by all means be silent," said the captain, as he stuck the first pick-axe into the ground.

Green and Tuttle commenced digging, as soon as the captain made a sign for them to do so. They dug three feet into the "bowels of the earth," when they struck a spring of water, which gushed out so fast that they became terrified. The captain promptly explained the cause of this, and they resumed their labors, the party all the rest of the time continuing within the circle, and as silent as death. Having dug to the depth of six feet, Crooker took one of the party aside, and had a serious conversation with him, which lasted several minutes.

He then exclaimed, with a gravity irresistibly ludicrous, that the spirit had been disturbed, and was near them, but he was visible to no one but himself, as he alone had disturbed him. "He has light complexion and sandy hair," said the captain. At this speech, the boys laughed heartily, when the captain flew into a tremendous passion, and, with uplifted hands, fell upon his knees, exclaiming—"The charm is broken! The spirit is still following me! Don't be surprised, my friends, if you see a phantom ship go up the channel within an hour!"

The laugh now became general, and the party retired—some of them heartily ashamed of the scrape into which they had been dragged by the captain, and others, who had no faith in the enterprise from its commencement, shaking their "unfed sides" at the folly of which they been eye witnesses.

Whether an account of an actual or imagined treasure hunt, this narrative overflows with riches. (The Mr. Brown, incidentally, is the afore-mentioned poet, and William Tewksbury was a heroic lifesaver on Deer Island.) It is clearly based on the Kidd legend, but the reference to monies from the American Revolution is a noteworthy update, as is the inclusion of a guardian ghost which only one victim could see—an inspired adaptation of the notion of "spectral evidence." What an amazing tale!

The destruction of the *Magnifique* on Lovells Island in 1782 summoned treasure seekers and their tales, and another tragedy in 1786 galvanized the imagination. Verifiable details are scant, but a few sources (including a journal kept by one John Ellis) contend that on December 9, several citizens from Wrentham, Franklin, and Sherborn perished on Lovells, having been shipwrecked during a snowstorm. Only one of the thirteen castaways survived, Theodore Kingsbury, but he perished in Boston and was buried in Franklin on December 25.

Frederick Brown memorialized the shipwreck in his valedictory poem—or at least drew inspiration from it—and introduced a "youthful pair," engaged to be married, who perish "locked within each other's arms." We should not assume that Brown's poetry is accurate history, of course, nor is it evident from the language if he is the inventor of this addition. He does not, for example, mention hearing the story from others as he does with the headless ghost.

Nevertheless, the tale entered the oral tradition. James Lloyd Homer, in a second volume from 1848, fleshed out some details. The vessel was a packet schooner bound from Maine to Boston. It struck Ram's Head, a drumlin on the island's northwest end, at midnight. Homer records fifteen passengers, all of whom sought shelter "from a piercing north wind behind a rock six or eight feet high." Thomas Spear of Georges Island came to the rescue the following morning, only to find all of them huddled together and frozen to death. "Two of the passengers," Homer recounts, "were clasped in each other's arms. They were about to be married, and were on their way to Boston to purchase furniture for house-keeping."

In the early 1900s, the boulder was well known as Lovers Rock and routinely visited by tourists invested in its mournful romance. Since the

1890s the bride-to-be has occasionally been identified as Sylvia Knapp, whose father, Samuel, moved to Maine from Mansfield, Massachusetts. But other genealogical studies purport that Knapp perished on October 20, 1798, alongside twenty-five others in a shipwreck off Boon Island.

Further complicating matters, Homer clearly states in 1848 that the shipwreck occurred "some twenty-five years ago," which would be 1823. Sweetser, writing in the 1880s, concurs that it happened "some sixty years ago." In other words, the pieces of this legend of Lovells Island do not quite fit. It is plausible that they are from different puzzles, mixed together from various shipwreck stories to make for a single, sorrowful romance.

Surviving anecdotes tease of a rich store of tales concerning the wealthy English gentlemen John Breed, who purchased the island that briefly held his name—now known as Spinnaker and connected to Hull—after his bride perished days before their wedding and he abandoned society a heartbroken hermit. Another unnamed hermit leaves even less intimation of rumors upon Slate Island. But no other tale of hermits in Boston Harbor could rival "Captain John Smith" of Grape Island.

Captain Smith's real name was Amos Pendleton, and according to Sweester he was "distinguished equally for his dangerous temper, his Munchausen stories of a past life of crime, and his complicated and ingenious system of profanity." Sweetser continues:

He claims to have been for many years an officer of a slave-ship, and afterwards of a smuggler on the Spanish Main; and, to the few visitors who could win his confidence, he told blood-curdling stories of battles with cruisers, and long flights over Southern seas, with English or Spanish men-of-war in hot pursuit, long-toms roaring, and slaves dying by scores in the hold. The scene would change from the coast of Africa to the bayous of Louisiana, or the lagoons of South America; but everywhere the story was of horror and bloodshed. Captain Smith has

a sinister reputation among the yachtsmen and fishermen of the harbor;
and many stories are told of his firing upon invaders of his ancient
solitary realm, and planting bird-shot in inconvenient localities.

By 1885, Smith had moved from Grape Island into a scow anchored in the Weir River. There he granted an interview to the *Boston Globe* and launched a career as a celebrity eccentric. In 1895 he was too feeble to continue his solitary existence on his floating home and was removed to the Hingham almshouse, where he died in 1897.

Pendleton re-created a fantastical life. He was born on July 4, 1804, in Lincolnville, Maine. At age six he was abducted by a peddler and stolen some forty miles away from his parents. He never saw either again. For one year he lived "like a dog," sorely abused by his captor. Eventually the boy summoned the will to escape, but nearly perished of hunger before being rescued by a farmer.

That farmer proved nearly as violent a taskmaster as the peddler, but Pendleton remained with him until age eleven, when he ran away to Bangor. There he learned his father had died in the War of 1812. With no family to return to, Pendleton turned to the sea. He became a sailor in the West Indies and scrimped enough money to purchase his own freighter to conduct trade on the Mexican coast.

Pendleton bragged that at one time he was worth $100,000, a massive sum in those days. But he lost it all to litigation, he said, and retreated to Boston to begin anew. There he learned the art of carpentry and set up shop on Merrimac Street. His first job was to construct a house, but fate had other plans. A fire devoured his shop, his tools, and all the supplies, leaving him "penniless and friendless" on the streets at age fifty-three.

Pendleton moved to Abington and labored as a carpenter until opportunity invited him to Hingham, where he packed mackerel on the fish wharves and worked the odd jobs he could find. But sunstroke felled him and, unable to continue a punishing pace, Pendleton agreed to watch sheep on Grape Island and live the hermit's life.

When ownership of Grape Island changed hands, Pendleton was forced into exile once again. He had prepared for that inevitability, constructing the scow while living alone, and sailed his mobile home safely into the Weir River. According to the *Globe* reporter, it was a veritable curiosity shop, ambitiously decorated with bowie knives, cutlasses, pistols, guns, and relics of the Mexican war.

Pendleton gave away few secrets of his early years—he knew how to leave an audience wanting more—but claimed in interviews with the *Globe* and the *Boston Herald* that he had sailed the globe. In twenty long voyages he shipwrecked thirteen times, seven of which left him with only the shirt on his back. But he had read the Bible straight through from Genesis to Revelation as often as he had survived.

In 1885 Pendleton claimed such health and strength as to lift a horse reclining on the ground. He was fond of tobacco—"I chew it, then smoke it, then use the ashes to clean my teeth"—but not of marriage, quipping that he never had much faith in mankind and even less in women.

Pendleton remained a fixture in local folklore for decades following his death. Edward Rowe Snow, for example, captured a few tales from those who followed in his wake, including his daring exploits as a slaver, smuggler, and pirate. Today Pendleton is all but forgotten, and given some of his predilections it is not difficult to see why, but few individuals can claim to have had such indisputable influence on the stories of Boston Harbor.

In the mid-1800s tales of Viking explorers—and rumors of a tomb with a skeleton and sword resting on Rainsford Island—titillated audiences, echoing a fad that erupted throughout Massachusetts when a "skeleton in armor" was unearthed in Fall River in 1832. Storytellers speculated that Thornvald Erikson, son of Erik and brother of Leif, had visited Cape Cod and Boston Harbor around the year 1000, where he was mortally wounded in an attack by Indigenous people. According to this tradition, his dying wish was to be buried with a cross at his head and at his feet. As with Kidd's treasure, the search for Thornvald's grave was a popular activity for several decades.

Similarly, a horrific story about a massacre of French traders on Peddocks Island by Indians and subsequent cosmic revenge in the form of a pox—a tale first told by Thomas Morton in the 1600s—continued to reinforce prejudices about Native hostilities toward Europeans.

No story of Boston Harbor, however, was more provocative in the nineteenth century than that of Nix's Mate Island. As the site for gibbeting pirates in centuries past, it was long known as a foreboding abode of the damned. The piratical body of William Fly flew there in 1726, but countless rumors also counted John Quelch and the treacherous survivors of the *Whydah* in that punished fraternity of malfeasance. Bird Island, now buried for the expansion of Logan Airport, was also regarded as a site for the gibbetted criminals of the sea. Ironically Hangman Island had no such purpose, and maps demonstrate that it was once named Hayman's.

Numerous legends and literary creations arose to explain the name of Nix's Mate. Among the earliest was that a certain Captain Nix was murdered while still at sea. His mate was charged and executed but protested to his final breath and prophesied the island where he hanged would prove his innocence by receding into the waves. (There are similar tales throughout the United States in which a natural sign, often a tree, testifies on behalf of the blameless.) Quarrying and erosion devastated the actual island, reducing it from a dozen acres to a mere bump in the water, so this apocryphal tale was often told in jest or lament of that irreparable decline.

A second story posited that Captain Nix was a pirate who buried treasure on the island—and his slain first mate atop it. Sweetser attributed this tale to the author James Jeffrey Roche, but it clearly borrows the basic components of a conventional Kidd treasure tale.

A third tale was unquestionably literary, but it made the rounds anonymously in newspapers of its time. In 1839 Boston author Rufus Dawes published *Nix's Mate: An Historical Romance of America*. His story involves the discovery of treasure in southern waters by William Phipps of Kennebec. Captain Nix makes a subsequent recovery, taking along as his mate Edward Fitzvassal. On the return to New England, Fitzvassal instigates a mutiny and thrusts Nix out to sea. The captain washes ashore and brings justice against his mate, who is executed on the island that takes his stained name to forever remember his crime.

Decades later a fourth explanation arrived as a letter purportedly penned in the early 1700s. It recalled the passing of the island by the *Jewel*, part of the Winthrop Fleet of 1630. Its pilot was a Dutchman, Dirke Stone. When William Coddington, one of the more illustrious passengers, inquired the name of the island where the winds howled and the surf roared, Stone mistook the question. Thinking he was asked the Dutch word for the weather phenomenon, he promptly answered "Nixie Shmalt," meaning the Wail of the Nixies, the water spirits. An Anglicized version stuck. (That is, incidentally, a false etymology.) And in the twentieth century, Snow collected yet another explanation that a man named Nix once owned both Gallop's Island and its mate.

Rather than search hopelessly for a solution, we should appreciate how all these increasing tales show fidelity to a disappearing island. That same admiration was surely on display in 1842 when the National Theater of Boston hosted a debut drama, *The Legend of Boston Harbor*. Although I regrettably cannot find the script, newspaper advertisements announced a promising theme and a splendid way to close out this chapter:

> Each island in our harbor tells,
> Legends of by-gone years;
> On some a tale of darkness dwells,
> To summon up our fears.
> One lonely pile a voyager sees,
> It tells of love and hate,
> Sad stories float on every breeze
> That fans old "Nix's Mate."

24

The Haunts of Boston Harbor: Part Two

I N 1862, AS the American Civil War raged on, Fort Warren stood ready on Georges Island. There it welcomed hundreds of Confederate guests into a labyrinth of prison cells.

One Confederate officer visiting Boston Harbor under these conditions had a faithful young wife who received the news of her husband's imprisonment with heartbreak that soon hardened into action. Against all good sense she traveled to the North until she could stare at the shadow of Fort Warren. The citizens of Hull were loyal to the nation but kind to this bride who risked her fate to be closer to her beloved.

What those citizens did not know was that the young woman came with rebellious determination. In the cover of darkness and dressed in disguise as a Union soldier, she rowed a boat to the lonely island. There, as she had conspired to do in coded letters to her husband, she began to dig in the sand. Her husband and his imprisoned comrades had done their part for several weeks. They had dug a secret tunnel from within the prison heading to the beach outside. Their laborious plan to escape was now nearly complete. And with a boat awaiting them on the shore, hope finally came to those supporting the cause of the Confederacy.

Perhaps it was the clang of a shovel. Perhaps it was the sighs of those desperate to be free. Or perhaps it was simply cruel luck that brought a patrol to the site where the young woman dug toward her husband's embrace. Upon seeing Union soldiers, her determination turned to desperation. A scuffle began in an attempt to capture someone the patrol took to be a uniformed traitor in their midst.

But the young woman was well prepared indeed. She had a pistol in her possession and fired without hesitation. The bullet struck, but not her intended target. Instead her husband, the cause for her private war, fell dead upon the wet sand.

The Union soldiers succeeded in capturing a new prisoner as she caressed her husband's lifeless body, anointing it with saltwater tears. After a quick trial she was sentenced to death as a spy. She asked to be hanged in a funeral dress rather than a Union soldier's garb. Another scramble ensued to fulfill her final wish. And with that complete, the young woman went to the gallows dressed in mourner's clothing.

The secret where the ambitious couple was buried went with those Union soldiers to their graves, but some say the soul of the mournful bride never left Georges Island. And some even say they see her phantom still, determined to fulfill her task, haunting the halls and tunnels of Fort Warren for eternity as the sorrowful Lady in Black.

Before we begin, I need to clear my conscience. As much as I relish sharing this tale, I know that it is has been told by a far superior raconteur, Edward Rowe Snow. Indeed, Snow is the very reason we are able to enjoy this and many other stories concerning Boston Harbor.

When he began interviewing informants for his 1935 *The Islands of Boston Harbor*, Snow struck a treasure trove of folkloric narratives. He recovered a tradition that the pirate Henry "Long Ben" Every buried treasure at Point Shirley and diamonds on Gallop's Island. From Billy McLeod, the caretaker of Grape Island after Amos Pendleton departed for the Weir River, he collected a tale of intrigue concerning gold diggers searching at the behest of a clairvoyant. (McLeod was able to enlighten matters by explaining that the real treasure of the island was its rich store of clams.)

From an unnamed informant Snow gathered an odious tale of Apple Island—another sacrifice to Logan Airport's extension—in which the lifeless body of a beautiful young woman, daughter of a colonial governor, was found drifting in its waters. A band of robbers inhabit the island, immediately raising suspicion of culpability. In order to infiltrate their ranks, her lover poses as a thief desirous of joining the murderous crew. But his vengeance would never succeed. Weeks later, a fisherman finds his lifeless body hanging from an elm tree. The ghosts of the crestfallen couple were said to haunt the island until the turn of the twentieth century.

The Lady in Black, unquestionably the most popular folkloric tale of the Harbor today, was utterly absent in the records of the nineteenth century. Yet when Snow first set it to print, he remarked that it had been "whispered for many, many years" at Fort Warren. How could that be?

"Whispered" is the essential word. It points to an origin in what folklorists call occupational folklore, in this case a ghost story shared by soldiers stationed at the fort in order to pass the time and in all likelihood to prank each other mercilessly.

As Snow reports, the earliest examples come from the lips of soldiers. A sergeant hears a sudden voice warn "Don't come in here!" Three soldiers witness footprints pass by in the snow without a body attached to them. Rumors circulate of soldiers court-martialed for firing weapons at unseen beings or deserting their post in fear. And then there is the small matter of a supernatural presence disturbing the routine poker games played by the soldiers, hopefully on their off hours.

In my educated guess the legend of the Lady in Black is the product of a group of men bonding over a demanding job in an unusual place that was ripe for ghost stories—imagine the initiation of a rookie made to explore Fort Warren's tunnels in search of the specter. Eventually their lore found its way to the greater public and the legend of the Lady in Black became a widespread sensation.

Historical evidence adds up. Construction on Fort Warren began in 1833 and was completed in 1861. During the American Civil War it served as both a Union training camp and a prison for Confederate soldiers, politicians, and supporters. Fort Warren had a relatively low rate of fatalities under the direction of Colonel Justin Dimmick. It remained in operation during the Spanish-American War and the First World War. Following the end of those hostilities, it was maintained but not fully active again until the Second World War.

The Lady in Black may have remained a soldier's story and passed into oblivion after Fort Warren was decommissioned in 1947 were it not for Snow's publications, public talks, and indefatigable activities to promote Georges Island. Snow spearheaded the drive to preserve the fort in the 1950s, an act of leadership commemorated today by a memorial plaque in his honor. As a well-respected lecturer and teacher Sow also attracted the attention of journalists, and eventually became a contributing writer for area newspapers.

All of this publicity had the effect of introducing the legend of the Lady in Black to wider audiences. Not surprisingly, the story continued to evolve over several decades. When Snow first spoke on the issue in 1934, she was better known as the "Black Widow" who haunted the "lonely outpost for soldiers." In the late 1940s her husband was called Andrew Lanier; by the early 1970s it had changed to Samuel Lanier, and by the late 1970s she was known as Melanie Lanier.

Snow regularly conducted tours of the island, often to schoolchildren, and would regale them with a puckish sense of humor. According to many gratified victims, Snow enlisted actors to jump out of the shadows and scare the youngsters—and the young at heart—at precisely the right moment in the tale. Through these enlivening performances, he assured that generations from Massachusetts and beyond would remember this legend and retell it often.

A particularly revealing version appeared in the *Boston Globe* just before Halloween in 1989. Snow had died seven years earlier, so the duty of chief raconteur fell to Alfred Schroeder, the historian of Boston's Metropolitan District Commission. Recognizing the inconsistency from earlier versions that Melanie managed to kill her husband despite their being separated by a wall, this new version proposed that Samuel escaped from his prison window on a rope of bedsheets and assisted his wife in digging a tunnel to free the other prisoners inside. This later version also updated the spectral footprints story, moving it to the Second World War.

Is there any truth to this tale? Not in the sense of a southern belle who attempted to free her husband and ended up in the hangman's noose. That simply did not happen.

But Moses Sweetser, writing in 1882, may furnish a clue to the inspiration for the story. He notes that in May 1862, a number of prisoners joined the ranks of the eight hundred already guarded there. These prisoners were from the South and unaccustomed to the cold winds of New England. But Sweetser also comments that many who protected the garrison in those early years were amateurs, ill-prepared for the "distressing climatic conditions," especially the relentless dashing of the waves upon the island. Standing guards were replaced by patrols in order to withstand the weather.

That weather, Sweetser surmises, played havoc with the imagination.

"No wonder that the unfortunate sentinels saw mysterious shapes," Sweetser suggests, "so that an order was posted at the guardhouse, 'denouncing severe punishment in any case where ghosts were allowed to pass a beat without challenge and arrest.'" One colonel, F. J. Parker, likened the fort to the Castle of Udolpho—a Gothic romance by Ann Radcliffe penned in 1794—"with its clanging sounds of chains, its sweeping gusts of air, its strange moanings and howlings, and the startling noise of some sudden clang of a shutting door reverberating through the arches."

Sweetser further explains that in 1863 "a daring attempt at escape was made." Four officers and two Confederate soldiers managed to squeeze through their prison and drop into the moat at night, evading the sentinels in the darkness. Two attempted to swim to Lovells Island, but the tide swallowed them and they were never seen again. Two others rafted to Lovells "intending to capture a boat, and return for their comrades." They achieved the securing of a ship, but their strength failed them and they washed out to sea. Those escapees were captured off the coast of Maine. The final two waited on the shore for their comrades who never returned and were recaptured in the morning.

A creepy granite fortress whose prisoners attempt to escape and free their fellow inmates? In all probability that is the originating seed for the legend of the Lady in Black.

Although it did not enjoy the accolades of the Lady in Black, Snow collected another ghost story in the early twentieth century concerning the Scarlet Lady of Long Island. This legend, without question, originates with soldiers stationed at Fort Strong. Snow attributes it to Bill Liddell, who shared the tale with him in 1950. The two men visited the island where Liddell had served, inspiring what folklorists would call a breakthrough into performance.

Liddell wove a compelling tale concerning Evacuation Day, that March 17 in 1776 when British soldiers and scores of Tory sympathizers fled Boston, delivering George Washington a major victory in the war. Not every ship sailed immediately, the story purported, and several lingered in the Harbor for months, just off Long Island. A mere thirteen remained when the Continental forces captured the island and began bombardment of the British ships in June of that year.

Among the Tory refugees were William and Mary Burton. A cannonball struck the ship. Mary Burton was mortally wounded and in her dying breath implored her husband to bury her on land rather than at sea.

A flag of truce was raised. William Burton was granted temporary permission to observe his wife's final wishes and bring her body to Long Island. Mary was wrapped in a scarlet blanket and lowered into a grave. Those fighting for the American cause graciously promised to leave a marker for her. Heartbroken but dutiful, her husband returned to the British vessel. It left the harbor for Halifax, never to return. A wooden marker soon stood over Mary Burton's grave. But wood is not permanent, and with the passing of the years the location of her body was lost to the vicissitudes of time.

In 1804 Long Island saved a group of fishermen shipwrecked in a storm. They climbed its cliffs and found shelter sturdy enough to survive the night. But they are unprepared for the unearthly wailing that cut through the rain and wind. Investigating the matter, they spied to their horror the specter of a woman draped in a scarlet cloak, blood slowly dripping down her forehead. She walked past them, absorbed in her agony, and disappeared beyond the hill.

The Woman in Scarlet again appeared during the War of 1812. And she was seen once more in 1891 by a young private by the name of William Liddell.

As with the Lady in Black, all of the elements are available for the Woman in Scarlet to become a sensational legend in Boston Harbor. Unfortunately, the city refused to cooperate. Unlike Georges Island, which fell into disrepair and was then transformed into a tourist destination, Long Island continued to be used for municipal social services. Throughout the twentieth century it housed the homeless and a campus of buildings including shelters, a hospital, a center for alcohol addiction treatment, and a chapel. A few summer camps and associated activity fields were the most recent additions. Although visitation was not fully restricted, Long Island did not become a tourist destination, and hence its resident ghost did not—or has not yet—entered the oral tradition with the same fervor.

In 2014 the city had to close the deteriorating bridge to Long Island, standing since the 1950s. All programs and residents were evacuated within a year, and as of this writing its future remains uncertain. But rest assured that were it to become a developed tourist site in the decades ahead, its restless dead in scarlet will surely enjoy newfound celebrity.

The final haunt of Boston Harbor is not a ghost story but a legend of a storied writer of ghostly tales. It begins innocently enough. In 1871, Nathaniel Shurtleff published a history of Boston, which included commentary on Castle Island and Fort Independence. Shurtleff noted that duels had occasionally been fought there and that one victim had a small marble monument erected in his honor. That young man was Lieutenant Robert F. Massie, who died on Christmas Day 1817.

Although that observation appeared in other tour guides throughout the 1800s and early 1900s, little more was made of it until Snow began to lecture on the topic. In 1935 he presented three independent tales to rapt audiences. The first concerned the discovery in 1905 of a skeleton in military uniform buried in a casement on the grounds of the fort; Snow attributed that tale to an unnamed elderly gentlemen. The second story told of a curse brought upon the island. Snow did not name his informant, but the tale was one of abiding revenge.

Sometime before the American Revolution, a young woman lived on the island with her father. She loved an American, but her father insisted that she marry a British officer. The suitors dueled for her hand, and the American lost his life. She committed suicide rather than accept her fate. (This story echoes some of the late Lovers Leaps tales associated with the Berkshires and may have similarly been composed in the early 1900s.) The British officer cursed the island so that no one who comes near would find happiness in their lives.

The third story—and again, regrettably, Snow did not name his informant—entailed a young Edgar Allan Poe, who served at Fort Independence in 1827. Poe investigated the marble marker to Massie and, learning how the body had been buried on the island, found atmospheric inspiration for his later tales.

Newspapers demonstrate that this initially mild suggestion of a correlation between Poe and Fort Independence was a hit with audiences. By 1940 the tale of the curse had given way to a fast-evolving legend surrounding Poe. The skeleton—which in its earliest narrations had no immediate connection to the author—became the key to bringing it all together. That skeleton became the remains of the officer who killed Massie, walled up by the lieutenant's comrades, a secret that Poe uncovered and used as the basis for "The Cask of Amontillado."

Snow continued to tell this tale for another half century. In time, it reflected his tastes and emphases. In the *Boston Herald* in 1970, for example, he identified the walled-up officer as John Drame and suggested that he was made drunk on four glasses of amontillado by Massie's vengeful companions. In 1972 Snow retold the tale in the *Herald*, returning to an earlier account in which the officer was named Greene.

Although Snow was a significant contributor to popularizing the Poe legend, he was not the sole progenitor. In 1957, for example, author Robert T. Reilly published an essay entitled "Poe and the Purloined Plot." Reilly, who was born in Lowell in 1922, recalled visits to Fort Independence as a boy that included the Poe story. His published version resembles but does not cite Snow directly. And others had their say as well. By the 1980s the name Gustavus Drane was the favored choice for the officer forever walled into the fort in an act of brutal revenge.

For the record, there is little in history or in Poe studies to substantiate this legend. Poe did serve at Fort Independence but not in the current structure, which was constructed with its sibling Fort Warren beginning in 1833. There is no chance a skeleton discovered in 1905 had any connection with the 1817 duel. Or, more appropriately, "purported skeleton." Recall that Snow passed along a tale about the discovery by another raconteur. Later archaeologists and Castle Island historians dispute that a skeleton was ever unearthed.

This is a delicious folkloric anecdote, but should we put any credence into a direct correlation between Poe's stories and Fort Independence? I have my doubts.

"I have my doubts." Where have I heard that before?

Legend Tripping

I don't mean to cheat here, but the best advice for those who wish to visit
and hike the available sites mentioned in the previous chapter and this one
is to consult the website of the Boston Harbor Islands National and State
Park: https://www.bostonharborislands.org/.

In addition to copious information, there is a very helpful interactive
map that shows which islands can be visited and which cannot. Of those
with legendary elements, Lovells Island, Georges Island, and Grape Island
are accessible, as is Deer Island (which does not require watercraft to
visit). Lovells Island offers a 1.5-mile loop. The best island hike is the 4
miles on Peddocks, but the legendary material is light there. The hike at
World's End is peaceful and an excellent way to see the area of Weir River
where Amos Pendleton spent some of his eccentric days. It is managed by
the Trustees of Reservations (https://thetrustees.org/place/worlds-end-
hingham/), which offers a map. **Trailhead GPS: N42 15.29 / W70 52.24**

Thompson and Spectacle Islands are accessible and equally worth-
while for hiking, although there is no significant folklore attached to
them. (Spectacle Island was occasionally referenced as Specter Island in
newspapers of the 1800s, but alas without unhinged yellow journalism to
spin a yarn.) The other islands associated with legends are not accessible or
have disappeared, although the boat rides to those with tourist attractions
pass by them.

25

On Springfield Mountain and Vicinity

I N OPENING THIS chapter I will share a folkloric story concerning Springfield Mountain by distilling all the elements upon which all raconteurs agree. Here is that tale in its reverberant glory:

A young person died.

Beyond that point of consensus lies endless variation regarding the identity, gender, location, and manner of the victim and the death. Arguably the best-known version of the ballad today concerns a young man who is bitten by a rattlesnake on Springfield Mountain the day before his wedding so that the anticipated happy celebration is replaced by sorrowful funerary rites.

There are worse ways to spend a day than tracking down and listening to as many variants of the ballad "On Springfield Mountain" as one may find. It is a devil of a task to try and collect them all. Throughout this book I have noted that when a folkloric tale appears in print it is often the signal that there were numerous narrations in the surrounding oral tradition. In the case of "On Springfield Mountain," print accounts reach back well into the 1800s and number in the high dozens to hundreds. By that equation, we can assume thousands upon thousands of live narrations—of actual singing of this tale—with incalculable variations over time.

If the sea serpent reigns as monarch of Massachusetts folklore, his emissary to the western part of the Commonwealth is surely "the pesky sarpent" of the ballad. (No offense is meant to the state reptile, the garter snake.) Indeed, as an editorial in the *Berkshire Eagle* from 1868 proclaimed, the ballad "will live as long as the Old Bay State itself."

Today the preponderance of folklorists agrees that the ballad was originally composed following the death of Timothy Merrick, who lived on the border of what is now Wilbraham and Hampden and what was a parish of Springfield at the time of his death in 1761. The entire area had been known as Springfield Mountains for some time. In the town records one finds this sad notice:

Timothy Mirrick, the son of Lt. Thomas and Mary Mirrick, was bit by a rattlesnake on August 7, 1761, and died within about two or three hours, he being 22 years, two months, and three days old and very near the point of marriage.

The ballad of his death, one of the—if not *the*—earliest American ballads (as opposed to English or Scottish ballads imported here), soon followed. There has been considerable debate as to when it first appeared, but it is very likely that the song originated as an obituary narrative poem. There was also debate concerning who composed it. In the early 1800s, many considered it the work of his brokenhearted fiancée. But by the mid-1800s, there was increasing acceptance that its original author was Nathan Torrey, an educator and poet living in Wilbraham at the time.

Several reputable town historians, especially those who favored Torrey as the author, presented the following as the most authentic version to the original (I have contemporized the language):

On Springfield Mountains there did dwell
A likely youth who was known full well
Lieutenant Mirick's only son
A likely youth, nigh twenty-one

One Friday morning he did go
Into the meadow and did mow
A round or two, then he did feel
A poison serpent at his heal

When he received his deadly wound
He dropped his scythe upon the ground
And straight for home was his intent
Calling aloud still as he went

Though all around his voice was heard
But none of his friends to him appeared
They thought it was some workmen called
And there poor Timothy alone must fall

So soon his careful father went
To seek his son with discontent
And there his fond only son he found
Dead as a stone upon the ground

And there he lay down supposed to rest
With both his hands across his breast
His mouth and eyes closed fast
And there, poor man, he slept his last

His father viewed his track with great concern
Where he had ran across the corn

Uneven tracks where he did go
Did appear to stagger to and fro

The seventh of August, Sixty One
This fatal accident was done
Let this a warning be to all
To be prepared when God does call

The pathos of the ballad holds centuries after it first comforted mourners. It continues to be sung and evolve even today. And within the first century and a half of its life, it had become subject to remarkable variation. In some versions the family name is not Merrick but Merrill or Murray or Curtis or Carter or Davis. In some the unfortunate event happens on a Monday instead of a Friday.

In an alternative version of the ballad the victim is a young woman, usually Sally and often Sally Carter, who is not bitten by a snake but who picks berries by a riverside, falls in, and drowns. This one is also set at Springfield Mountain, so it is plausible that the Connecticut River was the intended body of water, but there are other rivers in the area that could prove fatal to someone unable to swim. The young woman's lover finds her dead body and carries it back to her home, where her mother dies of shock. In a few rarer examples a jilted lover flees the object of his affection and, coming to Springfield Mountain, is bitten by the waiting serpent.

In what is often called the "comic" version of the ballad, a young man—frequently named Johnny but also Zerubbabel or Samuel or Joe—is bitten while mowing. He strikes down the snake with his scythe and is able to stumble back to his lover or fiancée, often called Molly Bland and sometimes Sally. In order to save him, she sucks the venom out from the wound but, having a rotten tooth, is then herself poisoned. The two young lovers die together, devastating the community, but the final image often depicts them as happy ghosts together in the afterlife.

The ballad soon proliferated throughout the United States. It is found virtually everywhere, each variant showing signs of local flavor. There are examples in which the fallen young man is a cowboy struck while haying—surely as far away from Massachusetts as it could be. Another variant invokes both Monterey and Mexico. Letters to the editors in the nineteenth century routinely mention its popularity in Ohio, Michigan, Virginia, Pennsylvania, and Wisconsin. I cannot do justice here to the wide range perpetuated throughout the nation or all of the variant groups, but they are formidable.

Returning closer to home, the ballad became so deeply integrated into the cultural life of the Springfield area that it spawned additional lore. When large snakes were killed throughout the 1800s, for example, there was a good chance that newspapers would describe it in relation to the serpent that killed Timothy Merrick. The *Springfield Republican* published a rich example in 1850 when one Dr. Hosford, hunting on Mt. Tom, "killed the largest black snake ever seen in this region." He struck it on its head and then began to pull out the monster from the woodpile where it was coiled. It measured seven feet in length and had seven full-grown red squirrels inside its belly.

"A grey squirrel was on a limb above, and would probably have followed the red ones," the article continues. "The snake had undoubtedly lain there, and charmed the unlucky seven into his insatiable jaws, as he was too full and dumpish to run at all. He is supposed to have been the identical 'pizen sarpint' that bit the heel of a youth who a long time ago dwelt on Springfield mountain."

It does not matter that Merrick was killed by a rattlesnake and not a black snake or that snakes do not live for a century—or that this entire tale is probably just fiction. It demonstrates the community's—and Massachusetts's—embrace of the ballad. It is similar to an 1886 essay by Charles Goodrich Whiting, a writer associated with the *Republican*, who joked on the scythe going out of fashion among farmers that the new riding machines would deny the world future ballads by denying future rattlesnake fatalities.

Rattlesnakes were a tangible and routine threat to colonial settlers and nineteenth-century farmers. Many places throughout New England that were branded with diabolical names—such as "Devil's Den"—have nothing to do with Satan; they were, rather, references to dens of snakes, often venomous ones. Western Massachusetts was an ideal environment for them. Sophie Eastman, a local writer, mused that it was "a common saying in Amherst College that no student was worthy of his diploma unless he had killed a rattlesnake," and a member of the class of 1830 joked that with only the seniors present for the commencement dinner, the campus would soon be overrun with serpents.

Snake lore entails some of the most fascinating—pun intended—folk traditions from Massachusetts and New England as a whole. In 1896 the eminent folklorist Clifton Johnson recorded numerous examples in *What They Say in New England*. I am pleased and eager to admit that Johnson— to whom this book is dedicated along with his grandson Charlie—is a far more engaging storyteller than I could hope to be, so I encourage readers to seek out those pages, and for that matter all of Johnson's books. You will thank me for the favor of recommending them.

In *What They Say*, Johnson commences his chapter on snake lore with the widespread belief that serpents, especially rattlesnakes and black snakes, had the power to charm, and not solely in the figurative sense. It was believed that snakes could fascinate—that is, mesmerize—their prey, such as the poor squirrels mentioned above, or birds, or even unlucky humans. Johnson provides a few examples of young people falling under a snake's spell in which the victims, having gazed into the serpent's eyes, see an array of beautiful colors and sights and become paralyzed. Fortunately, they escaped the hold upon them when a quick-thinking companion broke the charm.

Another threat lurked in brooks, Johnson observes, at least according to the superstition that one could swallow a tiny snake in the water, which would subsequently grow in the stomach and devour the poor victim's food. A particularly gruesome example appears of a child who, having swallowed a snake accordingly, also suffered it wiggling out of his mouth one day to investigate the scent of milk. When the child's father pulled the serpent out, its body was four feet long.

Hoop snakes were part and parcel of Massachusetts folklore. These legendary beasties were capable of grabbing their own tail in their mouth and, so forming a hoop, roll at tremendous velocity toward a victim. Upon reaching its target, the hoop snake would "blast" it—that is, whip its sharp pointed tail like a stinger, paralyzing its prey and causing it to shrivel up. The informant whom Johnson interviewed explained that not just flesh but anything struck by a hoop snake would deteriorate. Handles or hoes or shovels, for example, would break into splinters as if struck by lightning.

There is numerous other snake lore awaiting the reader of Johnson's collection, but these suffice to survey the folklore and to show how it reflects and shapes the genuine anxieties of an everyday reality from a different time than our own. Much of that lore was designed to educate children—and to remind adults—to be wary of the wooded environment into which their daily lives would take them, as well as to keep them from drinking unsafe water sources. It was propagated when snake populations were impressive. And although Johnson assured readers that many snakes were helpful, he recognized they had to be aware of their existence throughout the region.

Today, snake populations are in decline in the Commonwealth, and the timber rattlesnake has suffered the most. It is now found in only a few mountainous regions. Thankfully it is protected by the Massachusetts Endangered Species Act. They are very rarely seen by hikers who stay on trails, and despite that earlier admonitory lore which spoke to different experiences from a different time, rattlesnakes do not seek trouble if left alone. And take it on good authority that you will not be charmed or chased by hoop snakes out there, although you should still not drink brook water.

While exploring the trails between Mt. Tom and the Ashley Reservoir in Holyoke, hikers are in a section once known for Tim Felt's ghost. Johnson first collected this tale for *Picturesque Hampden,* published in 1892. I reprint it here in full to share with the reader the joy of Johnson's prowess as a storyteller, still shining 130 years after he set it down:

In the old days there lived on Back street a Mr. Felt. One fall he sowed a field to rye, which in the spring was looking green and thrifty, and he was much disturbed at the frequent visits of neighbor Hummerston's geese to the said field. Mr. Felt had a quick temper, and this sort of thing was too much for him. He caught the whole flock one day, killed them, and then wended his way to Deacon Hummerston to inform him what he had done and where his geese were to be found.

This and other acts, showing his hasty temper and savage disposition, brought Mr. Felt into disrepute among his neighbors. He often cruelly beat his horses and cattle, and there were times when he served the members of his family in the same way.

He had a son, Timothy by name, a dull-witted fellow, who was slow of comprehension and in his work made many mistakes. This was a frequent cause of anger to the father, who on such occasions would strike Tim to the earth with whatever implement he happened to have in hand—a hoe, a rake, or a pitchfork, perchance. These attacks sometimes drove Tim from home, but after a few days' absence necessity would bring him back again. At last, however, he disappeared and was seen no more, and a little later the Felts moved west.

In building the New Haven and Northampton canal, a great deal of limestone was used. On Mr. Felt's farm was a ledge of this rock, and the company soon had a quarry there. The overseer was a rough, ill-tempered fellow, and it was not long before he had trouble with his workmen and they all left him. That brought work to a standstill, and the overseer was at his wits' end to find some way out of the difficulty.

One night, shortly after the men left, the overseer, on his way home from the corner store, quite late, saw a dark figure standing on the ledge outlined against the sky. The overseer stood still, his frightened gaze riveted on the stranger. Presently he broke the silence by asking, "Who are you and what is your business?"

The specter replied, "My name is Timothy Felt, and my bones are under where I now stand. I was killed by my father four years ago, and if you will blast this rock you will find by bones."

This story ran through all the country round and created great excitement. Every day for some time thereafter, loads of people, not only from Ireland Parish but from towns quite distant, wended their way thither, inquiring the way to the "ghost place," and when night came on people would make a long detour rather than pass the place. Money was raised to continue the quarrying until Tim's skeleton should be brought to light, but no bones were found, and after the overseer had gotten out what stone he wanted, the work lagged and was discontinued.

Was this humbug or not? One good old lady used to say:

"Where folks believe in witches, witches are. But when they don't believe, there are none there."

In this case there was wide belief that Tim was murdered, and that his ghost did really appear.

There are so many things here to explore. The first and obvious is that it is a macabre tale of homicide of one's own child. In the folklore of Massachusetts—and New England—that is not as uncommon a theme as one might think. In 1901, for example, Lyman Powell recorded the existence of a tale—but not the story itself—circulating around Wellfleet of the "minister's deformed child, done to death by a dose from its father's hand," whose ghost flits about on moonlit nights around a certain rosebush. These dreadful acts speak volumes to domestic anxieties and the breakdown of family fidelity, laying an enticing if lurid stimulant for a horror narrative.

But the Tim Felt tale also raises questions about ghost stories, human gullibility, and the malleability of belief. After all, in the story tourists came to seek and see his bones. Money poured into the project. Did the overseer actually encounter Tim Felt's ghost, or did he merely say that he did to stir up interest and to accomplish his task—"to find some way out of the difficulty"? The moral of the tale hits it home, even as Johnson leaves a winking ambiguity in the narrative as to whether the source of the belief was humbug or not. It's sagacious commentary on the potential of folklore by one of the great folklorists of New England.

Legend Tripping

Unless one wishes to provoke a fight between Wilbraham and Hampden as to where specific events occurred in the untimely death of Timothy Merrick, it is best to hike in both towns. In Wilbraham one finds the Pesky Sarpent Conservation Area. As of this writing there are no formal trails, although there has been discussion concerning development and access. The Merrick house once stood nearby. Hiking is available at the Rice Nature Preserve, which connects with the Sunrise Peak Trailwalk. There is free parking at the end of Highmoor Drive. The highest point in Rice Nature Preserve is known as Rattlesnake Hill. The town maintains the property and maps (https://www.wilbraham-ma.gov/294/Hiking-Trails-in-Wilbraham); there are 3.4 miles to explore in Rice Nature Preserve. **Trailhead GPS: N42 06.08 / W72 25.34**

Although no one suggests that Minnechaug Mountain was Springfield Mountain, this impressive site has bragging rights for one of the nicest views of the area. The mountain has more than 3 miles of meandering trails. Minnechaug Land Trust (https://minnechauglandtrust.org/) has a map and summary information for each of the named trails. The free South Road parking lot is the most readily accessible. **Trailhead GPS: N42 03.26 / W72 24.51**

All of Mount Tom State Reservation deserves attention. It is managed by the Department of Conservation and Recreation (https://www.mass.gov/locations/mount-tom-state-reservation), which offers maps and suggested hikes. **Trailhead GPS: N42 16.07 / W72 37.00** And with a little creative work—the hardest part is locating parking—one could readily explore the New England Trail (formerly called Metacomet-Monadnock

Trail) between the Ashley Watershed and Whiting Reservoir in Holyoke. Consult https://newenglandtrail.org/ for further information.

Although not discussed above, Clifton Johnson lived in Hockanum, a village of Hadley on the Connecticut River. The Mount Holyoke Range stretches to the east, but the area closest to Hockanum comprises Skinner State Park, also administered by the DCR (https://www.mass.gov/locations/skinner-state-park). The hiking trails and views are striking, and there is local folklore attached to various natural features, all celebrated by Johnson. The Devil's Football, for example, is a large boulder purportedly kicked over from Amherst by His Satanic Majesty himself. **Trailhead GPS: N42 18.00 / W72 35.15**

In what will forever be the greatest day in my career as a folklorist, I was shown all of these sites by Clifton Johnson's grandson Charlie. Charlie was more than ninety years young at the time. He generously shared the folklore collected by his grandfather and created by his father, Roger (whose exploits promoting the glawackus are featured in the Connecticut *Spooky Trails* guide). He also shared family stories, including those of encountering snakes on the mountain. Charlie's enthusiasm and hospitality remain among the greatest gifts I have received. In sharing these tales and hikes with you, dear reader, I hope I have done justice to that favor bestowed on me by an illustrious storyteller from a legendary family.

Works Cited

In the interest of expediency, I have cited only the works for which direct quotation occurs or those that supply the source for a retelling in the chapters rather than every publication mentioned or consulted.

1 His Snakeship Returns
Anonymous. *Fall River Daily Evening News*, July 30, 1896.
Bentley, William. *The Diary of William Bentley, D. D*. Volume IV. Salem: The Essex Institute, 1914.
Brainard, John Gardiner Calkins. *The Poems of John G. C. Brainard*. Hartford: S. Andrus and Son, 1846.
"Cape Cod at the Head." *Boston Globe*, September 17, 1886.
Humphreys, David. *Some Account of the Serpent of the Ocean*. New York: Kirk and Mercein, 1817.
Josselyn, John. "A Report of Wonders." *A Library of American Literature*. Volume I. Edmund Clarence Stedman and Ellen Mackay Hutchinson, editors. New York: Charles L. Webster and Company, 1888.
Loomis, C. Grant. "Henry David Thoreau as Folklorist." *Western Folklore*, volume 16, number 2, 1957.
"Mermaid." *Nantucket Inquirer*, May 22, 1833.
"No More a Myth." *Boston Globe* (morning edition), July 30, 1896.
"No Serpent." *Boston Globe* (evening edition), July 30, 1896.
O'Neill, June Pusbach. *The Great New England Sea Serpent*. New York: Paraview, 2003.
"Provincetown's Town Crier." *Boston Globe*, September 12, 1915.
"Seeing Sea Serpents Slipping." *Boston Globe*, August 8, 1948.
"Two White Whales." *Boston Globe*, July 31, 1896.
"Where Has N. E. Sea Serpent Gone?" *Boston Globe*, November 15, 1923.
"White Humps." *Boston Globe*, July 29, 1896.

2 Ain't We to Provincetown?
"Beast of Truro Mystifying Cape." *New York Times*, January 17, 1982.

CapeCast: "Does the Legendary Pamet Puma Exist?" October 10, 2008. https://www
.youtube.com/watch?v=CUk6mdt0QAQ.

Digges, Jeremiah (Josef Berger). *Cape Cod Pilot*. Boston: Northeastern University Press, 1985.

"Old Timer Recalls the Days." *Brooklyn Daily Eagle*, February 13, 1928.

"On Land. Big Sea Serpent Caught at Last." *Boston Globe*, May 5, 1893.

"Out to Sea Again." *Boston Globe*, May 6, 1893.

Reynard, Elizabeth. *The Narrow Land: Folk Chronicles of Old Cape Cod*. Boston: Houghton Mifflin Company, 1934.

Vorse, Mary Heaton. *Time and Town: A Provincetown Chronicle*. New Brunswick: Rutgers University Press, 1991.

3 The Salem Witch Trials

Along the Coast of Essex County: A Handbook. Boston: Junior League of Boston, 1970.

A. J. R. "A Phantom Farm." *Minneapolis Journal*, September 17, 1904.

Barry, William. *A History of Framingham*. Boston: James Munroe and Company, 1847.

Davis, Rebecca. *Gleanings from Merrimac Valley*. Haverhill: Chase Brothers, 1886.

Downing, Margaret. "Summer Capital of the Nation." *Los Angeles Times*, July 30, 1911.

Drake, Samuel Adams. *A Book of New England Legends and Folk-Lore*. Boston: Roberts Brothers, 1884.

King, Caroline Howard. *When I Lived in Salem, 1822–1866*. Brattleboro: Stephen Daye Press, 1937.

Lowell, James Russell. *Letters of James Russell Lowell*. Volume I. New York: Harper and Brothers Publishers, 1894.

Mather, Cotton. *The Wonders of the Invisible World*. London: John Russell Smith, 1862.

Mednick, Amy. "Cave Lore Spurs Preservation Drive." *Boston Globe*, December 13, 1992.

Roads, Samuel. *The History and Traditions of Marblehead*. Boston: Houghton, Mifflin and Company, 1881.

Robinson, John. *Visitor's Guide to Salem*. Salem: The Essex Institute, 1895.

Sargent, Porter. *A Handbook of New England*. Boston: Porter E. Sargent, 1916.

Skinner, Charles Montgomery. *Myths and Legends of Our Own Land*. Volume I. Philadelphia: J. B. Lippincott Company, 1896.

"Summer Residences." *Boston Herald*, July 12, 1903.

Temple, Josiah. *History of Framingham*. Town of Framingham, 1887.

"The Ghost of Granny Hogins." *Whimwhams, by Four of Us*. Boston: S. G. Goodrich, 1828.

The WPA Guide to Massachusetts. New York: Pantheon Books, 1983.

Whittier, John Greenleaf. "Powow Hill: A Legend of Essex County." *New England Magazine*, volume 2, issue 5, 1832.

4 The Witch of Half Way Pond

Bodfish, Abbie. "Story of Tower Hill." *Hyannis Patriot*, January 5, 1933.

Kittredge, George Lyman. *Witchcraft in Old and New England*. Cambridge: Harvard University Press, 1929.

Otis, Amos. *Genealogical Notes of Barnstable Families*. Volume I. Barnstable: F. B. & F. P. Goss, 1888.

Otis, Amos. "Liza Towerhill." *Barnstable Patriot*, March 20, 1860.

Reynard, Elizabeth. *The Narrow Land: Folk Chronicles of Old Cape Cod*. Boston: Houghton Mifflin Company, 1934.

Swift, Charles Warner. "Tale of the Two." *Yarmouth Register*, October 7, 1896.

5 The "Witches" of Dogtown

Boston Evening Transcript, October 12, 1842.

Cheney, Ednah Dow Littlehale. *Stories of the Olden Time*. Boston: Lee and Shepard, 1890.

Crowell, Robert, and David Choate. *History of the Town of Essex*. Town of Essex, 1868.

Daley, Sarah. "Peg Wesson." *Fall River Daily Globe*, October 11, 1892.

Estes, Edith Perry, and W. M. D. Bodwell. "Cape Ann." *Boston Herald*, March 27, 1898.

MacKaye, Percy. *Dogtown Common*. New York: The Macmillan Company, 1921.

Mann, Charles Edward. *In the Heart of Cape Ann or the Story of Dogtown*. Gloucester: Proctor Brothers Publishers, 1896.

N. G. "Letter from Pigeon Cove." *Boston Traveler*, August 16, 1869.

Rosebault, Charles. "Haunt of Witches and Smugglers." *New York Times*, October 23, 1921.

Upham, Charles. *Lectures on Witchcraft*. Boston: Carter, Hendee and Babcock, 1831.

"Water Basin Operation Recalls Witch's Curse." *Boston Globe*, January 20, 1931.

W. E. S. "The Romance of History." *Cape Ann Advertiser*, February 12, 1869.

Wilkinson, Richard Hill. "Old Shag." *The Binghamton Press*, May 26, 1934.

6 The "Witches" of Hadley and Westborough

Atwood, Margaret. "Half-Hanged Mary." *Morning in the Burned House*. Toronto: McClelland and Stewart, 1995.

Du Bois, Constance. "Mary Webster, the Witch." *Demorest's Monthly Magazine*, June to July, 1884.

"Fishing at the Falls." *Springfield Republican*, January 22, 1868.

Forbes, Harriette Merrifield. *The Hundredth Town: Glimpses of Life in Westborough*. Boston: Press of Rockwell and Churchill, 1889.

Judd, Sylvester. *History of Hadley*. Northampton: Metcalf and Company, 1863.

Mather, Cotton. *Memorable Providences, Relating to Witchcrafts*. Boston, 1689.

More Old Houses in Westborough, Mass., and Vicinity. Westborough Historical Society, 1908.

"Two Hundredth Anniversary of the Settlement of Hadley." *Boston Transcript*, June 8, 1859.

The WPA Guide to Massachusetts. New York: Pantheon Books, 1983.

7 Hannah Screecher and Her Sister

A. L. (Adeline Hallett Lovell). "New England Superstitions." *Boston Journal*, June 8, 1877.

Avant, Joan Tavares. "Powwow, a Time of Community and Legend." *The Mashpee Enterprise*, July 8, 2018.

Avant, Joan Tavares. "Screecham Sisters' Strawberries, Crumpets, and Biscuits." *The Mashpee Enterprise*, April 2, 2019.

Johnson, Clifton. *What They Say in New England*. Boston: Lee and Shepard, 1896.

Reynard, Elizabeth. *The Narrow Land: Folk Chronicles of Old Cape Cod*. Boston: Houghton Mifflin Company, 1934.

Richards, Anna Matlack. *Memories of a Grandmother by a Lady of Massachusetts*. Boston: Gould and Lincoln, 1854.

Simmons, William. *Spirit of the New England Tribes*. Hanover: University Press of New England, 1986.

Stockton, Frank. *Buccaneers and Pirates of Our Coasts*. New York: The Macmillan Company, 1919.

8 The Screeching Lady, the Wizard, and the Pixies

Brittan, S. B., and B. W. Richmond. *A Discussion of the Facts and Philosophy of Ancient and Modern Spiritualism*. New York: Partridge and Brittan, 1853.

E. K. "Marblehead and Its People." *Springfield Republican*, May 24, 1869.

E. K. "Marblehead and Its People." *Springfield Republican*, June 7, 1869.

Nauticus. "Legends of Marblehead." *Columbian Centinel*, September 4, 1839.

Roads, Samuel. *A Guide to Marblehead*. Marblehead: Merrill Graves, 1881.

Roads, Samuel. *The History and Traditions of Marblehead*. Boston: Houghton, Mifflin and Company, 1881.

Story, Joseph. *Life and Letters of Joseph Story*. Boston: Little and Brown, 1851.

Upham, Charles. *Lectures on Witchcraft*. Boston: Carter, Hendee and Babcock, 1831.

9 The Mooncusser's White Horse

Digges, Jeremiah (Josef Berger). *Cape Cod Pilot*. Boston: Northeastern University Press, 1985.

Digges, Jeremiah (Josef Berger). *In Great Waters: The Story of the Portuguese Fishermen*. New York: The Macmillan Company, 1941.

Early, Elizabeth. *And This Is Cape Cod!* Boston: Houghton Mifflin Company, 1936.

Hawthorne, Nathaniel. *Twice-Told Tales*. Volume II. Boston: Ticknor and Fields, 1863.

Kittredge, Henry Crocker. *Mooncussers of Cape Cod*. Hamden: Archon Books, 1971.

Reynard, Elizabeth. *The Narrow Land: Folk Chronicles of Old Cape Cod*. Boston: Houghton Mifflin Company, 1934.

Sibley, Frank. "Down East." *Boston Globe*, December 14, 1926.

Snow, Edward Rowe. "White Stallion of Monomoy." *Boston Herald*, November 25, 1970.

"Tell It to Truro, and Get Lammed." *Boston Globe*, November 30, 1938.

Thoreau, Henry David. *Cape Cod*. Boston: Ticknor and Fields, 1865.

10 The Wild Man of Wellfleet

A General History of the Pyrates. Volume II. Mineola: Dover Publications, 1999.

Alden, Timothy. *A Collection of American Epitaphs and Inscriptions*. Volume III. New York, 1814.

Digges, Jeremiah (Josef Berger). *Cape Cod Pilot*. Boston: Northeastern University Press, 1985.

Fitzgerald, Michael. *1812: A Tale of Cape Cod*. Yarmouthport: C. W. Swift, 1912.

Hale, Edward. "Lord Bellomont and Captain Kidd." *The Memorial History of Boston*. Justin Winsor, editor. Boston: James R. Osgood and Company, 1881.

Hutchinson, Thomas. *The History of the Province of Massachusetts-Bay*. Boston: Thomas and John Fleet, 1767.

Reynard, Elizabeth. *The Narrow Land: Folk Chronicles of Old Cape Cod*. Boston: Houghton Mifflin Company, 1934.

Reynard, Elizabeth. *The Mutinous Wind*. Orleans: Parnassus Imprints, 1951.

Skinner, Charles Montgomery. *Myths and Legends of Our Own Land*. Volume I. Philadelphia: J. B. Lippincott Company, 1896.

Thoreau, Henry David. *Cape Cod*. Boston: Ticknor and Fields, 1865.

Whitman, Levi. Topographical Description of Wellfleet. Massachusetts Historical Collections, 1794.

11 Old Harry Main of Ipswich

Bell, Earnest. "The Wraith of the Winthrop Mansion." *Appleton's Journal*, November 28, 1874.

Brown, Abbie Farwell. "Old Ipswich Town." *New England Magazine*, volume 28, number 4, 1903.

Drake, Samuel Adams. *A Book of New England Legends and Folk-Lore*. Boston: Roberts Brothers, 1884.

Felt, Joseph. *History of Ipswich, Essex, and Hamilton*. Cambridge: Charles Folsom, 1834.

For Each Other: A Novel. New York: G. W. Carleton and Company, 1878.

Hill, Benjamin, and Winfield Nevins. *The North Shore of Massachusetts Bay*. Salem, 1881.

Morgan, James Appleton. "Ipswich Town." *Brooklyn Union*, February 24, 1873.

Morgan, James Appleton. "Old Ipswich Town." *The Magazine of Poetry*, volume 7, number 1, 1895.

N. E. "A Day in Ipswich." *Boston Journal*, July 28, 1863.

Skinner, Charles Montgomery. *Myths and Legends of Our Own Land*. Volume II. Philadelphia: J. B. Lippincott Company, 1896.

Waters, Thomas Franklin. *Ipswich in the Massachusetts Bay Colony*. Ipswich: Ipswich Historical Society, 1905.

Waters, Thomas Franklin. *Some Early Homes of the Puritans and Some Old Ipswich Houses*. Salem: The Salem Press, 1898.

12 The Treasure of Scraggum Woods

Ames, Paul. The Legend of Buried Treasure in Byfield! February 20, 2017. https://www.youtube.com/watch?v=Yyy_dhGQoWg.

Barry, William. *A History of Framingham*. Boston: James Munroe and Company, 1847.

Boston Evening Transcript, October 12, 1842.

Cardin, Sabrina. "Is There Buried Treasure in Byfield?" *Newburyport News*, September 27, 2007.

De Lue, Willard. "The Great Treasure Hunt." *Boston Globe*, December 26, 1951.

"Mystery of Scraggum Woods." *Boston Globe*, July 11, 1909.

Snow, Edward Rowe. *Sea Disasters and Inland Catastrophes*. New York: Dodd, Mead and Company, 1980.

Snow, Edward Rowe. *True Tales of Buried Treasure*. New York: Dodd, Mead and Company, 1957.

Temple, Josiah. *History of Framingham*. Town of Framingham, 1887.

"That Pirate Treasure in Scraggum Woods—Will It Ever Be Found?" *Boston Herald*, May 6, 1906.

Thoreau, Henry David. *The Writings of Henry David Thoreau*. Volume VII. Boston: Houghton Mifflin and Company, 1906.

13 Dungeon Rock

Ames, Nathan. *Pirates' Glen and Dungeon Rock*. Boston: Bedding and Company, 1853.

Bulletin of the Essex Institute, volume 1, number 9, 1869.

Ellms, Charles, editor. *The Pirates Own Book*. Portland: Sanborn and Carter, 1837.

Emerson, Nanette Snow. *The History of Dungeon Rock*. Boston: Bela Marsh, 1859.

Lewis, Alonzo. *The History of Lynn*. Boston: Press of J. H. Eastburn, 1829.

Newhall, James Robinson. *Lin: Or Jewels of the Third Plantation*. Lynn: T. Hebert and J. M. Munroe, 1862.

14 The Horror of the Bridgewater Triangle

Cadieux, Aaron. *The Bridgewater Triangle*. 2013.

Citro, Joseph. *Passing Strange: True Tales of New England Hauntings and Horrors*. Boston: Houghton Mifflin and Company, 1996.

Coleman, Loren. *Mysterious America*. New York: Paraview Pocket Books, 2007.

Coleman, Loren. "Mysterious World Name Game." 1998. http://www.bigfootencounters .com/articles/henry.htm.

Fritz, Jean. *The Good Giants and the Bad Puckwudgies*. New York: G. P. Putnam Juvenile, 1982.

Packard, Winthrop. *Woodland Paths*. Boston: Small, Maynard and Company, 1910.

Reynard, Elizabeth. *The Narrow Land: Folk Chronicles of Old Cape Cod*. Boston: Houghton Mifflin Company, 1934.

Russo, Bill. *The Creature from the Bridgewater Triangle*. CreateSpace Independent Publishing Platform, 2015.

Schoolcraft, Henry Rowe. *Algic Researches*. New York: Harper & Brothers, 1839.

Skinner, Charles Montgomery. *Myths and Legends of Our Own Land*. Volume I. Philadelphia: J. B. Lippincott Company, 1896.

Stewart, George. *American Place Names*. Oxford: Oxford University Press, 1970.

The WPA Guide to Massachusetts. New York: Pantheon Books, 1983.

Weston, Thomas. *History of the Town of Middleboro*. Boston: Houghton Mifflin and Company, 1906.

15 Dinglehole

Crate, P. T. "Questions Still Haunt Millis Dinglehole." *Medway and Millis*, volume 3, number 10, October 1, 2012.

Jameson, Ephraim Orcutt. *The History of Medway*. Providence: J. A. and R. A. Reid, 1886.

J. B. "Dinglehole." *Village Register*, January 19, 1826.

Muise, Peter. "A Scary Place with a Silly Name." August 27, 2010. http://newengland folklore.blogspot.com/2010/08/scary-place-with-silly-name.html.

Seventh Annual Report of the Trustees of Public Reservations. Boston: George H. Ellis, 1898.

Sixth Annual Report of the Trustees of Public Reservations. Boston: George H. Ellis, 1897.

Smith, Frank. *Narrative History: A History of Dover, Massachusetts*. Town of Dover, 1897.

"Strong Yarn." *The Youth's Companion*, May 7, 1891.

The WPA Guide to Massachusetts. New York: Pantheon Books, 1983.

16 The Dover Demon

Citro, Joseph. *Passing Strange: True Tales of New England Hauntings and Horrors*. Boston: Houghton Mifflin and Company, 1996.

Coleman, Loren. *Monsters of Massachusetts*. Mechanicsburg: Stackpole Books, 2013.

Coleman, Loren. *Mysterious America*. New York: Paraview Pocket Books, 2007.

"Gremlins in Dover?" *North Adams Transcript*, May 16, 1977.

Sullivan, Mark. "Decades Later, the Dover Demon Still Haunts." *Boston Globe*, October 29, 2006.

17 Rag Rock and Hoccomocco Pond

Botkin, Benjamin, editor. *A Treasury of New England Folklore*. New York: Crown Publishers, 1947.

Converse, Parker Lindall. *Legends of Woburn*. Woburn, 1892.

Converse, Parker Lindall. *Legends of Woburn Second Series*. Woburn, 1896.

Forbes, Harriette Merrifield. *The Hundredth Town: Glimpses of Life in Westborough*. Boston: Press of Rockwell and Churchill, 1889.

Parkman, Ebenezer. "An Account of Westborough." *Collections of the Massachusetts Historical Society*. Volume X. Boston: Munroe, Francis and Parker, 1809.

Skinner, Charles Montgomery. *American Myths and Legends*. Volume I. Philadelphia: J. B. Lippincott Company, 1903.

Skinner, Charles Montgomery. *Myths and Legends of Our Own Land*. Volume I. Philadelphia: J. B. Lippincott Company, 1896.

Stewart, George. *American Place Names*. Oxford: Oxford University Press, 1970.

"The Legend of the Hobomak." *Boston Globe*, September 10, 1893.

The WPA Guide to Massachusetts. New York: Pantheon Books, 1983.

18 Bash Bish Falls

"Bash Bish Falls Wildest Scene South of the North Country." *Berkshire Eagle*, October 26, 1935.

Bolté, Mary. *Haunted New England*. New York: Weathervane Books, 1972.

Coxey, Willard Douglas. *Ghosts of Old Berkshire*. Great Barrington: The Berkshire Courier, 1934.

Coxey, Willard Douglas. *Romances of Old Berkshire*. Great Barrington: The Berkshire Courier, 1931.

Perry, Clay. *Underground New England*. Brattleboro: Stephen Daye Press, 1939.

The Berkshire Hills: A WPA Guide. Boston: Northeastern University Press, 1987.

19 The Wizard's Glen, Wahconah Falls, and Monument Mountain

Brown, Ella. "Wahconah Falls—Their History and Traditions." *Collections of the Berkshire Historical and Scientific Society*. Volume III. Pittsfield: Press of the Sun Printing Company, 1899.

Bryant, William Cullen. *Poetical Works of William Cullen Bryant*. New York: D. Appleton and Company, 1894.

Greylock, Godfrey (Edward Adams Smith). *Taghconic: The Romance and Beauty of the Hills*. Boston: Lee and Shepard, 1879.

Lavin, Lucianne. "Mohican Memorabilia and Manuscripts from the Stockbridge Mission House Indian Museum: The Persistence of Mohican Culture and Community." 2011. http://wakinguponturtleisland.blogspot.com/2015/05/monument-mountain-and-other-indigenous.html.

"Monument Mountain: Strange Legend of an Indian Maiden." *The Berkshire Hills: A Historic Monthly*. Volume II. 1902.

Peters, Samuel. *A General History of Connecticut*. London: J. Bew, 1782.

Skinner, Charles Montgomery. *Myths and Legends of Our Own Land*. Volume I. Philadelphia: J. B. Lippincott Company, 1896.

The Berkshire Hills: A WPA Guide. Boston: Northeastern University Press, 1987.

Whittier, John Greenleaf. *Legends of New England*. Baltimore: Genealogical Publishing Company, 1992.

Whittier, John Greenleaf. "Powow Hill: A Legend of Essex County." *New England Magazine*, volume 2, issue 5, 1832.

20 Hobbomocko and Moshup

Bruchac, Marge. "The Geology and Cultural History of the Beaver Hill Story." *Raid on Deerfield: The Many Stories of 1704*. 2005. http://www.1704.deerfield.history.museum/.

Field, Phinehas. "Stories, Anecdotes and Legends." *History and Proceedings of the Pocumtuck Valley Memorial Association*. Volume I. Deerfield, 1890.

Pressey, Edward Pearson. *History of Montague*. Montague: The New Clairvaux Press, 1910.

Reynard, Elizabeth. *The Narrow Land: Folk Chronicles of Old Cape Cod*. Boston: Houghton Mifflin Company, 1934.

Sayet, Rachel. *Moshup's Continuance: Sovereignty and the Literature of the Land in the Aquinnah Wampanoag Nation*. Thesis, Harvard University, 2011.

Simmons, William. *Spirit of the New England Tribes*. Hanover: University Press of New England, 1986.

Temple, Josiah, and George Sheldon. A *History of the Town of Northfield*. Albany: Joel Munsell, 1875.

21 The Ghost of Mount Greylock

"Does Old Coot's Ghost Still Haunt Mt. Greylock Slopes?" *North Adams Transcript*, February 8, 1965.

Doherty, Rodney, and Richard Lodge. "Quick Camera Captures Coot." *North Adams Transcript*, November 1, 1979.

Durwin, Joe. "The Old Coot Continues to Captivate." *North Adams Transcript*, November 3, 2009.

"Ghost of Thunderbolt Photographed." *North Adams Transcript*, January 27, 1939.

"Ghost on the Thunderbolt." *North Adams Transcript*, January 19, 1939.

Groves, Alexander. "Old Coot Legend Haunts Curiosity of Transcript Staff." *North Adams Transcript*, October 13, 1988.

Groves, Alexander. "Spirit of Old Coot Captured on Film." *North Adams Transcript*, October 31, 1988.

Lanfair, Howard. "Down the Ski Trail." *North Adams Transcript*, March 3, 1939.

Leahey, Maynard. "Old Coot, Ghost of Greylock." *North Adams Transcript*, August 4, 1978.

Skinner, Charles Montgomery. *Myths and Legends of Our Own Land*. Volume II. Philadelphia: J. B. Lippincott Company, 1896.

The Berkshire Hills: A WPA Guide. Boston: Northeastern University Press, 1987.

"The Short of It." *North Adams Transcript*, December 2, 1972.

Trabold, Randy. "Transcope." *North Adams Transcript*, March 20, 1971.

Trabold, Randy, and Charlie Hoye. "Old Coot Gives Transcript Team the Slip." *North Adams Transcript*, March 9, 1971.

Whalen, Michael. "The Old Coot of Greylock." February 28, 2015. http://mysterioushills.blogspot.com/2015/02/the-old-coot-of-greylock-legend-in-full.html.

22 Popcorn Snow of Petersham

"Another Suicide by a Woman in Petersham." *Barre Gazette*, September 6, 1844.

Barber, George Warren. *History of the Hermit of Erving Castle*. Andover: Warren Draper, 1868.

Coolidge, Mabel Cook. *The History of Petersham*. Petersham: Petersham Historical Society, 1948.

"Deaths." *Christian Watchman*, December 12, 1872.

Gaines, Judith. "Recalling the Towns Drowned for Boston." *Boston Globe*, November 29, 1992.

Greene, J. R. *Historic Quabbin Hikes*. Athol: Highland Press, 1994.

Greene, J. R. *Strange Tales from Old Quabbin*. Athol: Highland Press, 1993.

"Lonesome Road Offers Weirdly Unusual Sight." *Springfield Union*, September 1, 1912.

"Minor Items." *Rutland County Herald*, December 12, 1872.

O'Hara, Maryanne. *Cascade*. New York: Penguin Publishing Company, 2012.

"Probate Court." *Boston Globe*, January 23, 1873.

Skinner, Charles Montgomery. *American Myths and Legends*. Volume I. Philadelphia: J. B. Lippincott Company, 1903.

Smith, John. *The Hermit of Erving Castle*. Erving: Lyndon Crawford, 1871.

"Snow Tomb to Be Closed." *Springfield Republican*, August 16, 1912.

"Strange Tale of Asa Snow, Embalming Wizard." *Boston Herald*, August 10, 1924.

"Western Massachusetts." *Springfield Republican*, December 3, 1872.

"Worcester County." *Springfield Republican*, December 29, 1857.

23 The Haunts of Boston Harbor: Part One

Brown, Frederick. *A Valedictory Poem*. Boston: True and Weston, 1819.

Dawes, Rufus. *Nix's Mate: An Historical Romance of America*. New York: Samuel Colman, 1839.

"Hermit Is Dead." *Boston Herald*, January 22, 1897.

"Hermit No More." *Boston Globe*, January 29, 1895.

"Hingham." *Boston Globe*, January 22, 1897.

Homer, James Lloyd. *Nahant and Other Places on the North Shore*. Boston: William Chadwick, 1848.

Homer, James Lloyd. *Notes on the Sea-Shore*. Boston: Redding and Company, 1848.

Jameson, Ephraim Orcutt. *The History of Medway*. Providence: J. A. and R. A. Reid, 1886.

"Moored in Weir River." *Boston Globe*, November 19, 1885.

"National Theatre." *Boston Post*, November 29, 1942.

"Origin of Nix's Mate." *Boston Post*, February 22, 1840.

Perley, Sidney. *Historic Storms of New England*. Salem: The Salem Press, 1891.

Snow, Edward Rowe. *The Islands of Boston Harbor*. Carlisle: Commonwealth Editions, 2002.

Snow, Edward Rowe. *The Romance of Boston Bay*. Boston: Yankee Publishing Company, 1944.

Sweetser, Moses. *King's Handbook of Boston Harbor*. Boston: Moses King, 1883.

Sweetser, Moses. *King's Handbook of Boston Harbor*. Boston: Moses King, 1888.

Sweetser, Moses. *King's How to See Boston*. Boston: Moses King, 1895.

The Bangor Historical Magazine. Volume VI. Bangor: Benjamin Burr and Company, 1891.

24 The Haunts of Boston Harbor: Part Two

"Boston Harbor Ghost on Patrol." *Berkshire Eagle*, March 4, 1948.

"Castle Island Legend Recalls a Dire Curse, Duels and Even a Sea Serpent." *Boston Herald*, June 9, 1935.

Fogarty, Michael. "Boston Islands Harbor Many Famous Ghosts." *Boston Globe*, October 30, 1973.

Howard, Marjorie. "The Man Entombed in the Wall." *Boston Herald*, October 28, 1984.

Johnson, Willis. "Established New England Ghosts Fare Well without Halloween." *Boston Globe*, October 31, 1971.

"Lore of Harbor Islands Abounds with Romance." *Boston Globe*, November 21, 1934.

Meier, Mary. "Treasure Islands." *Boston Globe*, July 7, 1977.

"Mysterious Boston." *Boston Globe*, October 26, 1989.

Reilly, Robert. "Poe and the Purloined Plot." *Omaha World Herald*, December 29, 1957.

"Romantic Tales of Boston Harbor Told by Historian Edward Snow." *Patriot Ledger*, January 10, 1940.

Shurtleff, Nathaniel. *A Topographical and Historical Description of Boston*. City of Boston, 1871.

Snow, Edward Rowe. "Buried Alive on Castle Island!" *Boston Herald*, August 16, 1970.

Snow, Edward Rowe. "Roving Skeleton of Castle Island." *Boston Herald*, July 5, 1972.

Snow, Edward Rowe. *The Islands of Boston Harbor*. Carlisle: Commonwealth Editions, 2002.

Sweetser, Moses. *King's Handbook of Boston Harbor*. Boston: Moses King, 1882.

Wilson, Susan. "The Case of the Roving Remains." *Boston Globe*, October 25, 1990.

25 On Springfield Mountain and Vicinity

"An Old Settler." *Berkshire Eagle*, February 20, 1868.

Coffin, Tristram. "On a Peak in Massachusetts: The Literary and Aesthetic Approach." *A Good Tale and a Bonnie Tune*. Mody Boatright, Wilson Hudson, and Allen Maxwell, editors. Dallas: Southern Methodist University Press, 1964.

Eastman, Sophie. *In Old South Hadley*. Chicago: The Blakely Printing Company, 1912.

"Editorial Notes." *Springfield Republican*, September 26, 1850.

Johnson, Clifton. *Picturesque Hampden West*. Northampton: Picturesque Publishing Company, 1892.

Johnson, Clifton. *What They Say in New England*. Boston: Lee and Shepard, 1896.

Peck, Chauncey. *The History of Wilbraham*. Town of Wilbraham, 1913.

Powell, Lyman. *Historic Towns of New England*. New York: G. P. Putnam's Sons, 1898.

Whiting, Charles Goodrich. *The Saunterer*. Boston: Ticknor and Company, 1886.

Index of Places

About the Author

Stephen Olbrys Gencarella is a tenured professor in the Communication Department at the University of Massachusetts, Amherst. He is a regular contributor to iCRV Radio and cohosts a new series *Nature Folk: Wildlife or Wild Myth?* with naturalist Russ Miller. He was the resident folklorist for the Connecticut River Museum in Essex, Connecticut, from 2014 to 2019. He served as the folklore consultant to the William G. Pomeroy Foundation's Legends and Lore Marker Grant Program, a national initiative. His previous books, *Wicked Weird and Wily Yankees: A Celebration of New England's Eccentrics and Misfits* (2018) and *Spooky Trails and Tall Tales Connecticut* (2019) were published by Globe Pequot and Falcon, respectively. He holds a joint PhD from the Folklore Institute and the Department of Communication and Culture at Indiana University. He has published numerous articles in academic journals and in venues for the general public. He is a board member of the Connecticut Eastern Regional Tourism District and regularly consults with Essex Steam Train and Riverboat to develop programs drawing from the folklore of New England. A native New Englander, he lives in Lyme, Connecticut, with his wife, Winnie, and their children, Cella, Antonio, Angeline, and Salvatore.

9 781493 060429